THE FIGHTING SOUL

THE FIGHTING SOUL

On the Road with Bernie Sanders

ARI RABIN-HAVT

LIVERIGHT PUBLISHING CORPORATION

A Division of W. W. Norton & Company

Independent Publishers Since 1923

For information about permission to reproduce selections from this
book, write to Permissions, Liveright Publishing Corporation,
a division of W. W. Norton & Company, Inc.,
500 Fifth Avenue, New York, NY 10110

For information about special discounts for bulk purchases, please
contact W. W. Norton Special Sales at specialsales@wwnorton.com
or 800-233-4830

Manufacturing by Lake Book Manufacturing
Book design by Lovedog Studio
Production manager: Lauren Abbate

Library of Congress Cataloging-in-Publication Data

Names: Rabin-Havt, Ari, author.
Title: The fighting soul : on the road with Bernie Sanders /
Ari Rabin-Havt.
Description: First edition. | New York : Liveright Publishing
Corporation, a division of W. W. Norton & Company, [2022] |
Includes bibliographical references and index.
Identifiers: LCCN 2021053185 | ISBN 9781631498794 (hardcover) |
ISBN 9781631498800 (epub)
Subjects: LCSH: Sanders, Bernard. | United States—Congress
Senate—Biography. | Presidential candidates—United States—
Biography. | Presidents—United States—Election—2020. |
Legislators—United States—Biography. | Socialists—United States—
Biography. | Progressivism (United States politics) | United States—
Politics and government—2017–2021.
Classification: LCC E840.8.S26 R33 2022 | DDC 328.73/092
[B]—dc23/eng/20211129
LC record available at https://lccn.loc.gov/2021053185

Liveright Publishing Corporation
500 Fifth Avenue, New York, N.Y. 10110
www.wwnorton.com

W. W. Norton & Company Ltd.
15 Carlisle Street, London W1D 3BS

1 2 3 4 5 6 7 8 9 0

To Julie, who sacrificed more for the Bernie campaign than anyone knows.

And to the Bernie advance team. You were my family on the road, always accomplishing the impossible with a smile on your face and a cold Diet Snapple Peach Tea waiting.

CONTENTS

Prologue

"ARI . . . GET ME A CHAIR."

At that moment I knew something was very wrong. Bernie Sanders never asked to sit down during a campaign event in the more than three years I'd traveled with him. There are, in fact, few things he detests more than sitting down when answering people's questions. He thinks it's disrespectful.

It was Tuesday, October 1, 2019, and Bernie was speaking at a low-dollar fundraiser in a Middle Eastern restaurant a few miles from the Las Vegas Strip. At the end of his stump speech, he asked for a chair. Once seated, Bernie answered only a handful of questions from the attendees, far fewer than normal. He then left the stage, skipping the selfie line that was customary at these events.

The day began with no hint of what was to come. We arrived in Las Vegas and headed to the "Healing Garden," a memorial honoring the victims of the deadliest mass shooting in American history, which took place outside the Mandalay Bay Casino. I took photographs of Bernie that afternoon, as I always did. Looking back, they revealed no indication of what was to come. He was genuinely moved by the experience and was somber but friendly with those gathered at the site to mourn.

Before heading to the fundraiser, we stopped at a Starbucks for a cup of coffee. Inside, Bernie and I got into an argument about the next day's schedule, which he claimed was too taxing. While it was not uncommon for Bernie to quiz me about the schedule, I should have paid more attention. We frequently argued about scheduling, but Bernie—even though he generally expressed his fatigue from having been on the road constantly for nearly three years—never complained about being too tired to campaign. In this case, Bernie told me he was too tired to meet with union members the next morning. Clearly something was off. In the moment, I missed it.

In the SUV leaving the fundraiser, I had no doubt something was very wrong.

Bernie and I were joined in the car by Jesse Cornett, who hours earlier when we arrived in Las Vegas had started working as the campaign's trip director and body man. Jesse was driving, the senator was in the front passenger seat, and I was in the back. A lead car with other staff drove ahead of us down the Strip toward our hotel.

"Are you OK, Senator?" I said.

"Yes, just a little tired," he rumbled from the front seat. "It's been a long day."

Bernie then called Jane, his wife of more than thirty years. I overheard him tell her that he was feeling a little sick and was headed to his hotel.

Once the call was over, I asked, "Do you want dinner?"

"No, I'll go right to my room."

This was another sign that something was off. Bernie rarely turned down dinner.

"Senator, would you like me to send a doctor to your hotel room?"

"You can do that?" he said, apparently shocked that such a service existed.

"Yes, but can we talk about what's wrong so I can tell them?" Even inside a complete circle of trust, Bernie remains one of the most guarded people I've ever been around. I would often have to repeatedly prod him with questions about his well-being.

"Ari, I'm just tired. I also have this pressure feeling in my lungs. It's not a pain, more like pressure."

"Anything else?"

"Nothing that bad, but over the past week, my left arm has hurt."

I glanced to Jesse, who turned to look over his shoulder at me. That was all it took—he pulled the car out of the motorcade. As he did so, I told the senator we were going to the nearest urgent care center. I went on Google and found one just a few blocks away in a strip mall, but when we got there, the nurse inside told me they could not take any more patients for the day. Then I suddenly remembered Elite Medical, an urgent care center located behind the MGM Grand. On one of many previous Vegas trips, I'd seen it out the window of my hotel room. I gave Jesse the address and he headed toward the facility.

During the five-minute drive, the senator's condition seemed to worsen. It was clear that he was extremely uncomfortable. His initial hesitance to seek medical treatment quickly turned to impatience as he repeatedly asked how far we were from the clinic.

When we arrived at Elite Medical, I found a nurse and told her that I had an extremely well-known patient feeling sick enough to require medical attention—asking if he could be swiftly triaged into a private room? The last thing I wanted was Bernie Sanders sitting in a busy waiting area in a Las Vegas urgent care facility. She asked who it was, and when I told her, she replied that she would need to see a driver's license. I ran out to the car and retrieved Bernie's license, and we rushed him into the clinic.

Once Bernie was in the exam room, I was handed a stack of admission and insurance paperwork to fill out, and started to make a round of calls that I would repeat over and over again for the next few hours. First Jane; then our campaign manager, Faiz Shakir; then Jeff Weaver, Bernie's longest-serving and closest aide, who had been with him on and off since the late 1980s. In between calls, I checked on Bernie. He was sitting up in bed, shirt off, anxious about the results of the CAT scans and other tests the doctors were performing.

I feared the worst. I was the deputy campaign manager of Bernie's presidential campaign, and I couldn't help but think about what this would mean for his candidacy—but he was also a friend. We had been constant travel companions for three years, sharing thousands of meals and tens of thousands of miles on the road.

Diving into the logistics and little details is how I prevent myself from becoming overwhelmed in challenging situations, so that's what I did. I just kept running through what needed to be done: fill out more paperwork, check on Bernie, talk to the doctor, call Jane again, call Faiz again, call Jeff again, repeat.

Eventually, a doctor told me that Bernie had a blocked artery in his heart and would need to be transported to a nearby hospital for catheterization. I dispatched staff to determine how to arrive at the hospital without making a scene: Jane and I had agreed that Bernie's children—Levi, Heather, Carina, and Dave—and grandchildren should hear about what was happening from her, and not from cable news. Unfortunately, it was already after midnight in New England, where most of them lived. I didn't want someone in the hospital snapping a picture on a cell phone that would quickly make news around the world.

Before the ambulance arrived to take the senator from the urgent care clinic to the hospital, the doctor told me I would need to grab Bernie's wedding ring and glasses because they could be broken or lost during the procedure. After some pushback, Bernie gave up the wedding ring, but the glasses were a different matter.

"No, Ari, that's bullshit, I'm keeping them," he barked. Jesse and I spent the rest of the evening nervously passing Bernie's ring back and forth—losing it became our greatest fear.

I rode in the ambulance with Bernie, while Jesse followed in the SUV. Bernie chatted with the EMTs about the job—Did they have health insurance? How did they view health care in this country?

A few minutes later, we arrived at the hospital, where we were met by Dr. Arturo Marchand, the cardiologist who would perform the procedure. He asked Bernie a standard series of questions.

"Senator, are you allergic to eggs?"

"Ari, you answer these questions."

"Senator, I have no idea if you are allergic to eggs."

"No, I'm not allergic to eggs."

"Senator, who here can make medical decisions for you in the case you are incapacitated, and we can't reach your wife?"

"Ari." It was the obvious answer, given that of the campaign staff at the hospital, I was both the highest-ranking staffer and personally the one closest to him. But it still shocked me.

"Senator, on a scale of 1 to 10, how much pain are you in?"

"That is a bullshit question. I have no idea." The doctor looked at him, perplexed, but moved on.

Bernie was wheeled into the catheterization room, and Jesse and I walked to a waiting area along with Charla Bailey, the staffer who had scouted the hospital arrival. I made another round of calls. Jane was booking a 6 AM flight from Burlington, Vermont, through Chicago, which would get her to Vegas by midday. Faiz would be on an AM flight from DC.

"This campaign is over," I told Jesse and Charla. "We work for a seventy-eight-year-old who is running for president. There is no way our campaign survives this. But we have to run through the bag," I said, using a Little League analogy. "We owe it to Bernie to do our jobs perfectly over the next few days." They nodded in agreement.

About forty-five minutes later, Dr. Marchand came into the waiting room. The blockage was only in one artery, and the procedure to clear it had been a success, he said. I put the doctor on the phone with Jane.

Charla, Jesse, and I soon found ourselves in Bernie's room. He looked at Charla and joked, "Why am I in the hospital every time we are together?" Charla had been in South Carolina back in March, when he banged his head on a shower door, an injury requiring seven stitches.

We all laughed, and I knew then he would be OK. I noticed that the color had returned to his face. It was a subtle change from the previous weeks—I hadn't paid attention, but now in hindsight I realized Bernie's complexion had grown progressively grayer, and he'd begun to look older than usual. Already a healthy pink hue was returning; I was relieved.

But I still didn't think the campaign would survive. The next afternoon, with Jane, Faiz, and me sitting in his hospital room and Jeff on the phone, Bernie made his opinion known:

"Look, there's no point in quitting now. If people aren't going to vote for me, that's fine, but we need to keep talking about the issues that matter. Without this campaign, that won't happen."

Bernie's campaign was always about more than just winning the White House. It was about creating a political environment conducive to the agenda he had devoted his life to: making health care a human right; reversing the impacts of climate change; and making higher education available to every American by ensuring that public colleges and universities were tuition-free.

For someone who has mastered many aspects of modern politics in the United States, Bernie is at best ambivalent about—in truth, hostile to—our current political discourse. He detests the focus on personality and process. His relentless focus on his core agenda blinds him to the desire of most people to truly know him, in the way they hope to know the politicians they elect to high office. To Bernie, that's all gossip. Issues are what matter, not personalities. That's why even after two presidential campaigns, the public, his supporters, and many on his staff don't really know who Bernie Sanders is.

While his agenda has caused a tectonic shift in our politics—

such that even a moderate like Joe Biden, as president, has overseen the largest nonmilitary expansion of the federal government since the New Deal—Bernie had waged a lonely fight for his central policies for years. In many ways his distance from the mainstream was a comfortable place for him. He would lament often on the campaign trail that, prior to 2015, he didn't have to watch what he said, because often nobody cared. He would joke about a press conference he once held on Capitol Hill with AFL-CIO president Richard Trumka that was not attended by a single reporter from a mainstream outlet.

Having brought the Democratic Party to him without compromising his principles, he will never be lonely again. Yet despite his influence and fame, he has remained the same person he was before. What was clear to all who witnessed it was that his heart attack was insignificant to him, compared to what our campaign meant to the working people of this country. We would press on, because for Bernie, there was no other choice.

* * * *

BERNIE SANDERS NEVER SOUGHT FAME or power for their own sake. In many ways, he is shocked by what has happened to him. "Ari, my parents would tell me I was crazy if I told them I would become a senator, much less could become president of the United States," he has said to me on a few occasions.

The difficulty in describing what Bernie is like in private is that, at first glance, he is not that much different from Bernie in public. Except for the four-letter words, specifically "fuck," articulated in a drawn-out way in his Brooklyn accent, his head leaning back on his shoulders as the syllables drag out of his mouth—FFFFFFUUUUUUUCCCCCKKKKK.

In public, Bernie is almost always prim, with the noted exceptions of the word "damn," most famously punctuating sentences at debates—"I wrote the damn bill"—"The American people are sick and tired of hearing about your damn emails."

In 2018, as New York governor Andrew Cuomo's primary campaign against the actress Cynthia Nixon heated up, the *Daily News* quoted one of the governor's spokespeople saying that he was "in lockstep" with Bernie Sanders on policy. This boast was laughable on its face, so I tweeted, "The idea that Andrew Cuomo and Bernie Sanders are lock step on policy is 100% Grade A American bullshit." Cuomo was incensed by the tweet and personally called multiple senior staff members in Bernie's office to demand that I be reprimanded or even fired. Bernie was on a plane from Burlington to DC as this was taking place. I went to the airport to intercept him before Cuomo could get ahold of him.

Bernie got in the car and asked me what was going on. I explained what I had tweeted. Bernie started laughing. Then he stopped. "Ari, you represent me when you tweet. You should not have used the world 'bullshit.' A better tweet would have said that if Bernie Sanders and Andrew Cuomo were in lockstep, then he would support Medicare for All."

Cursing might be the only area where Bernie's private words diverge from his public ones. Bernie truly believes every word that leaves his lips. And the times when we, his senior staff, asked him to say something for political reasons, he could barely keep it together, almost always failing.

Bernie loves rallies and is not a fan of Washington politics. He is not unpopular within Congress, but rarely socializes with his peers. He is a rabble-rouser and a street protester, but also someone who respects authority and rarely bucks party leadership. He loves media attention but has his limits. The attention has to serve his larger policy interests, or it's not worth it, or even worse, it's a "reality show."

One example that stuck in my head came in the lead-up to the government shutdown in 2018. I and a few other staffers came up with a plan for Bernie to lead a sit-in in Mitch McConnell's office. It would have been carried across the news networks, and we likely would have raised millions of dollars in online contributions. Bernie would not even think about it.

"Ari, that is a stunt. Go pitch it to another senator," he said. The subtext was clear: Governing is serious. People were in trouble. Act like it.

But Bernie is not serious all the time. One difference between public Bernie and private Bernie is the joyfulness of the latter. Beyond his family, Bernie gets excited about baseball and football and historical sites and monuments. Often, while on the campaign trail, we would stop just to stroll around landmarks without public notice. With no press or fanfare, we toured the Alamo and visited the Buddy Holly memorial in Lubbock, Texas. He lamented that following the 2016 campaign, any hope of anonymity was gone forever. Now, wherever he went, from airport terminals to restaurants, people would line up to ask for selfies.

Bernie can be seen as humorless, but in fact he has a superb sense of humor, dry and cutting. At the end of a nearly four-hour drive from Los Angeles to Desert Hot Springs, where he was vacationing at a spa, we passed a massive wind farm with several large windmills. Bernie had been silent for the better part of an hour, his head slumped as he took a nap. As we drove through the wind farm, he looked up and stared at a windmill. "That, Ari, is a giant motherfucking windmill." I could not stop laughing for the rest of the ride.

To the world at large, he is Bernie or Bernie Sanders (never just "Sanders"). In memos he might be referred to as SBS. But to senior staff on the campaign, he was also Earl. As in, "Earl is dead wrong about this"; "Earl was really funny this morning"; "Earl refuses to do debate prep." It's what we call Bernie in public—in taxis and restaurants, on planes, and even walking down the street, especially in Washington, DC, and Burlington, Vermont, where saying his first name out loud would cause more than a few ears to perk up.

I have no idea how or when senior staff started using Earl as a code name for Bernie, but it stuck. Earl was also the name of the encrypted Signal thread that senior staff used to communicate with each other.

Talk to any senior staffer in public and Bernie could do no wrong. "Earl," however, elicited a more forthright critique. Earl wasn't mean or abusive, and his dry humor would crack us up, but the truth was that Earl's superpowers were also his weaknesses—most glaringly, that he *hated* the political part of political campaigns. His 2016 campaign never hired a political director, the person primarily responsible for maintaining relationships with politicians and organizations for the candidate.

In 2020, our political department was run by Analilia Mejia, who had spent her career in New Jersey union politics, and Sarah Badawi, who had spent years working for major progressive organizations. Because of Earl, Analilia and Sarah had the toughest jobs on the campaign. They needed him to call important people—elected officials, union leaders, heads of progressive organizations. But Earl hated those calls. The idea that these people would need to be courted and have their asses kissed was at best an annoyance, and at worst exactly the kind of glad-handing he detested. Getting him to make these phone calls was a thankless task. And if he *did* make a phone call and it didn't immediately result in an endorsement, he would point to it as an example of our wasting his time. "Ari, I'm *busy*," he'd say. "I can't spend my life on the phone with everyone."

On the positive side, Bernie's reluctance to engage in this form of politics meant he could be a candidate who did not care about the traditional mores of the Democratic Party, because he never built bridges that he could burn. This allowed him to challenge the traditional power structures and take positions others might deem too radical.

There were other challenges we faced. Earl hated spending money on staff. Early in the campaign, he had walked into headquarters and seen about a hundred new faces. He lost it. *Why did we have so many employees? What were they doing all day?* He insisted on a hiring freeze that substantially damaged the campaign. In perhaps his biggest mistake, he demanded we send the campaign's policy director back to the Senate, hamstringing the campaign just as Elizabeth Warren climbed in the polls on the strength of her "has a plan for that" slogan. Our campaign, unlike Warren's, had no staff to produce policy plans that could be central to driving a media narrative.

Earl hated the process of scheduling. At times he would insist on approving every second of his day; at other times, he wouldn't engage in the conversation at all, leaving us hanging, sometimes for weeks on end, unable to plan future movements and often leaving me to go insane with frustration.

When Earl *did* get involved, it often resulted in last-minute changes because he didn't fully trust his staff. Scheduling on a presidential campaign is driven by two elements. First, there are the events the candidate needs to attend—debates, forums, party dinners, and the like. Then, there are the states, cities, and communities that need to be visited for strategic reasons. Once a general map is set—say, we decided to be in New Hampshire for a three-day visit—the state director and local staff create a schedule that included rallies, town halls, breakfasts, forums, interviews, and other events based on the needs of the campaign.

On the campaign's first trip to New Hampshire, the then–state director had sent me a perfectly reasonable schedule that included a mix of media interviews and rallies. Earl, however, wouldn't approve it. When I finally got him to talk about it, he pulled out a map of the state and questioned each stop on the tour, moving some rallies just one town over.

This micromanagement could focus on the minutest issues. At the start of the campaign Bernie was concerned about the quality of our bumper stickers. He stuck one to his desk and then peeled it up easily, to demonstrate his dissatisfaction: it lacked a firm hold on surfaces and would fall off people's cars. He immediately got on the phone with senior adviser Chuck Rocha and demanded higher-quality stickers.

There was the time he spent three hours on the phone with me and our director of advance—Jean-Michel Picher, who had produced some of the most memorable political rallies of the past decade—discussing the merits and costs of *purchasing* sound systems versus *renting* them. He had a similar conversation with Ben Cohen, the cofounder of Ben & Jerry's Ice Cream and a co-chair of the campaign. It's not that we didn't arrive at the right answers—it was just that Earl would waste time on these little decisions, overriding the expertise of staff who had been working on such matters for years. On campaigns you can always raise more money or hire more staff; a candidate's time is the only nonrenewable resource.

On a presidential campaign, "advance" are the staff who set up the rallies, plot the motorcade routes, make sure the press are properly set up and corralled at events, check the candidate and traveling staff into the hotel, and generally make sure that the campaign is safe and efficient while traveling. Responsibilities can extend to finding a hospital on short notice.

Yet Earl consistently pushed to minimize their presence. In part, this was because he hated entourages—they simply made him uncomfortable. But he also believed that in 2016 the campaign had overspent on events.

To Bernie, campaigning meant getting in a car with Jeff Weaver or Phil Fiermonte and driving around Vermont, holding town halls that could be scheduled a day in advance. He never fully appreciated the effort it took to set up a 5,000-person rally.

As far as principles go, Earl had a fairly modest set of requirements. The number one rule was no giant suites. He hated it when hotels would upgrade him to their biggest suite. This was not, as one might expect, a matter of principle for a left-wing politician. Earl simply liked to sleep in rooms that were cold, and large hotel suites did not cool down as well as small single rooms. In fact, advance would set the temperature in his room to 60 degrees before he arrived.

Earl's other comfort needs were likewise simple. Water in the room; red Gatorade or Vitaminwater; cough drops. Pre–heart attack, Milano cookies were a favorite; post–heart attack, clementines became ubiquitous. After he lost his voice in September 2019, a friend recommended a specific and hard to find brand of cough drop—Grether's Blackcurrant Pastilles. For weeks after the campaign ended, advance staff would text each other with pictures of tins and the tiny black candies they found in the crevasses of their bags. Other than that, Earl just needed his iPad and he was relatively content.

Without Earl's eccentricities, Bernie wouldn't be the leader he is. He never became accustomed to the trappings of power, and he figured out how to succeed in politics without compromising his core values. Unlike many politicians, he was not forced to stop being who he authentically is—which is one reason his supporters and staff love him.

* * * *

MY JOURNEY INTO Bernie's orbit was an unexpected one. I didn't work for him during his campaign in 2016. At the time, I was a host at SiriusXM, and my superiors were reasonably serious about maintaining neutrality in the primaries. When I was going to endorse Bernie, just before Super Tuesday, my boss sternly warned me against it, telling me that when Hillary inevitably won the presidency I could cause Sirius's progressive channel to be blackballed by the new administration.

The night Donald Trump was elected president of the United States changed everything for me. I was at the Javits Center in New York, under that giant glass ceiling that was the final overthought gimmick of the 2016 election. My job was to cover the night's proceedings that would ultimately end in Hillary Clinton's election as the 45th president of the United States.

Was I excited to see her as president? Not particularly. The defining moment of my political generation was the decision to go to war in Iraq—something she was on the wrong side of. The fact that Joe Biden was, too, and had led the effort to pass the war resolution in the Senate, was one reason I remained unenthusiastic about his administration during the 2020 election cycle. That night my responsibilities included interviewing a lineup of Clinton surrogates all expressing excitement about the prospect of her presidency. Michelangelo Signorile, Mark Thompson, and Nomi Konst, my colleagues on SiriusXM Progress, were in studio. As progressive hosts, we were all a bit cocky. Of course, Hillary was going to win. I even went on conservative commentator Tomi Lahren's television program early in the evening to boast about defeating Donald Trump.

I had my future laid out for me. In the coming weeks, I was going to launch a new think tank to push Hillary's administration to the left, arming progressive allies on Capitol Hill with the policy and communications weapons necessary to engage in that fight. Hillary would win, and it would be our job to force her administration to be more progressive.

Then it happened.

I was interviewing Mary Kay Henry, the president of SEIU, one of the country's largest unions. I then saw a Clinton campaign communications staffer enter the hall where the media was positioned and start nudging their surrogates out. It was a bad sign. The staffer came to my table and cut short the interview.

I ventured into the basement of the Javits Center to investigate, running into Tyrone Gale, a Clinton (and future Kamala Harris) communications aide who had worked for me at Media Matters years earlier, and who would tragically die of cancer in 2018. I asked him what was going on with Florida's numbers, which were heading south. He responded, "Got a lot of votes out there."

"Oh shit," I replied. "You lost."

"Still a lot of votes out there, Ari," he replied. I remained skeptical.

I went on air a few minutes later and said to my cohosts that I thought Hillary would lose. Donald Trump, I told them, was going to be the next president of the United States.

They responded with incredulity. An executive at Sirius texted me, "that's a bold prediction, Ari."

I remained at the Javits Center until one in the morning, by which point the result was clear, before staggering back to my hotel in Times Square, a few blocks from SiriusXM's studio. I would have to go on at 6 AM and explain to my audience what had gone wrong.

After barely two hours of sleep, I walked into the studio to be greeted by LGBT activist Joe Sudbay and Palestinian civil rights activist Linda Sarsour. After broadcasting from 3 to 6 AM, they were emotionally drained. I had been doing daily three-hour broadcasts for five years, and I don't know if I could have survived those particular three hours on air. As opposed to a celebration, they were presiding over a funeral. Linda and I hugged. What would we do next? The only thing we could: keep working, keep fighting, seeking the same goals as before.

But how? That was what drew me to Bernie Sanders. At that moment my only personal contact with Bernie had been a selfie taken with him at the White House Correspondents' Dinner earlier that year and an interview on my radio show. In early 2015 I profiled Bernie in his new role as ranking member of the Senate Budget Committee for *The American Prospect*, and during the 2016 campaign I wrote another profile, this one for the *New York Observer*. In the latter piece I noted that, far from a strange European form of socialism, Bernie Sanders took his ideological cues from President Theodore Roosevelt, after he left the Republican Party and ran as the candidate of the Progressive (Bull Moose) Party in 1912. That party's agenda, which was written by the formerly Republican president, lined up perfectly with Bernie's, even though they were separated by more than a century.

My decision to work on the Sanders campaign was a personal one, in the end. I came to Bernie's campaign for much of the same reason others did: pain. When Bernie talks about his childhood—an infrequent occurrence—he usually mentions his parents' arguing due to their lack of money. It wasn't the fact that they were materially poor that haunted Bernie, but the fights that financial instability caused. I believe Bernie is uncomfortable telling his own story, in part, because he is embarrassed by it. Like any kid listening to his parents fight about money in a small apartment, he was worried about what the neighbors would hear. Yet in other ways he is incredibly proud of his parents' story.

His father, Elias Sander (the final "s" of "Sanders" was added after his arrival), came to the United States, in Bernie's words, "without a nickel in his pocket." In 1921, at age 17, he had left Słopnice, a small town in southern Poland; most of his family remained, although one brother would also make the journey to America. The family, along with most of the town's Jewish population, including Eli's family, would be murdered by the Nazis.

There is a sense of pride in Bernie's voice when he talks about the courage it took for his father to leave Poland for America. One of the few times Bernie was seen getting emotional in public was when his older brother, Larry, cast his ballot as a Democrats Abroad delegate at the 2016 Democratic Convention. Bernie had tears in his eyes, but a smile on his face, as Larry spoke from the seats of the Wells Fargo Center in Philadelphia, "I want to read before this convention the names of our parents: Eli Sanders and Dorothy Glassberg Sanders. They did not have easy lives and they died young. They would be immensely proud of their son and his accomplishments. They loved him." Casting his vote, Larry told the convention hall that his parents "loved the New Deal of Franklin Roosevelt and would be especially proud that Bernard is renewing that vision."

Eli Sanders eventually became a paint salesman, but struggled financially throughout his life. Bernie's mother, Dorothy Glassberg, was born in the United States. She had seven siblings, some of whom found some financial success in the garment industry. His mother's dream was to one day move out of their rent-controlled apartment on East 26th Street near Kings Highway in Midwood, a Brooklyn neighborhood, and own her own home, something she never achieved.

Larry explained to Vermont Public Radio, "I think what Bernard and I took from that is that financial problems are never just financial problems. They enter into people's lives at very deep and personal levels."[1]

The struggles of Bernie's family drew me to him. I grew up in a mostly one-income household, with my father unemployed for much of my childhood and adolescence. Like nearly everyone who worked for Bernie, I came to his office with a story connecting my political beliefs to personal pain.

Still, after I started a job in Bernie's Senate office, I was not further motivated by a personal tie to him or love for him as a person, even though we ultimately became close friends. On the Bernie team this was not unusual. Beyond Jane and Jeff Weaver, most of us came to Bernie's 2020 campaign not for the man, but for the cause. And he liked it that way. Bernie would speak in terms of a war, and he wanted unsentimental warriors on his side. Those allied with him wanted to build the fundamentally just society that we all believed, and still believe, is possible.

* * * *

FOR THREE YEARS, I spent more hours with Bernie Sanders than I did with my wife, and he spent more hours with me than he did with Jane. We visited thirty-six states, attended hundreds of events, drove thousands of miles, flew enough to earn me hundreds of thousands of frequent flier miles on American Airlines alone, and ate in countless stomach-churning restaurants.

My first call in the morning would be from him: "Hey Ari. How ya doing? Any gossip I should know? Want to go get breakfast in fifteen minutes?" I walked him to his hotel room in the evening to make sure he was OK and there were no last-minute issues to discuss.

Discussions over evening meals would focus primarily on the work of the day: what needed to be done and how it needed to be done. Once we finished for the night, Bernie would sit with his iPad watching old episodes of *Saturday Night Live* ("Ari, do you know who Gilda Radner is? She was funny"), old boxing matches, and movies. I later learned he also enjoyed watching flash mob videos, seeing them as fun cultural and community events.

While I started as a staffer in his Senate office, I eventually became one of three deputy campaign managers for his 2020 presidential run. Everyone knows how that portion of my journey with him—and how Bernie's 2020 campaign—ended. We lost. I wish we hadn't. Our country would be better today with Bernie Sanders in the White House. Still, despite a heart attack four months before the first caucus, Bernie ended up winning the popular vote in Iowa, New Hampshire, Nevada, and, by a considerable margin, the largest state in the country, California.

If not for centrists consolidating behind Joe Biden in an extraordinary forty-eight-hour period between the South Carolina primary and Super Tuesday, Bernie Sanders would likely have won the Democratic nomination. But this book doesn't tell a story about losing. Nor does it tell a story about winning *despite* losing: while Bernie has shaped this country more than any other losing candidate has since perhaps William Jennings Bryan in 1896, 1900, and 1908, campaigns have a singular goal, and the radical transformation that Bernie fights for will only happen if the occupant of the Oval Office shares his politics. Nor, finally, is this book an argument for progressive policies or an extended think piece about the state of the country and its politics.

It is, instead, a more intimate story, told largely through Bernie's last presidential campaign, from the perspective of someone who was by his side at almost every moment. My ambition in this book is at once simple and daunting: to explain who Bernie Sanders—an elderly Jewish socialist from Vermont who managed to capture the imagination of the young people of America and transform our country—really is.

CHAPTER 1

Waiting Game

BERNIE SANDERS'S 2020 PRESIDENTIAL CAMPAIGN BEGAN in the living room of my apartment in January 2018, even if the candidate didn't know it yet, and even though he wasn't sure he wanted to run. The meeting came after weeks spent by Jeff Weaver and me trying to get Bernie focused on the potential of another presidential campaign. While his mind was still not made up, Jeff and I, along with digital guru Tim Tagaris, felt the need to start preparing.

Presidential campaigns are insane endeavors. Ultimately, within the span of thirteen months, we would launch a corporation and hire nearly 1,000 staff, raise and spend $200,000,000, and then shut down. We would have operations in more than a dozen states simultaneously, and host events attended by more than 500,000 people in total. All this had to be carried out while under intense media scrutiny as cable news panels judged our every move.

In 2015 nothing had been expected of Bernie when he launched his campaign. Most people in the political establishment and the media believed he would garner support equivalent to Dennis Kucinich's in 2004—which is to say, very little. Bernie was an unknown with zero expectations surrounding him, which gave his campaign time to ramp up while no one was paying attention.

Obviously, 2020 would be different. Bernie would be a top-tier candidate, if not the front-runner. If tens of thousands of people did not attend our launch events, it would be a disappointment that could doom our media narrative—and by extension, the actual campaign—from the start. Furthermore, for most of the 2016 cycle the only two candidates in serious contention in the Democratic primary were Bernie Sanders and Hillary Clinton. In 2020, nearly two dozen Democrats would run, with at least ten treated as serious candidates by the media. Because of Bernie's prior success, many of our opponents would themselves adopt significant parts of our campaign's agenda. While Hillary had attacked Bernie's policies in 2016 as a naïve wish list, between Elizabeth Warren, Kamala Harris, and Cory Booker, among others, every one of his significant initiatives had the support of other candidates in the race.

As Bernie struggled to make up his mind about running, other campaigns were moving forward. Staff was being hired, endorsements solicited; and most of all, other campaigns were spending massive amounts of money on building up their email lists and social media followings. Tim Tagaris, in weekly, sometimes daily calls, fretted about losing our clear advantage if we did not act quickly.

For Bernie, it all seemed a bit premature. He had not decided whether he truly wanted to try again for the presidency, and feared any moves we made might lock him into a run. Jeff would consistently retort with the story of Mario Cuomo's aborted 1992 campaign, where aides were driving to New Hampshire at the moment that the New York governor decided not to enter the race. Bernie could always choose not to run, but we would soon lose any opportunity to take advantage of our head start.

Also weighing heavily on Bernie was his Senate race in Vermont. There was never any doubt that he would win reelection. He was not only the most popular political figure in the state but he was also the most popular among his constituents of any member of the United States Senate. Yet while building a national platform over the previous four years, he felt that he had been neglectful of his home state and that his prominence was now competing with his work as a senator.

He wanted to run for reelection, and to focus on the race and his state while doing so. Of course, any national aspirations would be an issue, but unlike most politicians in a similar situation, he would not be deceitful about them. When asked if he was running for president, he would answer honestly that he had not made up his mind, but he would do what he believed was best for the people of the state of Vermont.

Jeff, Tim, and I, and occasionally Mark Longabaugh, the media strategist from his 2016 race, continually pushed on Bernie to let us begin work on the presidential campaign or at least let us convene a meeting. Finally, in early 2018, he signed off on the gathering. But we would have to keep it quiet.

That is how Bernie ended up in my condo in Adams Morgan, in Washington, DC, on a Saturday in late January 2018, to discuss how a new campaign for president might take shape. In the room along with Jeff, Bernie, Tim, Mark, and me were future campaign deputy campaign manager Arianna Jones, strategist Chuck Rocha, Our Revolution president Nina Turner, former NAACP president and Maryland gubernatorial candidate Ben Jealous, pollster Ben Tulchin, and Mark's business partner Julian Mulvey.

Calling in to two separate cell phones were Jane, in Burlington, and RoseAnn DeMoro, the former executive director of the nation's largest nurses' union, National Nurses United, and a close political ally of Bernie's, who joined us from her home in Northern California. Because of the odd logistics, Bernie spent the meeting holding both phones, pointing them in the direction of whoever was speaking.

In the weeks before the meeting, Ben Tulchin had run a poll in Iowa to test the state of the race. In our minds, there were two other candidates who could affect Bernie's standing and challenge his status as a front-runner: Joe Biden and Elizabeth Warren. We didn't know whether either of them would get in the race.

If neither ran, Bernie would be the clear leader in Iowa from the start. If Biden ran, he would be the front-runner, and if all three ran, Bernie would be in the weakest position. The dynamics between the three candidates were not in line with conventional wisdom. The voters most likely to support Bernie in the 2020 primary also liked Joe Biden. Warren might be perceived as ideologically similar to Bernie, but her voters were less likely to support Bernie than Biden voters. We would shorthand this distinction as "beer track" vs. "wine track." Bernie was a beer track candidate, as was Joe Biden. Warren and Pete Buttigieg were wine track candidates. Beer track voters were less wealthy, less educated, and more working class.

One of the main takeaways from Ben's polling was that Bernie's 2020 support in Iowa would be immediately cut in half from 2016. A large portion of his vote in the 2016 primaries was from people who did not particularly believe in him or his ideology, but merely did not like Hillary Clinton.

Presentations centered around polling were always dicey with Bernie, who has a complicated relationship with polls. He would obsess about every public poll, good or bad, asking if we could get the full crosstabs to see the ratio of younger-to-older voters that would often be the key determinant of his standing in the race at any given moment. If a poll had a high percentage of voters under forty-five, it would look good for us; with a high percentage of voters over sixty-five, he'd fare much worse.

At the same time, he hated conducting his own polling. He never wanted his message, issue focus, or policies determined by numbers. Bernie would often comment derisively about other politicians, even ones he liked, for their overreliance on polls. I remembered a time in the summer of 2017, when Bernie and I were sitting next to each other on a flight from Washington to Chicago, on our way to Missouri. He was reading on his iPad, and every few minutes, he would start laughing. I asked what was so funny, imagining that his loud guffaws would draw attention on the crowded plane. It turned out he was reading *Shattered*, Jonathan Allen and Amie Parnes's book about the 2016 race, and he was laughing at the chapter on Hillary's campaign launch on Roosevelt Island and the preparations for her speech at the event. "Ari, imagine needing that many people to tell you why you are running for president. That's unbelievable."

Furthermore, Bernie often fundamentally mistrusted the science behind polling, and therefore its accuracy. To Bernie, crowds and rallies were focus groups. He used them to test which lines would work, which wouldn't. You could see him becoming more comfortable with certain policy elements of his legislative agenda—for example, student debt cancellation and the legalization of marijuana—based on the reactions from crowds.

In addition to Ben's polling, during the condo meeting we went through various fundraising, organizing, and television presentations, sketching what his second campaign for president would look like. How would we structure a staff? How many people would we need in the states that held the first primaries and caucuses—Iowa, New Hampshire, South Carolina, and Nevada? What was our path to victory, and, most important, what was the story the campaign needed to tell?

We also chewed over several strategic issues that we expected to confront. While Bernie would win young voters of all races, older African American voters who dominated Democratic primaries in southern states, most notably South Carolina, remained a challenge. And how would we address the problem of Russian interference in US elections?

One important strategic decision made in my living room that day was to treat California like an early state. It was the biggest delegate prize and was likely moving its primary up to Super Tuesday. The preponderance of mail-in voting in the state meant voters would receive ballots the same week as the Iowa caucus. To us, the strategy for winning the nomination was clear. In many ways, though nobody said it at the time, our path to the nomination was similar to Donald Trump's path to the GOP nomination and then the presidency in 2016. We would use our built-in advantages to win Iowa, New Hampshire, and Nevada. We would need to finish at least second in South Carolina and move into Super Tuesday with the Democratic field divided. If we could dominate California and win several other states, we could emerge with a delegate lead that would be insurmountable. It was unlikely we could win a one-on-one showdown with an establishment candidate before Super Tuesday, but the proportional allocation rules of the Democratic Party meant that if we emerged with a lead in early March, it was probable we could hold it and then unite the party behind us.

At that point in time, we were optimistically hoping that Cory Booker and Kamala Harris would perform well enough in Iowa to stay in the race along with Biden and Warren through Super Tuesday.

*   *   *   *

THOUGH THE CONVERSATION that day in January 2018 involved the strategy and scale of a presidential campaign, Bernie had another concern on his mind. "You guys do the technical stuff," he said, "you know what you are doing and are good at it." But he wanted a second run for the White House driven by momentum, *not* engineered through traditional campaign tactics. Accordingly, he challenged all of us with a simple question: "How do we create the magic?"

Bernie's core thesis about 2020 was that with Donald Trump in the White House, only a campaign built on energy and enthusiasm that brought new voters out to the polls would create the electoral coalition necessary to defeat him. This was his North Star. If Bernie Sanders did not believe he was the best candidate to take on Trump, whom he regarded as the most dangerous president in American history, then throwing his support behind the candidate who could win would be an easy decision. The stakes were too high.

Trump was dangerous on a policy level, but Bernie was also scared of his erratic nature. In the spring of 2017, Bernie and I ran into Arizona senator John McCain and South Carolina senator Lindsey Graham on the subway that travels between the Senate offices and the Capitol. After negotiating a giant Veterans Affairs reform bill with McCain—the meetings often devolved into screaming matches—Bernie and the Arizona senator had become friends, even chummy. Bernie and I had returned from a weeklong tour of the country with Democratic National Committee chair Tom Perez. We had held a giant rally in Mesa, Arizona.

"Look at this guy," McCain said, turning to Graham. "He just had 7,000 people out in Mesa. Bernie, I can't get 7,000 people in Mesa."

"Well, John," Bernie replied, "maybe I should move to Arizona and run for Senate?"

"Better not. I would lose," McCain joked.

The conversation became serious. Bernie leaned over to McCain, and the two turned their backs so the rest of the car, which included some journalists, could not hear. "John, I'm really concerned about the president. This isn't a political thing. Is he really this nuts?"

"Bernie," McCain replied, "have you ever met the president?"

Bernie replied he hadn't.

Without a hint of irony, McCain said, "The guy's a fucking wack job."

At the beginning of 2018, when Bernie looked at the field of potential Democratic presidential candidates, he did not believe any of them would put the party in the best position to defeat Trump. In his eyes and ours, all were too beholden to big money, focused on elites rather than working-class Americans, and too set in an old-style politics, more concerned with attending events on the Upper West Side and Beverly Hills than with talking with workers on picket lines. While Bernie truly detested Trump, he also saw the president as someone who genuinely excited a segment of the Republican Party. He believed no other candidate on the Democratic side could consistently bring out crowds with the same energy while galvanizing young and working-class voters.

Bernie very much believed he would have beaten Donald Trump in 2016. His argument was simple. Hillary Clinton had lost because in three states—Wisconsin, Michigan, and Pennsylvania—Democratic voters did not turn out at the expected levels in the general election. These were people who felt they had been screwed over by the system: by trade deals and outsourcing that sent well-paid jobs overseas, by large corporations who got away with paying no taxes while treating their workers poorly, and by banks and health insurance companies whose business model denied families their basic needs. Bill Clinton's presidency had ushered in many of these changes: NAFTA, permanent normal trade relations (PNTR) with China, mass incarceration, and welfare reform, to name a few. Bernie had spent decades fighting against that system and felt he could win back some of those voters who saw establishment Democrats as part of the problem.

Bernie also regarded Hillary Clinton's "deplorable" gaffe as a stunning example of elitism and political malpractice. Were there racist, sexist, homophobic, and xenophobic Trump supporters? Of course. But when a candidate for president describes a group of voters as deplorable, she's telling their families and their friends that she has no interest in engaging at all. While many people would not vote for Trump, many of those chose not to vote at all.

Nevertheless, and despite what many people believe, Bernie worked hard to elect Hillary Clinton. The truth is, Bernie knows only one approach to campaigning. He isn't a fundraiser and doesn't have relationships with the high-dollar donor community. Sending him to the Hamptons or Martha's Vineyard would be an exercise in futility. All he knows, in his words, is how to "rally the people." By which he means, in practice, public events. Bernie ended up doing thirty-nine events for Hillary in September and October 2016. He traveled to more than a dozen states, headlining more than three dozen rallies along with countless TV appearances on her behalf. During the last week of the campaign, he held more public events, in more states, for Clinton's campaign than she held herself. No surrogate, apart from her vice-presidential nominee, Tim Kaine, did more events for her from Labor Day to Election Day, the height of campaign season.

The blame Bernie took for Hillary's loss was unfair for this reason and others. Beating Trump was supposed to be easy. He wasn't running a real campaign. He had no field operation to turn out voters. Hillary was out-raising him by tens of millions of dollars. His support among the Republican establishment and the operative class was tepid at best. His "campaign" was so chaotic he brought Breitbart's chairman Steve Bannon to run it. Hillary's team, in contrast, was supposed to have been staffed with the best and the brightest.

Part of the reason no candidate other than Bernie could run in 2016 was that the Hillary campaign had sapped every available ounce from the Democratic Party's talent pool. Among these, as chair of the campaign, Hillary tapped Clinton and Obama White House chief of staff John Podesta.

In 2017, Bernie asked me if I could set up a meeting with John. Even though they were opponents in 2016, Bernie always had the utmost respect for him personally and professionally. During the conversation, which centered on what Bernie could do to help lead an effective opposition to Trump, he asked Podesta what he thought cost them the election in 2016.

Podesta did not hold back. His analysis was simple, and it was the same one many informed observers had arrived at, though he could speak with greater authority and experience than most: the Clinton campaign spent too much of their time letting Trump and his campaign wag the dog. They chased after his every offensive act and let him lead their movement. They had ceded the media narrative, good and bad, to the Trump campaign—a fatal mistake. They allowed the campaign to be dominated by the kind of chaos that Trump embraced.

John was pointed and honest, not blaming Bernie, at least to his face, for Hillary's loss. Understandably, others did not take the same approach. Bernie was an easy scapegoat. He was not of their world and had no shared relationships at the donor or operative level. Because if the fault was Bernie's or the Russians' or any other third party's, it wasn't their ineptitude that sent Trump to the White House.

The talk with Podesta contributed to Bernie's thinking as he asked himself, was he the best candidate to defeat Donald Trump? To answer that question, he had to know whether he could re-create the "magic" of 2016.

Months before the January meeting where his second campaign effectively began, he was raising this topic with Jeff and me constantly. To Bernie, "magic" meant energy and enthusiasm. It meant big crowds. It meant the unpredictable moments in a campaign, like when a bird landed on his podium mid-speech, inspiring thousands of memes online. It also meant the creative force of his supporters.

As Bernie and I traveled the country in 2017–18 on numerous trips for rallies and other events, I could see him always looking for signs that the spark of 2016 was still there. When thousands of people showed up at packed rallies on our trip to Montana in

May 2017, he was clearly encouraged. After a rally in a half-empty theater in New York with Bill DeBlasio later that year, Bernie was filled with doubt.

The biggest test would come during our final tour of the midterm cycle in October 2018, when we were trekking around the country campaigning for Democrats. Bernie would go out on the road one last time before Election Day. We would spend a week on the road, holding more than twenty-five events. In the middle of the tour, we added two Florida events, to campaign for gubernatorial candidate Andrew Gillum.

The tour was a test. With only a skeleton crew of advance staff, could we pull off presidential-level events? We crisscrossed the country, heading from Indiana to Michigan to South Carolina to Iowa to Wisconsin to Arizona to Colorado to Nevada to San Diego before finishing in Northern California. Each day was filled with as many as four rallies, which we would livestream to a large online audience, as well as numerous interviews. In tow would be a dozen members of the media. We also had a full social media team with us while on the road.

When first planning the tour in the early fall, we discussed a few goals. We would campaign with progressive candidates who were longshots, like Liz Watson, who was running for Congress in a conservative Indiana district. But requests came in to do events with more moderate Democrats who also felt they could benefit from Bernie's support. The tour ended up including rallies with gubernatorial candidates like Gretchen Whitmer in Michigan and Jared Polis in Colorado. We also would head to Nevada for rallies with Jacky Rosen in both Reno and Las Vegas.

Rosen was perhaps the most conservative candidate we would hold an event for. The ask came in September, directly from Harry Reid. The retired senator from Nevada—and my former boss—noted there were two groups in the state, young people and Latinos, among whom Bernie was particularly popular. His support could significantly boost Rosen's standing in the race.

Jacky is not a progressive. Among Bernie's core issues, the only one she supports is a $15 minimum wage. When she and Bernie got on the phone, there was no chemistry between them. The call was dry and substance-free. But getting off the phone, Bernie said, "If Jacky Rosen wins, it will help Democrats take the majority, and that will stop Trump. If Harry thinks that will help, that is exactly what we will do."

I told Bernie I would let them know we were coming to Nevada in the fall. But I was going to affix a price to the visit. If Bernie were to run for president, something he had not decided yet, Nevada would be critical. Reid would never support Bernie's campaign, but would he stay out of the primary fray both publicly and privately, and not take steps to interfere in our campaign if it looked like we would win Nevada? In 2016, Reid had rescued Hillary's campaign in Nevada, according to the dean of the state's press corps, Jon Ralston, by calling the Culinary Union and asking them to organize their workers for Clinton's campaign. Reid then called casino executives, to ensure they would give their workers time to vote. Hillary won the caucus by 5 points. We needed to prevent something similar from happening to Bernie in 2020. From prior conversations, I knew Reid was at best lukewarm on the idea of Bernie running for president. I had worked on his staff from 2005 to 2008, but once you work for Reid you never really stop. He is constantly on the phone with former staff, eliciting gossip and occasionally asking for assistance.

In March 2018, when I was in Las Vegas for March Madness, I texted Reid and asked if we could have lunch. A few weeks earlier, he had lightly scolded me for not calling him to get together the previous times I was in the city. A basic lesson of Washington, DC, is that when Harry Reid lightly chides you, don't let the reason happen again. At his request, we met at Veranda, a restaurant inside the Four Seasons on the Strip.

Reid walked into the restaurant, his security detail, provided by MGM, in tow. We were escorted to a private room in the back. The large room was almost comically set with a single table for two. His security detail positioned themselves outside. As the sliding doors were closing behind us, I caught the eyes of other restaurant patrons clearly wondering what was happening in the room.

One thing Harry Reid and Bernie Sanders have in common is they don't like sitting in restaurants for an extended period of time. As soon as we'd sit down, Bernie would always politely tell the wait staff we were in a rush, whether we were or not. Reid took a bit of a different approach. He called over the restaurant manager and told her, "I really love this restaurant, but I don't eat here because you guys are slow. Speed up."

Reid's mind was focused on the University of Nevada, Reno men's basketball team and their game. He always liked underdogs. Reid also wanted to talk about Bernie. When he was Democratic leader of the Senate, Reid read *People* and *Us Weekly*. Now in Las Vegas, he had to rely on former staff for information about his own former workplace. He quizzed me on what the Democratic caucus was doing in the Senate and if Bernie was going to run. I didn't know, I told him truthfully.

In July, I was back in Las Vegas to play in some World Series of Poker tournaments, and we again had lunch, though this time our conversation had a different tone. I took a cab all the way out to his home in a gated community in Henderson. He had returned there to undergo chemotherapy after being diagnosed with pancreatic cancer a few weeks earlier and having had surgery at Johns Hopkins.

Coming to the door with a cane and a bit of a hobble, he still looked like the Harry Reid I had long known. His mind was just as sharp as ever. He again quizzed me about whether Bernie was running. I was honest with him again. Right now, I said, flip a coin. If he runs, he wants to be sure he is the best candidate to beat Trump. Nothing else matters. Reid noted that he was now concerned Bernie and Biden were too old, and their health could get in the way of successful campaigns. Confronted with his own mortality, the issue was clearly something he had given some thought to.

At the same time, he thought the other likely candidates simply had too many flaws. He told me that one prominent Democrat had asked him for a meeting. While together, this person had told Reid he was running. "What a joke."

Reid believed Warren and Bernie should not run against each other in the primary because they would compete for the same voters—a common view at the time—and take each other out of contention. His main concern was that Bernie was committed to keeping his supporters engaged in the process, whether he ran or not. "He can't just go have a nice life up there in Vermont."

As our conversation was coming to an end, he said something that only a former Harry Reid staffer would take as a compliment. "Ari, you're weird, that's why you're one of my favorites. You see the world differently. I think it's because you had some struggles growing up. My struggles were different. But now we understand that being a little weird is a bit of an advantage."

After Bernie made the decision to campaign for Rosen, I called Reid, telling him Bernie would do the events in Nevada as he had requested—on the condition that Reid pledge to stay out of the Nevada caucus and not do anything to otherwise shape the 2020 campaign. He eagerly agreed. Reid was completely trustworthy. If he made a commitment, he always kept it.

* * * *

THE MOST MEMORABLE EVENT of Bernie's fall 2018 tour took place in Bloomington, Indiana. That morning began with an uncomfortable moment for him. The hotel, as a courtesy, had brought a full breakfast to his room, waking him at 7:30 AM. He was not happy, in part because he was already disturbed that our advance staff had left four large bottles of water in his room. He said to me, "Ari, I'm not the president of the United States. I don't need four bottles of water in my room."

The rally would take place on the Indiana University campus. Bernie would then drive to a polling place a mile away and meet with voters. But he had a change of plans. He decided not to get in the car and instead led rally attendees on a march from the event to the polling station. During the short walk, reporters fell over themselves, couldn't keep up with Bernie, and ended up winded by his pace. One CNN reporter was huffing and puffing, sucking on a Juul, and looking like he was going to pass out when we reached the polling station.

The next day we were in South Carolina. It was perhaps the scariest moment of the tour: when we arrived at the venue, there were only fifty people in the 1,000-person auditorium. It was looking like it would be an embarrassment. While Bernie was at breakfast with ministers and other local leaders, I kept checking on the empty hall. When the breakfast was over, he asked me how the crowd was. I said, "Not good. There were only a hundred people in the room." Yet somehow, by the time we had walked down the hallway, the theater had nearly filled up. The event went from a probable disaster to an unmitigated success.

In every city we visited, crowds packed in. We were there to support other candidates, but people turned out to see Bernie. There were hitches, as there always are. In Arizona, with a thunderstorm coming in over the horizon, I asked the gubernatorial candidate to speed up his stump speech. Instead, he droned on for thirty minutes. When Bernie went up to the stage, I watched the clouds, timing lightning strikes to see when we would have to pull the event down. I signaled Bernie to leave the stage just as drops of rain began to hit.

When we arrived in Southern California, we had the morning off at a hotel right on the water. But we soon heard that a UNITE HERE local in San Diego was picketing outside another hotel, this one downtown. That was all Bernie needed to know. We might have all been tired from nearly a week on the road at a torrid pace, but we were going to walk that picket line. We drove to downtown San Diego where workers were gathered, and joined their protest in front of the hotel. This was Bernie's ethos boiled down to its essence. Rallies were great, but the opportunity to stand with hotel workers fighting for a decent standard of living was even more important.

After spending some time on the picket line with UNITE HERE workers, we held a rally with congressional candidates in Southern California, and one with Barbara Lee in Berkeley. After the event, we flew back across the country. Bernie asked me why we needed to fly that leg on the charter. We had leased the plane to give us the ability to hold twenty-five events in less than a week, something that would have been impossible if relying solely on commercial flights. But now, he was worried about the expense. Why spend the money? I asked him if he wanted to take a red-eye or burn an entire day in transit. He grumbled but agreed.

On that flight, Jeff Weaver, Josh Orton (who would go on to be the campaign's policy director), and I spoke. We had proven our team was capable of assembling a presidential-level tour, and the excitement was real. Bernie would make one more trip, to Florida, added at the last minute a few days later, but our run-through was a success. We were ready. The question remained, was Bernie? As it turned out, he still wasn't sure.

By this point, nine months after the crucial January meeting, Bernie had been seriously considering running in 2020 for at least a year. His lack of clarity was concerning. If Bernie wasn't sure about this, should he run? There could be no second-guessing the decision, and his confidence would be critical to the campaign's success. We were thinking about a single campaign. Bernie was thinking on a bigger scale.

The "magic," as he saw it, wasn't only about him. He was worried that in the age of Trump, the younger generation would lose hope in the possibility of progressive change—that politics would become something entirely cynical, leaving no room for the notion that if millions of people came together, they could fundamentally better their lives through the political process.

On that flight Bernie would ask Jeff and me for ideas on how to create that sense of possibility. He wouldn't accept that he was the key factor, the foundation of everything. We could perform the functions of the campaign, but the spark was never going to come from staff. It was always going to come from Bernie. Even after everything that had taken place during the 2016 cycle, Bernie would not believe that he had a special quality that inspired people.

*   *   *   *

WHILE THE CONDO MEETING didn't lead to any decisions, it did succeed in focusing Bernie on the potential of a second presidential run. A crucial component was the presentation by Tim Tagaris on Bernie's current and potential digital presence, compared with his competitors. Bernie was the dominant digital candidate. He already had an email list of millions of people. In January 2018, many of these people were still actively engaging, reading emails, signing petitions, and donating to Bernie and to candidates he supported.

Tim looked at our online competition and ran a competitive analysis. He saw three people as primary threats to Bernie's online dominance. First among them was Beto O'Rourke. While he was still in the midst of his Texas senatorial campaign, he had already spent nearly $12 million building a top-tier digital operation. It had already resulted in more than $30 million in contributions. Could he take that energy and convert it into a presidential run? Beto's online and field efforts were run by two former Bernie staff members, Becky Bond and Zach Maltz, both of whom we regarded as first-rate.

Tim viewed Kamala Harris as an equally potent online threat. She was not running for reelection to the Senate, yet had spent $4.2 million building her digital infrastructure. Analyzing ActBlue data, we could see her list was three to four times more powerful, in fundraising terms, than Elizabeth Warren's. Harris was also a candidate with the strength to raise money from both high- and low-dollar donors, something that previously only Barack Obama had done during his primary campaign.

Finally, there was Warren. She had built a large online following, but we were surprised at how weakly she was performing. The data told us that, compared to the rest of the field, she was in distant fourth place behind the other potential candidates.

Tim noted Bernie's significant advantage. While the other candidates were building their online armies, they tended to be made up of Democrats signing anti-Trump petitions after clicking ads on social media sites. Although this was a cheap way of achieving growth, it meant they were building a generic Democratic list. Bernie's online presence was comprised of individuals dedicated to making him, and only him, president. But the longer Bernie waited to decide to run and the longer we waited to reactivate these supporters, the greater the chance they would flock to another candidate. We knew that if a supporter were to donate to one of our competitors' presidential campaigns, they were unlikely to return.

Like all of us, Tim wanted to get to work. Bernie was not ready yet.

After the meeting in my condo, the questions became more and more pointed. Most Sunday evenings, a group of us would convene over the phone. Always participating in the call were Bernie, Jane, Jeff, and me. A mix of other individuals, including Tim Tagaris and Mark Longabaugh, also attended at various times.

In many ways, these calls felt like the movie *Groundhog Day*.

Bernie would ask a series of questions about how to structure the still-prospective campaign. About budgets and staffing. We would answer. While he allowed us to take minor steps and make a few hires, he remained, infuriatingly, undecided.

Bernie bases decisions on instinct, yes, but he is at the same time being incredibly deliberative. Important decisions take time. If there is a deadline, he will meet it, though he hates to be reminded of it and pushes back hard when someone sets artificial limits on his thought process.

Bernie is always writing—typically, longhand on yellow legal pads. This practice goes back decades, and his scribbled-on pads from his time as mayor of Burlington are now housed at the University of Vermont. These notes show a side of Bernie rarely seen—a politician who clearly grasped his own flaws and shortcomings. One of the central themes is his self-doubt. On one sheet from the mid-1980s he wrote, "It seemed to me this morning that planning and decision-making were two of the biggest weaknesses that I have. Not only do I not pay bills every month—'What, every month?'—I am unable to plan vacations or intelligent 'leisure time activity.' It would be fun going white[-water] rafting or sailing down a Maine river or on a sailing trip, or traveling, etc. etc. Actually, I am better now than I used to be—but pretty poor." He went on to write that his house "looks like shit because I don't hire someone to clean for $15 a week." Because of this, he did not want to have guests over.[2]

Now he was a potential presidential candidate, confronted with the most significant decision of his political life. He had begun the 2016 campaign in a car with longtime aide Phil Fiermonte, driving through Iowa, meeting groups of people, the meetings set up by local progressive organizations and labor leaders. Bernie's first presidential campaign had no pollster until the fall of 2015.

Now the world—and his world—had changed. Bernie would often talk about how hard it was to realize that every word of his was analyzed by the media. Pre-2016, nobody noticed a slipup. This was no longer true. It wasn't just about his words in public. He was often shocked at how private comments made to rooms of people he trusted would leak into the press. Just about everything he said was effectively on the record.

He had already built and established a legacy. The books he wrote following his 2016 campaign had also allowed him to put away a nest egg for Jane and his children. He could continue writing and speaking to millions, and he could continue pushing the Democratic Party to take an interest in the issues he cared about. If he ran for president and embarrassed himself in any way, he would be risking it all.

So, Sunday after Sunday, Jeff and I would get on the phone. Together we set deadlines for ourselves, only to be frustrated time and time again. Months were passing without a decision. In early December, I told Jeff that if we didn't get an answer by early January, it would be over before it began. We would simply be too far behind to assemble the operation we needed. But Bernie—deliberative to a fault, perhaps fearful of planning and of what could be lost in another run—just wasn't ready.

* * * *

CONVERSATIONS WITH BERNIE are often repeated over and over again. Bernie wants to talk through every detail and make sure he is correct. This can be incredibly exasperating. Once he asked me for my opinion on a staffing matter. I told him that the only bad decision was not making a decision. "No, Ari," he pointedly replied. "A bad decision is a bad decision."

Throughout the fall of 2018, it was clear that Bernie would, in fact, make the decision. A fear that spread through our small staff was that he would choose to run again and then expect the campaign to launch in a matter of days—which would be logistically impossible.

The role Jane would play was critical. She was not simply a spouse or partner; she was the political advisor who had been with him the longest. Above anyone else, Bernie trusted Jane. She had guided his career from the mayor's office in Burlington, to the House of Representatives, the Senate, and ultimately to his emergence as one of the best-loved politicians in the world. For Jane's part, their relationship and Bernie's mission in life were intertwined.

They grew up in the same neighborhood in Brooklyn but met only in 1981, during Bernie's first mayor's race in Burlington. Jane, a community organizer, set up a forum at the local Unitarian church. She had never met Bernie, but looking at him up on stage from the second row, she recognized that he was someone who shared her values and political beliefs. In that moment, in her own account, she knew that she wanted to be a part of what he was trying to build. After Bernie won the race, she ran youth programs for the city, and they began dating. She has been a part of every campaign since, serving at times as his campaign manager, chief of staff, and media buyer. "My wife has the best eye for detail of anyone I know, Ari. She can see things in ads nobody else can," Bernie often told me.

While we waited for the decision, we knew he and Jane were involved in an intense series of conversations. She would be the one person truly looking out for both his political and personal interests.

In 2016 Bernie had launched his presidential campaign by walking outside the Capitol and telling a group of assembled media he was running. That could not happen again. While Bernie hadn't decided to run yet, he had made a decision about how he wanted to launch his campaign if it did happen. Over the summer, Tim and I pitched the concept of beginning the campaign not by asking for money, but by asking for one million people to stand with us. Every other campaign would launch by asking their supporters to donate money. Ours would instead focus on grassroots action. This would have several advantages, including immediately refreshing the email list, adding up to a million supporters ready to back the campaign. What if we couldn't hit one million? Then it would be a sign that our campaign was doomed from the start. While we would raise less money than if we pushed a financial ask hard during the opening of the campaign, we were confident we would make up the difference in the following few days.

Bernie loved the idea. In our conversations in the lead-up to his decision, it seemed to be the one thing he was confident in.

As Bernie and Jane mulled, Elizabeth Warren launched her campaign for president in late December. At that point in the cycle, ActBlue released daily fundraising totals in six-month increments, and we were able to see very quickly what she had raised. It was immediately apparent the launch of her campaign had been a financial bust—it appeared she had raised a meager few hundred thousand dollars. This followed her botched attempt to explain away a right-wing attack that she had falsely claimed Native American ancestry. We saw two weaknesses in her team. First that they believed they were smart enough to think their way out of any problem. (The truth was, they were very smart.) Second, they were too responsive to the whims and desires of both the political media class and random activists on Twitter. While a significant part of Bernie's base is online, he also consistently tells staff to shut out the noise and not let decisions be guided by what was trending at the moment on Twitter. While others in Bernieworld counted her out after her dismal start, Bernie disagreed. "Elizabeth is very smart, and a number of Democratic voters will like what they see in her. She can still win." Later in the campaign, of course, she would infamously accuse him of telling her that he didn't believe she could win because she was a woman.

Right after the new year, Bernie and I spoke at length about what it would look like if he didn't run. We felt, at the time, that his influence in the party would increase during the primary, as candidates competed for his support or tried to block others from getting it. I also laid out a plan in which we could spend time in Europe and South America in 2019, working with progressives in foreign nations and helping to fight against rising right-wing authoritarianism. We could travel around the country talking about our issues. But I cautioned that while his influence was high at that moment, it would decline precipitously after the primary ended.

Finally, in early January 2019, Bernie sent an email to Jeff, Mark, and me scheduling a conference call. I phoned Jeff.

"He's not running."

"Why do you think that, Ari?"

"Just a feeling."

"We'll see tonight, I guess."

In truth, I was not feeling doubtful about Bernie, but rather about the entire enterprise. It reminded me of the first time I went sky diving. I was in a plane fifteen thousand feet in the air, strapped onto an instructor. My college friend Kabir went in front of me. I thought, hey, I'll wave when I get to the door. By the time I was at the edge, Kabir was thousands of feet below, free-falling. If I had had a moment to think, I wouldn't have jumped. But before I could say anything, I was outside the plane, falling through the sky. Yet it was the greatest feeling in the world.

That evening the five of us got on the call. Bernie dove right in.

"Guys, Jane and I have spent a lot of time thinking about this decision. I know you have been frustrated that we haven't moved forward yet, but I wanted to make sure it was the right decision. In many ways, it would be easier not to run. Ari laid out a pretty good alternative, but we've decided this country is in a place where we need to do this. This election needs to have a progressive voice in it. It is the best way to defeat Donald Trump."

And with that, we jumped.

* * * *

THE FIRST QUESTION WAS WHO WOULD SERVE AS CAMPAIGN MANAGER. Jeff had publicly stated he did not want the position. Bernie and Mark Longabaugh discussed the idea of him running the campaign, but there was a gulf between them.

Bernie interviewed a few other individuals, but none was the right fit. Ultimately, during a conversation with Bernie in his office, I proposed Faiz Shakir. Faiz had introduced me to Bernie in the first place. He certainly was an ideological match, believing whole-heartedly in Bernie's vision for a democratic revolution. Bernie is not, however, quick to trust people, even people he knows, and he wanted to make sure that Faiz and Jeff would work well together. A week of conversations ensued, and ultimately Faiz agreed to take on the role.

Meanwhile, we were putting the campaign together, aggressively interviewing and hiring staff and going about mundane tasks like office hunting. At the same time, Jean-Michel Picher and I began planning the rollout tour. It would be a big moment. We wanted to show the breadth of the campaign but also to say something original and true about Bernie. Vermont would have been the natural choice for the place to begin the campaign. The senior team had pitched to Bernie a launch tour that would tell his story, not only as a politician but as a human being.

This was a substantial difference between the 2020 and 2016 campaigns. Bernie is loath to tell his personal story. When the suggestion gets raised, he describes anything that might result from it as gossip. In his mind, people should vote for candidates based on what they stand for, not on self-aggrandizing personal anecdotes those candidates may tell. Here was another of Bernie's blind spots: he could not quite see that his story is what actually connects him to voters. His childhood, growing up in a working-class household, gives him and his beliefs a rare authenticity. His father's story—as someone who came to this country as a penniless immigrant unable to speak English—is part of the reason why his connection with first-generation Latinos is so strong. The deaths of family members in the Holocaust is why he feels so strongly about the rise of authoritarianism, and allows him to speak on the issue with such force.

We hoped the first weekend of the campaign would take Bernie to Vermont (where he lives), followed by giant rallies in New York (where he grew up) and Chicago (where he became an activist while attending the University of Chicago). But our campaign launch dates slid a bit, hampered by a government shutdown after Donald Trump refused to sign a bill to fund the government that did not contain money for a wall along the southern border.

The shutdown was the longest in history, dragging on for weeks. That's why I found myself in Bernie's Senate office one Saturday watching the Patriots' playoff game on a small TV behind his desk. As a lifelong Giants fan, I generally am offended by the Patriots. Bernie, after years in New England, had shifted his loyalties to his adopted home team.

Watching a football game with Bernie Sanders is a trip of its own. At one point, with the Patriots charging down the field, Bernie remarked how unfair this was to Tom Brady, who now was simply expected to win the game—it would be unimaginable if he didn't. Bernie would stress about every play the Patriots made. When the commercials came on and a trailer for an action film starring The Rock ran, he remarked on the stupidity of advertising within mainstream culture.

When the government shutdown ended, we determined the campaign would announce Bernie's presidential run with a video on February 19, followed by a tour beginning the first weekend in March. The second weekend we would go to Iowa and New Hampshire, followed by South Carolina and Nevada. We would conclude with a run of three events across California, highlighting the importance we believed the state would have in the nominating process.

Bernie views his own words as sacrosanct. There are few things more important to him than what comes out of his mouth. Speech writing for Bernie is an iterative process. A good response to a first draft was, "This is 85 percent of the way there." This would mean he would rewrite every word but use the draft as a framework for his final product. Less than 85 percent, he would throw the whole thing out and start from scratch. If Bernie said it was more than 90 percent of the way there, much of what you wrote would survive.

Bernie is only really able to deliver a speech if he is comfortable that the words are his own in every way. Warren Gunnels has been writing for Bernie for more than twenty years, and he only gets it right about 60 percent of the time. That is far better than the rest of us. The challenges involved in Bernie's writing process would come to a head during the launch process.

Mark Longabaugh and Julian Mulvey set about making two videos for the launch. The first was several minutes long and featured a montage of Bernie's accomplishments in transforming the country's political discourse, explaining why he was running for president. The second was a direct-to-camera video with Bernie speaking to voters about why this campaign was important.

The week before the launch, Bernie was scheduled to tape the second video. Mark and Julian wrote a script. It was strong, and did everything we needed it to do. But it clearly wasn't Bernie. When I read it, I knew he would never speak those words into the camera. He arrived at the shoot at Julian's house in DC, with a crew on standby, and insisted on rewriting the entire script, which slowed the process.

A few days later, the team received from the DML team the montage video, and we came back with several notes, the most detailed from Jane. She was unhappy with several elements, and she was right. For example, in the original version, during the passages about women's rights, they used stock footage. Jane pointed out we had great video of Bernie at the Vermont Women's March. The DML team was, not surprisingly, unhappy with the criticism.

The direct-to-camera video Bernie taped was equally problematic. Bernie and Jane both hated it. They didn't like the look, the feel, or his words. Bernie wanted to reshoot the entire thing. At this point, it was Friday, and I was on my way to Burlington for the launch of the campaign on Monday. Bernie would do an interview with CBS that would air on their national programs in the morning and afternoon.

Bernie decided he would retape the video at Polaris, a small studio located just off Church Street in Burlington, where he went to film TV appearances when he was at home. While fine for cable TV, the studio had neither the camera nor the lighting equipment we needed to produce a high-quality video. On top of this, his new script was more than ten minutes in length. I was one of only two staffers in Burlington with him. Everyone else was in DC managing the launch's technical aspects out of a small townhouse on Capitol Hill. We were worried the new video would look cheap. Unlike the softly lit house it was originally filmed in, the lighting at Polaris was harsh. Because Bernie wanted to deliver the speech standing up, the Polaris crew and I had to rig a giant flat-screen TV behind him with an image of the inside of a home on it, precariously balancing it on some crates. But Bernie was happy, and Tim Tagaris once told me that when Bernie was happy, things just seem to work out.

At the same time, we were struggling to find locations for our launch rallies. Bernie and Jane insisted on Vermont, but the amount of ice on the ground meant holding an outdoor rally was impossible. The best indoor site, the Champlain Valley Expo Center, was booked, leaving the gym at the University of Vermont as the only option. But it was not the right choice, because of its size and space limitations, and the idea was vetoed.

Bernie and Jane kept on me to look for parks in the downtown area, but the answer was always no. No one wanted to risk people injuring themselves, tripping and falling on the layers of ice accumulated on the ground. Bernie got irritated with me at one point, telling me on the phone, "Ari, I never want to hear the word 'ice' out of your mouth again."

Eventually, we convinced Bernie and Jane that we should come back to Vermont when the weather was better, delivering a much safer rally for his constituents. The first weekend of the tour would now involve two rallies, one in New York and one in Chicago, with a stop in between at an event in Alabama honoring John Lewis and those who had marched across the Edmund Pettus Bridge in Selma in 1965.

After a period of eight months spent deciding whether to run again for president, Bernie Sanders and his campaign were gearing up for what we all understood would be a massive fight—within the party and then, ideally, against Donald Trump and the GOP.

CHAPTER 2

"We're gonna win."

BERNIE SANDERS IS HUGELY COMPETITIVE. HE GETS FRUS-trated with himself when he misses a shot on the basketball court or doesn't hit a baseball as hard as he would like. During a mid-term campaign event in Iowa in 2018 he was filmed after play-ing basketball with congressional candidate J. D. Scholten. Bernie was disappointed he didn't match the young hopeful's ability, not accepting that the other man was half his age—and a former pro-fessional athlete.

Bernie would approach the 2020 campaign in the same way. If he was going to run, he wanted to win. He would not run for the sake of running or to make an ideological point—to merely drag the Democratic Party to the left. If Bernie embarked on this endeavor, there was one only goal.

By early 2019, we knew that Elizabeth Warren's launch had been underwhelming. Not only had she raised just a few hundred thousand dollars, but her first event in Iowa was at a small venue in Council Bluffs that held only a few hundred people. While most people assume Des Moines would draw the largest crowds in the state, in fact Council Bluffs boosts your turnout with much of the audience crossing the Missouri River from Omaha. Her advance team did an excellent job in picking a venue whose small size cre-ated an overflow crowd. However, we viewed the mediocre turn-out as a bad sign for her campaign.

While Warren was off to a sputtering start, Kamala Harris's launch was extremely successful. She raised $2 million in the first twenty-four hours of her campaign, after announcing on January 21, 2019, and then held a 20,000-person rally in her hometown of Oakland. Not only that: as a reporter for a major network confessed to me later, his bosses wanted Harris to be the nominee and were intentionally shaping their coverage to support her.

Two million dollars was now the fundraising milestone we would have to beat, or our campaign's launch would be looked at as a failure. Kamala had the advantage of high-dollar givers who flooded into her campaign on the first day. Could we match it?

* * * *

FEBRUARY 19, the day Bernie announced his campaign, went better than anyone within our tight circle assumed it would. Bernie's interview with CBS was near perfect. It was taped the day before. I stood in his kitchen as John Dickerson and a massive TV crew invaded Bernie's house. John began his queries:

"So, Senator Sanders, you're going to run for president."

"I am going to run for president. That's correct."

"What's going to be different this time?"

"We're gonna win."

I finally felt we had arrived. I had more than two years already invested in this project, and with those words, all the heartache, all the struggles were worth it. The campaign was real.

We managed to make sure Vermont Public Radio broke the news first, followed by an email blast. Bernie personally wrote the draft, which was more than 1,500 words long, mammoth for an email. The website launched perfectly, and donations flooded in through ActBlue. Millions of people watched our launch video.

One important element of that day was essentially an accident. Tim Tagaris had remembered a graphic created by a Bernie supporter in 2016 that had the words "Not Me, Us" on it. Tim loved the phrase and stuck it seemingly as placeholder text on the campaign's website and style guide. We debated a few slogans, but none seemed quite right. When we launched the campaign website, "Not Me, Us" was emblazoned across the top. It became more than a slogan. It became the ethos of our entire operation.

By the end of the day, we had raised an astronomical $5 million. Only twenty donors had contributed the legal maximum of $2,800. We were well on our way to our million-supporter goal. A few days later, we announced we had raised more than $10 million. The *New York Times* ran a long story about our early success, and Bernie pulled me aside to discuss one of my quotes in the article. "Our second day," I told the *Times*, "was bigger than anybody else's first day."[3] Bernie thought this bragging was not aligned with the spirit of our campaign.

We felt good. But a few days later, on February 26, back in DC, Jeff Weaver assembled an emergency conference call. Mark, Julian, and their firm were pulling out of the campaign. As we were on the call, our phones began to ring and buzz. Reporters were calling to confirm the news. It seemed as though our former colleagues not only had decided not to participate in the campaign but would make as big a show as possible about their departure. "We just didn't have a meeting of the minds," Mark told the press. We did not disagree.

As usual, I was tasked with sharing the news with Bernie. Bernie was matter-of-fact about it and called Jeff to talk. Jeff was apoplectic, telling me he thought their departure would cost us ten percent of our vote. I felt that was a bit of an exaggeration. Bernie had a different point—he didn't understand how they claimed to have quit a campaign that had not yet hired them.

None of us held a grudge against Mark for quitting. Our staff and the DML team never really did agree on the right approach. The disagreement revealed a fundamental aspect of Bernie Sanders's view of himself and his role. The DML team were not simply media strategists but in 2016 served at the strategic center of the campaign. Even if Mark wasn't going to run the 2020 campaign, we still expected them to play an important role. From DML's perspective, they should run the campaign, while Bernie should simply be the candidate. Other politicians might accept this arrangement, but Bernie scoffed at the idea. He would want to play an active role in most areas of the campaign operation. Another point of contention was that Mark repeatedly argued with Bernie that he should begin to identify himself as a Democrat.

Being an independent is central to Bernie Sanders's political ethos. For his entire time in Congress, he had been a member of the Democratic caucus. In all his Senate elections, he was supported and endorsed by the DSCC and other party vehicles. To get on the ballot in Vermont, he would pull a bit of political jujitsu. In the state, Bernie Sanders runs in the Democratic primary and overwhelmingly wins. He then withdraws his name from the ballot line and runs as an independent in the general election, while the Vermont Democratic Party chooses not to replace him on the ballot.

Bernie's independence is buttressed by the fact that Vermont has no individual party registration. Some of his hesitancy to declare himself a Democrat in 2020 came from a basic feeling he got while attending Democratic Party events. As Bernie told me, "It always was amazing to me. Whenever we would attend one of those county party dinners during the 2016 campaign, how the room felt. You would go and speak, and people would sit around the tables, and the room was dead and lifeless. We would then go across the street to our event, and the room would be packed with enthusiastic young people."

Of course, the lifelessness he spoke of was partly a result of the fact that Bernie Sanders rejected those parts of the Democratic

Party, so in return, they rejected him. Longabaugh was correct in observing that politics was a team sport, between and within the parties. By not putting on his team's jersey, Bernie Sanders rejected a team whose support he would need to become their captain. Bernie's bet was that he could fundamentally change the team's makeup.

Longabaugh was likely right, politically, in suggesting that Bernie was hurting himself among a certain set of voters who would otherwise support him by not officially embracing the Democratic Party. But he was also arguing that Bernie shouldn't be Bernie, and that just wasn't going to happen. While DML's departure was a low point amid a significant week, things were going well: those who doubted Bernie's political strength or ability to compete could see that the revolution was, in fact, proceeding.

* * * *

AFTER DML LEFT THE CAMPAIGN, our work turned to the launch rallies, which were at the center of our rollout. Every day Bernie would call asking for the RSVP counts. How many people would be attending? What did we think that number meant? He was clearly thinking of the success of Kamala Harris's first event. She was in Oakland in mild weather. We would be hosting an outdoor rally in New York—a risky move in early March.

The night before our rally, there was a major snowstorm, which we worried would clog traffic and prevent supporters from coming out to the rally. The next morning, at the site—a courtyard at Brooklyn College, which Bernie had attended for one year before transferring to the University of Chicago—I and other staffers shoveled snow, and people started to line up. There were easily several thousand people waiting to get into the event. As the crowd began to pack into the courtyard, a staff member from the college pulled me aside. The school had done some research, and it turned out that the courtyard we were in held some significance for Bernie. When he enrolled at Brooklyn College, Bernie had not yet developed his political views. In a 1985 interview with writer Russell Banks that appeared in the *Atlantic*, Bernie described his political "naivete" while attending the college's orientation. "There's this fair in the gymnasium where all the sororities and fraternities and student organizations have their literature and their people out." He continued, "There was this table and this group called the Eugene V. Debs Club, and I said, 'What's that? I never heard of Eugene V. Debs.' and they said, 'Oh, we're the local socialists,' and I said, 'Socialists!' I was shocked. Not that I was against it, you understand, but I was amazed. Here were real live socialists sitting right in front of me!"[4]

His development as an activist began his freshman year. The college official handed me a letter Bernie had written demanding access to the courtyard and athletic fields for students.

Headlined "Grassroots," the letter began by stating that Bernie was "very appreciative of the amount of natural beauty our campus possesses in the midst of a large and crowded city," and he could "well understand the administration's feelings when they ask the public to keep off the grass. . . . Although the reasoning is valid, I am not quite certain that the sight of students stretching out and reading on the grass might not add a type of beauty to the school which is more important than pretty grass."

Reading this letter, it was remarkable to me how little Bernie's voice had changed. And while he didn't get access to the courtyard fifty years ago, he returned to launch his second presidential campaign and would fill that space with more than 12,000 people. For the staff, it was another sign. The energy and enthusiasm critical to our strategy—the magic—still existed.

Right after the rally, Bernie took off for Alabama to attend events honoring the Bloody Sunday march across the Edmund Pettus Bridge in 1965. The trip presented one of the hard choices a campaign faces. I wanted to book a charter plane, to make things easier. Bernie balked at the trip's cost. Instead, he would arrive at the Montgomery airport on a commercial flight after 11 PM, take an hour's car ride to his hotel, and have to be up and ready for a breakfast event at 6 AM, only to fly to Chicago that night, again commercial, for the giant rally.

The rally in New York on February 19 was the start of two incredible months on the campaign. After the launch rallies, further rallies in Iowa and New Hampshire the next weekend easily eclipsed the crowds any other candidate brought out. But next, we went to South Carolina, where we would face our first major, unexpected test.

* * * *

AT NINE O'CLOCK on a Saturday morning in March 2019, on the third week of Bernie Sanders's 2020 presidential campaign, I found myself on my hands and knees on the floor of a hotel room in Columbia, South Carolina, mopping up a pool of his blood using a pile of towels and a spray bottle of cleaning solution I snagged from a maid's cart.

Two and a half hours earlier there had been a knock on my door. Terrel Champion, a recent Morehouse graduate who was then Bernie's body man, was standing outside. It took me a few minutes to get out of bed. Bernie was almost never up that early. He runs late and sleeps late. We often wouldn't be back in our hotel rooms until midnight, and days rarely started before nine. Before answering the door, I looked down at my phone and saw I had missed about half a dozen calls from Bernie starting at 6:00 AM.

"There is an emergency," Terrel said in his usual even tone. "You need to come to the Senator's room." Despite Terrel's demeanor, I knew this was a fairly serious situation.

Entering Bernie's room at the airport DoubleTree, I found him sitting upright on the edge of his bed in a T-shirt and underwear, with a blood-soaked towel pressed up against his head.

"Let me see it," I said.

"How bad is it?" Bernie asked as he removed the towel.

I didn't answer that question, as "bad" would have been an understatement. A slice ran down nearly the entirety of his forehead above his left eye. The skin had split wide open to the point where it looked as though his skull was exposed. As soon as he took the towel off, blood pooled into the cut and ran down his face.

"We need to get you to a hospital," I said.

"Ari, Ari, Ari," he replied. When he wanted to make a point, he always said my name three times. Jeff Weaver, his longest-serving and closest aide, would get his name twice. "Terrel" he would only say once. I never could decipher the meaning behind the variance. "Let's not make any quick decisions. Going to the hospital could be the end of the campaign."

"Senator, you need stitches."

"Are you sure?" he replied.

"One hundred percent," I told him. "Can you stand up?" The cut was not my first worry. That was easy to fix. I was worried about a more significant injury. Bernie got to his feet on his own, demonstrating that his balance was OK.

"Senator, could you please get dressed in your normal pants, a collared shirt, and your sports coat. We are going to get you out of here with nobody noticing."

I asked Terrel to stay and help Bernie while I went down the hallway and woke up Charla Bailey, one of our campaign's most experienced advancers, who has spent years working for Bernie producing events large and small all over the country, and who had been responsible for setting up the current trip. Charla loved Bernie, and Bernie both loved and fully trusted her.

We plotted how to get Bernie out of the hotel incognito. It was approaching 6:45 AM. Taking an elevator to the main lobby would have meant walking through the hotel's breakfast area, which was sure to be crowded. The other option was a back exit requiring Bernie to walk down six flights of stairs. That didn't seem wise, considering the size of the cut on his head. Charla and I decided the lobby was our only option.

Charla would pull a rented minivan around to the front of the hotel while Terrel and I ran Bernie as fast as possible through the lobby. While we prepared to leave the hotel, Charla would figure out the best medical facility for him.

I went back to Bernie's room. He was now fully dressed, sitting on the bed. I told him we would be walking through a packed lobby. He needed to fold up the towel to fit in his hand, so that it could cover the cut without peeking out. We would not stop in the lobby for any reason. Terrel would take the lead and open the doors. I would glue myself to Bernie's side, obstructing the diners' view of him as best I could. When the elevator doors opened on the lobby, we popped out, and, miraculously, we made it to the car without stopping once.

"Is that Bernie?" we heard as we slammed our doors and sped away.

Charla had found an urgent care facility a few miles from the hotel. When we arrived, I told Bernie to wait in the car while I went inside to assess things. Thankfully the waiting room was empty. I spoke to the nurse at the reception desk, explaining that Bernie Sanders had cut open his head and I needed them to triage him to a private room immediately. She looked at me as though I was hosting a hidden camera show but agreed that she would take him in back immediately if it was, in fact, Bernie.

With Bernie inside the examination room, I made my first mistake of the day. I didn't call Jane. In my defense, Bernie told me not to call her. He said this was not a significant issue and I shouldn't wake her up and worry her. We would meet her in Las Vegas that night. Stupidly, I listened to him. I would never make that mistake again. When Jane spoke to me later that day, I felt a real sense of shame. She was more than Bernie's partner. She was the person he trusted most in the world, including on all matters related to his career. She had been his principal political advisor longer than anybody and knew Bernie better than he knew himself. After decades together, they were still deeply in love.

While I didn't contact Jane, I did call both Faiz and Jeff, to keep them apprised.

In between calls, Bernie asked me to come in the back to the hospital room. He said he would need seven stitches, but otherwise looked fine, remarkably. The doctor told me there was no concussion or any other deeper issue. While we waited for Bernie to be discharged, the urgent care center's security guard walked up to Charla and me.

"Well, I'm voting for him now," he said. "If he can walk into here with a cut like that and still be on his feet, he will kick that motherfucker in the White House's ass."

Charla and I were relieved, of course, that Bernie was going to be fine. But now we had a new set of problems. His schedule for the day was almost as full as it could possibly be. It was 8:30 AM and Bernie was due to have breakfast with a large group of Black pastors in an hour. While they were, and represented, a vital constituency, and while Bernie would be meeting these particular pastors for the first time, I thought there was no chance he could make it now. I called the campaign's political director, Analilia Mejia, and Chairwoman Nina Turner, who had arranged the event, which was to take place at a Brazilian bakery thirty minutes from the clinic. I explained that something had happened, Bernie couldn't show, and they would need to handle things. They pushed back. Canceling would be a disaster, they each explained. Bernie struggled to persuade enough people in South Carolina's African American community in 2016. Now, on his first trip to the state of the 2020 campaign, he would stand up a group of Black pastors? But there was nothing we could do. I conveyed that the reasons for his absence would become evident in a few hours. Annoyed, Analilia said she would make it work.

Five minutes later, Bernie walked out of the facility with a giant bandage on his head. As we got into the car, I told Terrel to drive us back to the hotel, because I had canceled the pastors' breakfast.

"Why?" Bernie asked. "I'm fine. Let's go back to the hotel, clean up, and apologize to the pastors for being late." When I called Analilia to let her know, I could hear the joy and relief in her voice.

Back at the hotel, we had to deal with the mess in his room. The bathroom looked like a scene from the serial killer show *Dexter*, with blood pooled all over the floor. Bernie had cut himself on the corner of the glass shower door, which opened right in front of the toilet. The blood was not only covering the floor; it had also spread across the glass of the door and all over the sink. We couldn't leave it that way, imagining photographs of the bloody mess appearing online, connected to Bernie.

Jean-Michel Picher, the campaign's director of advance, liked to tell potential staff during job interviews that our campaign was different: we were all willing to scrub toilets if that's what was required. This was literally true. Before the campaign's first big rally in Los Angeles in March 2019, someone went to the bathroom of the RV we had rented to serve as a hold area for Bernie and his family, and left a mess. So before Bernie's arrival, we cleaned the toilet.

As Bernie got dressed, Terrel and I were on our hands and knees scrubbing the floors, the glass, and the fixtures. And yes, we cleaned the inside of the toilet. After about ten minutes, we were left with blood-soaked towels. These would have to be disposed of as well.

I scooped the towels up and brought them down to Charla's room, stopping at the maid's cart to return the cleaning supplies I had taken. I dumped the towels in Charla's bathtub and went back to my room to get dressed, while Charla drove the towels away from the hotel and burned them. To this day she will not tell me where she did this.

Having emerged from the urgent care center only about an hour before, I was so tired I could barely stand, after the early wakeup and the stress of the morning. Not Bernie. He was ready to go through his full schedule, even with a comically large white bandage on his head.

On the way to the breakfast with the pastors, I recognized just how good our team was. We worked for a presidential candidate who was seventy-eight years old and at that moment polling ahead of every declared candidate in the race. He had just suffered a major medical incident. This would have been a significant national story, yet there had been no leaks to the press—one of the clearest signs I ever saw of the loyalty Bernie engendered, not just to him, but to the larger cause. Outside the breakfast event, I paced in the parking lot on the phone with Jeff, Faiz, and then communications director Arianna Jones, discussing how to make the injury public and what kind of statement we would release.

Transparency is the basic principle to follow in such moments. In truth, the press is going to find out, anyway. In this case, they would see Bernie with a giant bandage on his head that afternoon and likely a black eye the next day. We would have to explain what had happened. Bernie's first public event would be a health care town hall before we flew to Nevada. The event was at around noon, and we would need to inform the press before then.

Our other central axiom in this situation was: Show, don't tell. It would be essential to release the information as close as possible to the health care town hall. Without pictures of Bernie onstage behaving normally, there was sure to be speculation on cable news about his condition.

During a 1991 interview with Judy Woodruff at Harvard's Kennedy School of Government, the late founder of Fox News, Roger Ailes, offered enduring wisdom about how the media acts: "Let's face it, there are three things that the media are interested in: pictures, mistakes, and attacks. That's the one sure way of getting coverage. You try to avoid as many mistakes as you can. You try to give them as many pictures as you can. And if you need coverage, you attack, and you will get coverage." Ailes summed it up by saying, "It's my orchestra pit theory of politics. You have two guys on stage, and one guy says, 'I have a solution to the Middle East problem,' and the other guy falls in the orchestra pit, who do you think is going to be on the evening news."[5]

In South Carolina, we had fallen into the orchestra pit. We released a statement shortly before he took the stage—and the incident was nothing more than a blip in the campaign news cycle.

That day, Bernie didn't miss a single event. He attended the breakfast with Black ministers and the health care town hall, performing well at each. Our flight to Las Vegas was canceled and resulted in a sprint through the airport to make a connection, but we made it to our rally in Henderson, Nevada. While fewer than half a dozen reporters attended out event in South Carolina that afternoon, the press riser in Nevada was packed with cameras.

Bernie, despite his age, has an inhuman amount of energy, an almost maniacal desire to always move forward, and a stubbornness that would not let a quart of blood on the floor of the Charleston Airport DoubleTree disrupt his day.

As for the cut itself: a week later, we were in San Francisco, and a member of National Nurses United met us at his hotel to remove the stitches. There wasn't even a hint of a scar on his head. "You are fucking Wolverine," I told him, referring to the Marvel superhero with incredible healing powers. He did not understand the reference.

* * * *

AFTER LAS VEGAS and three mega-rallies up the California coast, in San Diego, Los Angeles, and San Francisco, our first tour of the campaign had ended. Already, in less than a month, more than 75,000 people had come to see Bernie, he had stitches put in his head and removed, and he was steadily rising in the polls. Our fundraising also took off. While Beto O'Rourke had narrowly out-raised us the first day, it soon became apparent that he would not endure. Our supporters continued to donate in large quantities. We would end the first quarter of 2019, six weeks into our campaign, with a notable financial advantage.

We knew the one question—the only question—still remained to be answered: Could Bernie win?

* * * *

COULD BERNIE BEAT DONALD TRUMP? This question was constantly asked in the news media; and how to establish the answer as "yes" was also a topic among the campaign's senior staff. Our own answer was yes—obviously. We firmly believed that Bernie was the ideal candidate to take on Trump. In our minds, this election hinged on two main factors: geography and trust. Hillary Clinton's 2016 map showed the base of blue states that we believed every Democratic candidate should be able to win. There were a handful of other states we thought would put us in contention.

To start, we pretty much wrote off Florida. Bernie didn't mind that strategy. He is, in his words, "not a great fan" of the state. Based on the numbers and our research, we believed that winning the state was a near impossibility for us—and, for that matter, for any Democratic candidate. For Bernie, the state was an amalgamation of our worst-performing demographic groups: elderly voters, Cubans, and upper-class, middle-aged voters.

Arizona was, in some ways, the exact opposite. Latino voters were critical to our campaign. While the image of the typical Bernie voter in some quarters—including on social media—was a bearded, white, college-educated socialist, our most likely supporter was actually a young, working-class, first-generation Latina. But while we thought picking up electoral votes in Arizona was possible, the true path to victory was through the old blue wall in the upper Midwest.

Working-class, white voters in Wisconsin, Michigan, and Pennsylvania who voted for Trump, or more likely sat home, in 2016 were a winnable demographic for us. Our research bore this out. In internal Sanders campaign polling conducted in April 2019, Bernie beat Trump by 11 points in Michigan, 10 points in Wisconsin, and 8 points in Pennsylvania. Bernie was over 50 percent of the vote in each of these states, with remarkably high favorability.

Yet the national media narrative was hostile to our prospects. Pundits, many of whom had an ideological interest in our losing, consistently cast doubt on the idea that we could win nationally. We were too far from the mainstream, too far left to win. Handing Bernie the Democratic nomination was too risky and could guarantee a second Trump term. We knew this notion was our most significant electoral challenge. For the most part, Democratic primary voters agreed with Bernie on the issues. But their biggest concern was, "Could Bernie win?" If the answer was yes, we would win their votes. If the answer was no, they would flee to someone they perceived as a safer candidate.

It was with this obstacle in mind that, following our visits to early primary states, we would launch the first bus tour of the campaign, heading through the upper Midwest, in order to demonstrate Bernie's popularity among those states' electorates. We would not only hold large rallies along a route that took us from Illinois to Pennsylvania, with stops in Indiana, Michigan, and Ohio; we would visit areas devastated by trade policies that Bernie had opposed, but that had been promoted by some of our Democratic opponents. Beginning in Madison, Wisconsin, we would make our way through Gary, Indiana; meet with union members in western Michigan; rally in Macomb County, Michigan, which had swung from Obama to Trump; and talk to union members in Lordstown, Ohio, where GM had recently closed a large auto plant and moved production to Mexico. After a rally in Pittsburgh, we would move across the state for a town hall on Fox News in Bethlehem, Pennsylvania.

That particular media appearance was a critical, and controversial, part of our strategy. I had spent a significant portion of my career prior to working for Bernie running research and communication at Media Matters, a nonprofit dedicated to combating the conservative media's lies. I had written a book called *The Fox Effect* in 2012, arguing that the network was a propaganda arm of the Republican Party. In articles and TV appearances, I criticized their hosts, producers, and executives.

Now, as an intentional part of our strategy, we would use the network. Bernie loved the idea. A town hall on Fox was just the opportunity he needed to demonstrate how his ideas could resonate even in hostile environments. My former colleagues at Media Matters were not pleased. They believed that the appearance provided the network with legitimacy it did not deserve. Yet in our minds, we were using Fox. Bernie would not be shy about calling out the network and its propaganda while making his case to its audience.

Bernie had been invited by Fox—after the idea emerged from conversations between the network and our campaign. Elizabeth Warren, who we thought at the time had been extended the same invitation, responded by proclaiming she would not appear on Fox. I believed, and still believe, that this was a critical mistake. Activists and politicians play different roles. A politician's job is to reach out and talk to as broad an audience as possible. Going on MSNBC and CNN was necessary, but it could only help someone like Bernie so much. The Fox audience wouldn't be with us, but appearing on the network was a demonstration that our campaign was not simply after traditionally liberal voters—there was no audience Bernie was afraid of speaking to.

The negotiations over Bernie's appearance were complex. We needed to make sure we could set the room properly. First, we requested as many of the seats as possible. In the 400-person theater, about 100 of the seats were set aside for our supporters. We also quizzed network executives on how they would fill other seats. With that limited information in hand, quietly, so as not to arouse any public awareness, I reached out to people in the area we knew were supporters and told them ways they could possibly get tickets from Fox. Excited to see Bernie, they did so, further helping stack the room with a friendly audience.

At a hotel a few blocks from the venue, at an event space that looked out on the smokestacks of an old steel mill, we prepped with Bernie. Though he had wanted to appear on Fox from the moment we first discussed it with him, now that the town hall was approaching, he was worried, even more than usual. While normally he resisted preparation for town halls, in this case he felt like he needed more time. What gotcha questions could be asked? We worked with him for a few hours. "I don't know, guys," Bernie, feeling doubtful, said as we left the hotel.

As our motorcade arrived at the venue, about a hundred Trump supporters were protesting and waving flags outside, some voicing anger that they did not have tickets. I was nervous myself. While I had cordial conversations with Jay Wallace, the network president, among the other Fox staff in attendance was Washington Bureau Chief Bill Sammon, whose private emails I had included in my book. For me, it was like a mission behind enemy lines. When the program began, Bernie's worries appeared to dissipate, and he hit his stride. In the kind of moment Bernie staff had hoped for, host Bret Baier asked the audience to raise their hands if they got their insurance from work. He then asked, how many of those people would be "willing to transition . . . to a government-run system?" The audience cheered as nearly every person kept their hands in the air. This clip was not only aired on Fox but also on national network shows including ABC's *World News Tonight*.

We also clearly disturbed Fox's then number one fan. Donald Trump tweeted, "So weird to watch Crazy Bernie on @FoxNews. Not surprisingly, @BretBaier and the 'audience' was so smiley and nice. Very strange."

This was how we needed to make the case—to Democrats. Bernie is generally anti-theater. He wants to communicate with people in the most natural way possible and always pushed back on attempts at stage-managing him or, in his words, "just putting on a TV show." In this case, however, he understood the drama of the moment.

Bernie was so pleased by the notion of new media opportunities. Too much of the campaign was spent talking to the same ten outlets, who reached the same audiences. He wanted to break out. He instructed Faiz and me to start looking for other opportunities for unique appearances. At dinner the night after the town hall, two ideas surfaced. One was *The Howard Stern Show.* The other was Joe Rogan's podcast. The *Howard* booking never happened. I repeatedly pitched their producers throughout the summer and fall. They first claimed that it wouldn't make sense because the election was so far away and the interview would be perceived as "political." They suggested we try and find a date closer to the election. After continuing to pitch Bernie every time we had a trip planned to New York, we made a final ask in early 2020, and we were again turned down. I wish that interview had happened: I believe Stern would have had the unique ability to get Bernie to open up in public and reveal himself to the American people. Many would have seen a personal side of Bernie that few get to witness. By contrast, the Joe Rogan interview did happen, and, in terms of audience, became one of the most significant interviews of our campaign.

* * * *

AS BERNIE SAW IT, to win, we would have to reach out to new audiences. That didn't only mean going on Fox or Rogan. Bernie wanted to create his own media. For that reason, probably no development was more important to our campaign than something that had occurred nearly two years before it launched.

In February 2017, Donald Trump would deliver his first address to Congress. While the Democratic Party would have an official response, Bernie decided to do one of his own as well. We had a massive audience on Facebook and the ability to stream live from the studio on the sixth floor of the Hart Senate Office Building. And we knew millions of supporters from the 2016 campaign would want to hear what he had to say.

During Tom Daschle's time as Democratic leader, he built a fully functioning television and radio studio for the caucus. The Senate has a facility that all members can use, but the one Daschle built is just for Democrats. The facility includes a full soundstage and a modern control room. Most members used it only to beam back into their local TV stations.

We would do something different. Following the Democratic response to Trump's address, Bernie would offer remarks focusing on the issues he cared about. We would stream it on Facebook, in part as a test to see what type of audience we could attract. Convinced we could execute the broadcast technically, Bernie signed off on the plan.

Warren Gunnels, Bernie, and I spent the day in Bernie's office writing his speech. We went back and forth over drafts, me sitting on a chair, Bernie reading the speech, and Warren pecking away at the keyboard, one key at a time. Bernie's idea was to respond to Trump not by talking about what he did say but about what he didn't, and we drafted a speech along those lines.

About twenty minutes after Trump finished, Bernie walked through the labyrinth of reporters outside the Senate chamber and made his way back to the office. It was clear that he was nervous. Despite having spoken countless times in front of millions of people, Bernie is still anxious in the moments before he steps up to the microphone. Once he is onstage—and paradoxically enough, especially with a large crowd—he finds his comfort zone. But until then, particularly in big moments, you can sense, even see, the tension. Speeches are often practiced repeatedly, with Bernie concentrating on every word, chasing a self-imposed standard of perfection he never seems to reach. The writing process, in fact, is more about him rehearsing the speech than it is about writing. Bernie fights for every word as if the fate of the world hangs on it. Speeches, regardless of audience, are serious matters, not something to be done casually. This speech was even more critical.

In many ways, this moment was a demarcation point for the country. The 2016 election was over. Donald Trump was now president. The first political battles of the administration were behind us—most notably, the lying about the number of people who attended his inauguration and the Muslim travel ban.

The loose movement that some called, at least on social media, #TheResistance, was coming together. Where would Bernie fit? Many of the Women's March leaders had been prominent Bernie supporters in 2016, but many others were of course supporters of Hillary Clinton. Among a portion of her supporters, there was still a deep and abiding anger aimed at Bernie. They blamed him for losing the 2016 election, as did Hillary herself.

Now Bernie had to figure out where he fit into the party with Trump as president. It would mean working with people who had been a part of his movement as well as those who were deeply enmeshed in Hillary Clinton's world. Bernie's speech following Donald Trump's address was Bernie's first foray into positioning himself as a leader of the resistance.

In his office, Bernie began to rehearse the speech, making changes along the way. The process was slow-moving, and the minutes ticked by. We needed to head up to the television studio. Another staff member poked his head in and asked if Bernie was ready. "No," he barked. He needed more time. But a few minutes later, he recognized he had to go. Bernie, in his usual refrain, looked at Warren Gunnels and me and said, "I wish I had more time."

In the studio, the speech was already loaded in the teleprompter. Bernie sat down and proceeded to give the perfect version of his speech, like a great athlete rising to the occasion in a crucial moment. Nearly 10 million people watched Bernie's livestream that evening—a staggering number, well beyond even our rosiest expectations. For Bernie, this moment indicated that he had a new medium through which to get the word out. Leaving the studio, Jane kissed him. "See, guys. That is what you get when you give a good speech," Bernie said as we triumphantly headed back to the office. Jane's performance reviews were critical to Bernie. She was his biggest supporter, but also would deliver a blunt and honest assessment of his performance. If he hadn't done well, she would have let him know. Having seen Bernie speak thousands of times over the years, she also was one of his best judges—certainly the person whose views he took most seriously on this question (and every other).

At one point in working for Bernie, it occurred to me that he would have rather been a media mogul instead of a politician. This may sound odd, given his dim view of much of American media. But while his brief career making educational film-strips ended when he became mayor of Burlington, he remained obsessed with the power of television and other media. As mayor of Burlington, he hosted a cable access show. During the 2020 campaign, *Politico* paid to digitize the program's entire run so a historical record would be available. *Politico* was, of course, primarily trolling for embarrassing clips. While the production quality was not high, you can see a Mayor Sanders becoming Bernie, doing what he loved to do. He held conversations with real people, whether they were elementary school kids, small business owners, or punks hanging out at the local mall. Bernie is fundamentally a storyteller who is at his best when explaining complex problems and helping other people tell their own stories. That is what his TV show focused on. But now there was more to be done than TV shows.

From the livestream Bernie did on the day of Donald Trump's budget address, we started producing a raft of videos and other content out of the Senate office. It was around that time that Armand Aviram joined Bernie's Senate office. A huge Bernie supporter, Armand came to the office from NowThis, where he pioneered the techniques used to make viral political videos. Armand has no formal training in shooting or editing, but he had a real sense of what people on the internet like to watch and, more importantly, share, and he would skillfully hone Bernie's message in these online videos.

Bernie Sanders had always dreamed about having a television network, and now he saw it manifest before his eyes. After a suggestion to a network anchor that they do a roundtable on Medicare for All was ignored, Bernie decided to produce his own town hall, which more than one million people tuned into. This became a regular occurrence, as we put on town halls on a variety of topics, from income and wealth inequality to foreign policy, with guests ranging from Michael Moore to Elizabeth Warren to Alexandria Ocasio-Cortez. Bernie treated these like television programs, and often we had a live audience of as many as 400 people, with millions more watching online. The shows demonstrated to him the power of livestreaming, and our staff acquired expertise in producing such events once the campaign began.

Bernie's only disappointment was that other Democratic offices weren't emulating what he was doing. We were stretching the boundaries of what a Senate office could do to communicate with the American people. Bernie hoped that other members of his caucus would see this as a new way to communicate with their constituents and the American people. It doesn't seem like anyone did.

In 2017, as our online presence grew, Bernie took a personal interest in the distribution strategy behind our videos. He spent time each week thinking about the content he wanted to create and how many people were tuning in. At one point, we began to notice weird traffic patterns, with spikes and drops on Facebook that were seemingly unrelated to any obvious factors. Facebook was apparently out of sync with other social media platforms. While our audiences on other platforms were growing, all of a sudden people stopped "liking" our Facebook page. We quickly realized that the social network had changed its algorithm and was no longer serving our content. Later on, we recognized this happened to nearly all progressive outlets. The *Wall Street Journal* subsequently reported in October 2020 that Facebook had intentionally adjusted their algorithm to the benefit of conservative outlets over progressive ones.[6]

Bernie demanded a series of meetings with Facebook executives. One involved a sit-down with Adam Mosseri, the head of Facebook's newsfeed (and soon to become head of Instagram). He also had a phone call with the company's COO, Sheryl Sandberg. On the call, which took place in 2018, Sandberg was oddly obsequious, talking about how much she admired Bernie and inviting him to join her for coffee in Northern California. In these meetings and in public forums, the company always denied that it was doing anything to restrict progressive content, and that it was just serving its customers as best it could. During the meeting with Mosseri, it was revealed that Facebook had changed a setting on its back end that essentially shut off the pipeline of new subscribers to Bernie's page. They could not come up with a reasonable explanation for the changed setting.

In the fall of 2018, during the lead-up to the election, we noticed a flurry of Facebook pages running ads claiming Bernie was encouraging people to vote against Democratic candidates in swing House districts. Believing these ads were violations of the company's policies, we filed a complaint. The ads were initially taken down, but then they were put back up a few days before the election. A reporter from Vice looked into the ads' origins but when he went to the listed address of the company that produced them, he found that the group that claimed to be running the ads did not exist there: according to the building superintendent, there was no tenant in the building that fit the description.[7] Even when presented with this information, Facebook claimed the ads were legitimate and refused to take them down.

At a post-election meeting with Facebook in his Senate office, Bernie pressed Facebook representatives about how the company was making content decisions. A mid-level lobbyist told him he should be running specific types of content on particular subjects, perhaps changing how he talked about climate change or more prominently featuring AOC. Bernie asked if Facebook thought it should determine how he should communicate with his constituents. The Facebook staff said yes. Actually, as they saw it, it would be more effective for senators to simply outsource their constituent communications strategy to Facebook, which would decide who would receive his messages. Bernie got up and left the meeting at that point, leaving staff to talk.

The most junior Facebook employee in the room tried to make the case to me and other Bernie staff that we should shape his policy messaging around what Facebook thought would work on that platform. When we responded that that wasn't going to happen, she replied, "That's because your boss is a miserable old coot." I immediately asked the Facebook representatives to leave and never come back. In apologizing, the staff member then said, "I used to work for Chuck Schumer. I think he is a miserable old coot too."

This level of ego was what Bernie despised about the company. Yet we were also dependent on Facebook. Our campaign needed Facebook to communicate our message, even as they ultimately were trying to stand in our way. While we fully grasped the potency of social media platforms—they had the ability to stream hundreds of millions of views to the American people—Bernie saw something else: the ability for real people to use him as a vehicle to share their stories.

Bernie's theory was simple. Capitalism causes people to believe the problems they are facing in life—the inability to afford health care for their families, the debt they racked up getting an education, the failure to get ahead while making minimum wage—are all things to be ashamed of. They sit alone in their despair, assuming that these society-wide problems are due to their personal failings. But when people tell their stories publicly, they become aware that their pain is shared and that we can only solve problems through collective action. It is then that people can recognize their power and be inspired toward action.

Our use of social media to tell the stories of ordinary Americans started when blue-collar workers would come into the Senate office for meetings. In the spring of 2017, we started filming them talking about their lives, and sharing these videos on social media, where some were viewed millions of times. Perhaps the most emotional interaction occurred with a group of port truck drivers from Long Beach, California. These primarily immigrant workers had been told by the companies handling port transportation that they could "buy" trucks and thereby lift themselves and their families out of poverty. Yet the companies would deduct voluminous charges from their paychecks, meaning they often were left very limited income. Failure to pay these charges meant the drivers would lose their trucks and the entirety of their investment.

Their job was to move goods from ships to the terminal building where the goods were transferred to long-haul carriers. After working hundreds of hours in a single month, some of these drivers would go home with literally nothing in their paychecks. These companies were simply taking advantage of vulnerable immigrant populations. The Teamsters brought these workers to our office, and we filmed them telling their stories and posted the results online.

Employees at Disneyland had also contacted us. Their stories were equally heartbreaking. Working in the park for decades, some of these people lived in dire poverty in an area where the cost of living, including rent, was soaring. They needed our support.

In June 2018, eight months before the campaign began, Bernie decided he wanted to go and rally with the drivers. We planned the trip around a speech Bernie was to give at a retirement event for National Nurses United president RoseAnn DeMoro in Los Angeles, but we would also visit both the Disney workers in Anaheim and the drivers in Long Beach. Our schedule would also include a Black Lives Matter rally in LA with Shaun King and Patrisse Cullors, along with an appearance on *Real Time with Bill Maher.*

The point of the Anaheim and Long Beach rallies was to put direct pressure on both Disney and the port transportation companies by letting the workers' stories drive a narrative. This trip would also test our strength as a team. Could we successfully organize these events?

We had initially planned the rally on Terminal Island in Long Beach with both the Teamsters and the immigrant port truck drivers. But I got an angry phone call from the Longshoremen's Union. They had endorsed Bernie in 2016 and were relatively progressive. But while we viewed the rally as a way to help workers, specifically the port truck drivers, the Longshoremen's Union saw this as the Teamsters encroaching on their territory. In no uncertain terms, the Longshoremen's Union would not allow the rally to take place in the Port of Long Beach, nor would they allow us to use a park a few miles away in view of the *Queen Mary*, which has been turned into a landmark and a floating hotel. Within a few hours, we were able to move our venue to a Teamster facility a few miles away.

Then I got a call from René Spellman. René, who would eventually become deputy campaign manager and lead the massively successful California campaign in 2020, was helping manage the Black Lives Matter rally with Shaun and Patrisse. René was also someone who I could always rely upon to solve problems. Now she had a big one. When the vendors came to drop off the sound and lighting equipment, they were not satisfied with the insurance policy secured for the event. With no insurance, the vendors would not drop off the equipment.

We called around to try and secure insurance, but none of the providers we would typically use for our events would insure a Black Lives Matter rally. While this was problematic from a justice perspective, it was also a practical issue, of course. Bernie's flight was taking off for LA from DC, and we still hadn't solved the problem. As the plane left the ground, I called Jeff Weaver and asked if he could take care of it. By the time we landed, we had secured a policy for our campaign committee that would cost more than the entire BLM event itself. We never told Bernie that fact, because sometimes we just needed to get the work done, and he might have hesitated at the cost.

We landed in California, ready to go. That weekend in early June 2018 turned out to be one of the busiest all year, with three large public events spread throughout Southern California.

Our trip to California led to dozens of problematic political phone calls. Most politicians considering a presidential run spend hours on the phone. A lot of that time is spent talking to donors, which, thankfully, Bernie did not have to do. There are also "grass tops" leaders: heads of organizations, prominent community members, and other political influencers. The calls can be time-consuming; but even though they often result in nothing, if you don't make the calls, these well-connected individuals will usually complain about it later. Consider how many stories appear throughout the campaign cycle in publications such as *Politico* with often anonymous sources claiming candidate X has not reached out to Y community. Most often, these articles are not based on outreach to the voters themselves but on the fact that a particular influencer was not contacted, and decided to vent.

The politics in California, more than in any other state, are shaped by these dynamics. It's not only that California is a giant state. Its party structure creates dozens of local leaders, each with their own fiefdom. Additionally, the vast numbers of ethnic and social communities all have their own leaders. Each of these people expects to be reached out to and placated in some fashion. They want the conversation and, ultimately, the handshake photo for the wall behind their desk.

The standard politician recognizes the need to make these calls and just does the work. Bernie is not a standard politician. He does not want to do calls that have no purpose. And he does not want to talk to local potentates who, in his words, "think they are important because they sit on some committee, but don't do any actual work for people."

Manual laborers? Young people? Maids in hotels? He has all the time in the world for these groups. He asks them about their lives and how different policies affected them. But when it comes to the professional political class, he just does not care. "Are they going to endorse me? Then why am I wasting time with them?"

Our trip to California was all about the ordinary employees and blue-collar workers. When we arrived at the church where the Anaheim rally was going to take place, just outside the walls of Disneyland, thousands of people were there. They filled the theater, wearing union shirts representing different jobs within the park.

The stories these workers told were shocking. Some were homeless. Some lived in their cars. One woman who had worked for Disney for decades and was a waitress in one of the fanciest restaurants in the park talked about how she was starving, unable to afford to eat. She would get in trouble if she snagged leftover food off a customer's plate before throwing it in the trash.

Watching along with me and other staff in the back of the auditorium stood a group of Disney executives, in expensive suits, sticking out like sore thumbs while monitoring the proceedings.

After the event, we got in the car, and Bernie turned to me and said, "We are going to stay on this. Get more attention for these workers, and Disney will not be able to afford not to give them a raise."

With that, we headed west to Long Beach. At a rally positioned in between giant storage containers, port truck drivers told their harrowing stories about what their lives were like, being exploited by their employers. They would work hundreds of hours, yet, after the companies deducted expenses, would be left with almost no money in their paychecks.

Returning to the car after the event, Bernie had a thought. One of the drivers who spoke, Daniel, had made a particularly strong impression on him. A giant of a man, at least 300 pounds, he told his story and the story of his fellow workers with passion and a sense of solidarity.

"Did you see that guy Daniel, Ari?"

"Of course I did, Senator. He is hard to miss."

"That is the type of person I want on our campaign."

He was referring to the need for real diversity on our staff. Campaigns tend to attract young people who can pick up their lives and move anywhere, to work long hours for low wages. It is not a job conducive to people with families and childcare needs. To Bernie, racial and ethnic diversity were crucial. But he felt class and experiential diversity would also be critical to a successful campaign.

We set off for the Black Lives Matter rally in LA. The theater Shaun and Patrisse had booked held 2,000 people. There were already around 3,000 in line. It ended up being one of Bernie's best appearances of the year. In addition to the 2,000 people in the auditorium, another 2,000 filled the streets outside, so we ended up holding two separate rallies, one for each group.

Following the event, Bernie was slated to speak at the retirement dinner for RoseAnn DeMoro. The event, hosted by a public interest nonprofit whose funders were wealthy lawyers, would take place at the Beverly Wilshire Hotel. It was not exactly Bernie's scene. In the end, he decided we would not attend the dinner itself; he would give his speech and then leave. As for where we would eat, he said: "Anywhere reasonable to eat, Ari." The problem was that it was Saturday night in Beverly Hills. It would not be easy to find moderately priced fare. Instead of a meal in a room with high-priced LA attorneys, we ended up eating at the Cheesecake Factory.

Bernie had promised Disney workers that he would fight for them, and he kept his word: his office kept hammering Disney for its poor treatment of its theme park employees. Video after video showed the plight of these workers. In the middle of July, Bernie held another town hall event, in the US Capitol Visitors Center. This time he invited employees from Disney, McDonald's, Walmart, and Amazon. He also asked the companies' CEOs to attend. They, of course, declined.

The event again showcased the struggles of low-wage workers in the United States. One former Amazon worker, a Navy veteran named Seth, told an incredible story. He talked about the utter hell of working in an Amazon warehouse. No matter how hard he tried, he could never keep up with their quotas or the pace that his bosses required. It was almost painful to watch him speak. Stories like Seth's were resonating online, with these videos garnering millions and sometimes tens of millions of views.

A week after the DC town hall, Disney struck a deal with its employees' unions. As part of the agreement, they would pay all their workers at least $15 per hour. It was a huge victory. Bernie wanted one thing to be clear: while we had played a role, the workers' courage should be front and center. They were the ones taking action, putting their livelihoods at risk, and telling their stories—not just in front of hundreds of people in the room, but also for millions of people online.

The victory over Disney showed just how effective our livestreaming could be. And it only inspired Bernie to go harder at Amazon. Amazon is one of the country's largest employers, and forcing them to raise their wages would have reverberations across the entire economy. As we campaigned against Amazon, the company extended an invitation to Bernie to visit a "fulfillment center," yet we could never get the event scheduled. We proposed visiting a center in Wisconsin in July, before a Janesville rally with congressional candidate Randy Bryce. Amazon declined the request because it was "Prime Week" and they were apparently too busy with those celebrations.

In the fall, we would introduce legislation targeting Amazon: the Stop BEZOS (Bad Employers by Zeroing Out Subsidies) Act. The bill was straightforward. Large employers whose employees are on public benefits should pay for those benefits. For example, because Walmart underpays its workers, they are often on Medicaid and receive SNAP benefits. In this way, the American people subsidize Walmart and other companies that do not pay their employees a living wage. The legislation was never going to become law. Instead, its goal was to send a message.

The reaction from the establishment was swift. The Center on Budget and Policy Priorities, an ostensibly progressive think tank, released a report from its president attacking the bill. A Twitter spat ensued when Warren Gunnels pointed out that the think tank took money from Walmart. Other progressives cried foul: how dare the integrity of this institution be questioned?

In Bernie's Senate office, we could only laugh. The incoming criticism from the left was having no impact on the public debate but did give Bernie a franchise on this politically popular issue. Other senators and presidential candidates shied away from working with us because of the critiques. This, too, was to our advantage.

A few weeks later, on October 2, when Amazon announced that it would raise the minimum wage for all its employees to $15 per hour, Bernie Sanders was in a position to receive credit from the media. That morning I received an email from my contact at Amazon letting me know about the announcement shortly before it was made, asking if Bernie would issue a positive statement. Of course we would, as long as it was really happening. I called Bernie, who was still at his home on Capitol Hill, and gave him the news.

"No shit," he replied. "This is enormously important." He set to work writing a statement and asked if he could get on the phone with Bezos. Bernie and Bezos never had that conversation, but he did speak with former White House press secretary and current Amazon vice president Jay Carney, communicating how important he thought this move was. I was later told by a mutual friend that Bezos "fucking hates" Bernie.

CHAPTER 3

"No middle ground"

THE MEDIA ONLY KNOWS HOW TO TELL THREE STORIES when writing about political campaigns. The best analogy is a biblical one. Here is Jesus. Jesus is dead. Jesus came back to life. While my candidate was a Jewish carpenter—Bernie had worked as a carpenter in the 1970s, though he admits he wasn't a very good one—we could sense the downswing coming and that it would be painful. What we didn't know was whether we could make it to the resurrection.

Following the Fox News town hall on April 15, I received a call from a prominent progressive politician. "You guys are going to win this thing. You ready to be White House chief of staff?" There were two problems with this. First, I would never have been White House chief of staff. It is not a job I would ever want. Second, we had a very long way to go.

At this point Joe Biden had not entered the race but was still first in the polls. And Elizabeth Warren was making gains. A series of three events now facilitated our decline. First, Biden formally entered the race. The former vice president was our biggest threat, as we knew at that early point. While the media focused on liberal versus moderate candidates, we remained focused on the beer track versus the wine track, and Biden and Bernie were both beer track. And most of the other candidates were wine track. Reporters would often remark to me about the sheer number of

Bernie/Biden swing voters they met. They would act shocked, but it was no surprise to us.

The gains we had been making in national polls since we entered the race were from likely Biden voters migrating over to our campaign as Bernie attracted more and more attention. But a third of them went right back to Biden the day he announced.

The next thing that knocked us down was two bad performances at presidential forums. The Democratic National Committee tightly controlled debates, where all the candidates were onstage, and it sets the rules dictating which media outlets would host the events, the venues, the dates, and which candidates would be invited. But forums could be held by any organization that could entice candidates to do the events. Normally, the format of these events was not ideal for Bernie: the candidates would go up on stage one at a time, and take questions. One of the first forums on the schedule was held in Houston in April, by an organization called She the People, which describes itself as a "political home" for women of color.

While Joe Biden could skip it without repercussions, all the other candidates would show up. Among Bernie's staff, there was no question that we would have to participate in the forum. Women of color made up a significant percentage of Democratic voters, and the criticism from passing on the event would have been intense.

Bernie had already drawn criticism numerous times, sometimes unfairly, for his interactions with African American voters. The previous year, in the spring of 2018, Bernie had joined Al Sharpton, Martin Luther King III, and several other African American leaders to march in commemoration of Dr. King's assassination in Memphis. To Bernie, a Jewish man from Brooklyn, this event carried deeply personal meaning. He had attended the March on Washington in 1963 and saw King as his most significant role model, not only for his civil rights activism but for his struggle for economic justice and his brave opposition to the Vietnam War.

At this Memphis march, Bernie planned on hanging back after he gave his remarks, letting African American leaders take visible positions in the front row. He felt it was important to let others lead, and was sensitive to the criticism that could be leveled if he was seen as forcing his way on camera. However, Sharpton insisted that Bernie stand with him and others in the front.

After the march, we went out for barbecue. At the restaurant, Bernie saw a group of students sitting and eating. He decided to join them, engaging them in a conversation about the issues that mattered to them and what they wanted to see in an elected official. No cameras, no press. Bernie insisted that we not record the interaction in any way. He would often engage in these talks with young people, wanting to hear them speak truthfully about their experiences and dreams.

Briahna Joy Gray, then an African American columnist for the *Intercept*, had hitched a ride with us to Memphis. She and Bernie spoke continuously about the intersection of race and class and the need to work in both areas simultaneously. At the end of the ride, I called Briahna's editor, Ryan Grim, and told him that he shouldn't plan on having her around next year. If Bernie ran, we were going to try and steal her away.

After the march in Memphis, Bernie held a town hall meeting in Jackson, Mississippi, with Chokwe Antar Lumumba, who followed in his father's footsteps to become mayor of the city. A young African American progressive, his politics closely aligned with Bernie's. It was a beautiful event, but controversy erupted. Ruby Cramer, a reporter for Buzzfeed live-tweeting Bernie's speech, noted his remark that Barack Obama was a "charismatic individual," but that Democrats had lost thousands of seats across the country. A Twitter firestorm ensued, with one prominent commentator declaring it the end of Bernie Sanders's presidential aspirations. The issue, as people online saw it, was that Bernie had used the occasion of a significant historic milestone in African American history to criticize the nation's first Black president.

The reaction in the room was quite different from the response on Twitter. "He immediately won applause by declaring that the party's business model had 'failed' and then recalled, as he and many Democrats often do, that the party had lost about 1,000 state legislative seats in the last decade," wrote Jonathan Martin in the *New York Times*.[8] And as Briahna observed on Twitter, "From the audience, I watched the crowd of a 85% black city give Bernie Sanders a standing ovation both before & after his remarks. The crowd responded positively to Sanders's point that the Democratic party has failed to retain seats – even w/ a leader as charismatic as Obama."

Bernie left the room happy, unaware of the critical conversation online. Bernie and the mayor went for dinner at one of his favorite restaurants in the city. Bernie was decades removed from immersion in the day-to-day minutiae of city government, but you could tell how much he still loved it. They spoke about managing city services and Lumumba's community outreach methods. What Bernie loves about city government is the feeling of close connection to people's lives, and the way that a mayor's office could do so much to directly help constituents.

When Bernie encountered a city like Jackson and a mayor like Lumumba, it gave him hope. Here was an elected leader genuinely committed to making change in his community—this was Bernie Sanders's model for leadership. Change could take place from one block to the next—led by a mayor who walked the streets of his city and knew its residents and its business owners. Lumumba spoke about meetings he would have with the city's various constituencies and how to balance their needs. They talked late into the evening, even though Bernie had an early flight the next morning.

The controversy continued on Twitter over the next few days. When we returned to Washington, Bernie called the mayor, concerned about any backlash he might be getting for associating with Bernie. Lumumba told him it was unnecessary. The people in the audience had understood what Bernie had been saying, and in his view, the event had been an unmitigated success.

Bernie understood he could not miss the She the People forum that would take place in April. We would have to go to Texas during a period in which Bernie was still working in the Senate, and only holding campaign events on weekends and during congressional recesses. We were flying commercial, so getting to Texas meant burning half a day getting there and half a day getting back to Washington, DC.

Before the event, our campaign co-chair Nina Turner, deputy campaign manager René Spellman, political director Analilia Mejia, and national press secretary Briahna Joy Gray led a prep session for Bernie. These sessions with Bernie were always tricky because of his resistance to prepping for forums and debates. He therefore tends to delay these meetings until the last minute, creating a harried atmosphere. Bernie is also generally defiant to any attempt by staff to script his answers. Making it more challenging was that the moderator of the event was MSNBC's Joy-Ann Reid.

Reid hated Bernie. To her credit, she wasn't a phony and did not attempt to hide her contempt. In the past she had made disparaging remarks not only about Bernie but also about Jane, even questioning the stability of their marriage, tweeting that he engaged in "physical dismissal of women in his presence (including his own wife)." Jane had tweeted a reply, "Don't ever use me to demean my husband. I am very happy & very proud to be Bernie's wife. Your perception couldn't be more wrong."

Instead of rising to the occasion as he had on Fox, Bernie failed to follow the advice Turner, Spellman, Mejia, and Joy Gray gave him in the prep session, and his performance was mediocre; he fell back on some of his standard platitudes, and did not, despite advice, speak to issues impacting African American women in particular. At the same time, Elizabeth Warren gave a superior performance, getting plaudits for her ability to connect with the audience—to answer questions directly and bolster her statements with specific plans. The only positives of that trip to Texas were the two rallies Bernie did, each for several thousand people.

This was the dilemma we faced, in a single weekend. While other candidates would struggle to bring out crowds in the mere hundreds, Bernie could easily attract thousands anytime he wanted. And while the presidential forums were often the largest crowds many other candidates would see on the campaign trail, they were often among the tiniest for us.

While the She the People forum had not gone well, true disaster had struck a few days earlier, at a CNN town hall at Saint Anselm College in Manchester, New Hampshire. All presidential candidates face questions from the press that have nothing to do with the policies they hope to institute as president, but that will make a splash in the media, generating clicks and controversy. With Bernie riding high in the polls, one of those questions did a considerable amount of damage.

A Harvard student asked Bernie if his belief that felons should not lose their right to vote means that the imprisoned Boston Marathon bomber should be able to vote. This was the second time he faced this question. After talking about Republican attempts to suppress the vote, Bernie noted that Vermont is one of two states where the incarcerated can vote. "If somebody commits a serious crime, sexual assault, murder, they're going to be punished. They may be in jail for ten years, twenty years, fifty years, their whole lives. That's what happens when you commit a serious crime." Bernie continued, "But I think the right to vote is inherent to our democracy, yes, even for terrible people, because once you start chipping away and you say, well, that guy committed a terrible crime, not going to let him vote. Oh, that person did that, not going to let that person vote. You're running down a slippery slope."

He concluded: "I do believe that even if they are in jail they're paying their price to society, but that should not take away their inherent American right to participate in our democracy."

The audience applauded, but the moderator, Chris Cuomo, zeroed in on the point, asking, "My follow-up question goes to this being like you're writing an opposition ad against you by saying you think the Boston Marathon bomber should vote not after he pays his debt to society, but while he's in jail. You sure about that?"

Bernie replied, "I think I have written many thirty-second opposition ads throughout my life. This will be just another one. But I do believe, look, you know, this is what I believe. Do you believe in democracy? Do you believe that every single American eighteen years of age or older who's an American citizen has the right to vote?"

Always on message, he added, "Once you start chipping away at that, believe me, that's what our Republican governors all over this country are doing. They come up with all kinds of excuses while people of color, young people, poor people can't vote, and I will do everything I can to resist it. This is a democracy. We've got to expand that democracy, and I believe every single person does have the right to vote."

It's hard to think of more than two or three other politicians in our era who would've responded as Bernie did. He saw the matter as a fundamental question of democracy, and of morality.

Three days after the town hall, on April 25, Joe Biden officially entered the presidential race. Over the next two weeks, we fell in the polls from 23 to 15 percent. Almost all that support migrated from Bernie Sanders to Joe Biden. We would not recover for nine months.

While Biden was always going to siphon support from Bernie, Bernie's position on voting rights for incarcerated people was a political disaster. The very voters we were targeting, in particular working-class men, were highly unsympathetic to Bernie's stance.

Furthermore, this public stand reinforced the idea that because of views like this, even if it was the correct one, Bernie was too risky to nominate when Donald Trump would be the Republican candidate. A poll from HarrisX at the time found that 69 percent of voters and 61 percent of Democrats disagreed with Bernie's position. (By contrast, polls indicated that the vast majority of voters of both parties favored the restoration of voting rights to those who had already served their time.) But the fact that he would make a difficult moral argument was precisely why many of us were working for his campaign. As Bernie would remind us, our job was not merely to win a presidential election but to, in Bernie's words, create a "political revolution" and try to remake society along the lines of justice and equality. We were not there simply to win the White House; we were campaigning to shift public discourse and change the country.

In the days that followed the CNN town hall, numerous reporters asked me why we couldn't "walk it back." Bernie would never do that, obviously. And the idea that a presidential candidate in 2019 could "walk something back" without paying a price was ridiculous. If nothing else, we believed from the start of the campaign that authenticity was the key to victory, and inauthenticity would be deadly. It would be no surprise to us that the last two candidates standing in the Democratic primary would be the two most authentic in the race.

When I spoke to Bernie after the town hall about his stance on felon voting, he was adamant. If incarcerated individuals in Vermont had voted since statehood in 1791 without causing any problems, he did not understand why the rest of the United States could not follow suit. He also focused on the racial undertones of the issue. Clearly, the prevailing policies were designed to disenfranchise African Americans and other racial minorities—who were more likely to wind up in prison after committing the same crimes as whites—as well as poor people of any color.

* * * *

WE REMAINED IN SECOND PLACE after Biden's entry, but had dropped significantly in the polls. Now we would begin the grind. In what we saw as our path to victory, in early 2020 we would have to win the first three contests: the Iowa caucuses and the New Hampshire and Nevada primaries. While the race would be nationalized on Super Tuesday on March 3, 2020, the way we could convince Democratic voters that we could beat Donald Trump was simply by winning.

That meant, for Bernie, doing event after event. He would not focus on giant rallies, but rather on a slow grassroots buildup. In the late spring and summer of 2019 we found ourselves traveling across Iowa and New Hampshire to one small town after another. Bernie would often judge the success or failure of a day by how many voters he had spoken with, necessitating a packed schedule. We were traveling commercial, forcing us to methodically schedule our travel between airports that we could easily reach from Washington, DC, or Burlington, Vermont. The campaign didn't want to burn up hours at a time sitting in restaurants at Chicago's O'Hare.

Along with travel, the other thing that was difficult for Bernie, in this period, was watching the campaign scale up so quickly. In 2016, much of the staff worked out of an office in Burlington, where Bernie rarely traveled during the campaign. In 2020, the campaign office was in Washington, and in spring 2019 he returned to the city to vote in the Senate. While in town he would come to the campaign office for meetings and to film videos. By April the office had grown from a few dozen people to desk after desk of staff, covering two large open spaces. Bernie was shocked. Who were all these new faces, and what did they do?

Bernie does not have a large circle of friends and confidants, but especially after 2016, he was very wary of trusting new acquaintances. I never understood how I moved into his inner circle so quickly. Now he was faced with hundreds of new staffers, most of whom he had no role in hiring.

After his initial shock at the size of his operation, he wanted to institute a hiring freeze on national staff to make sure we were not overspending, just at the moment we needed to ramp up.

I had a conversation with one of our co-chairs, Ben Cohen, one of the founders of Ben & Jerry's. I asked him if he could speak with Bernie. Surely, Cohen understood what it was like going from a small operation to a massive organization—his company had started as an ice cream parlor in a onetime gas station. He sympathized with my dilemma and did speak to Bernie, relaying to him that when Ben & Jerry's was growing, he felt similarly bewildered, but ultimately understood that while expanding his company meant some additional inefficiency and a larger staff, it also was necessary to grow. Bernie was also concerned about expenditures. He worried I was spending too much on advance staff and rally expenses and became obsessed with the cost of events.

It seemed that Bernie was mostly upset about what he perceived as a lack of momentum. This was epitomized by his disappointment in the crowd at our rally at the Vermont Capitol in Montpelier that took place at the end of May. When he launched his 2016 campaign, 6,000 people came out to see him in Burlington. Four years later, fewer than 2,500 joined him at the state capitol, even though we had A-list talent joining us.

In April, we were in Las Vegas for less than twenty-four hours, to attend the Machinists Union Convention. Bernie spoke in the morning at the convention, and we headed to McCarran Airport for a flight back to Washington, DC. Only Terrel Champion and I were with him. As we went through security, a woman in a cowboy hat and her partner approached, very excited to see Bernie. After getting a picture, the woman gave us her cell phone number. She said she was a musician and would be happy to play an event for Bernie.

It wasn't until a day later that we realized that the woman was Grammy Award–winning country star Brandi Carlile. It turned out she would be playing a show near Montpelier around the time of our rally there, and so agreed to play before Bernie spoke.

For a number of reasons, the rally turned into an abject disaster. Responding to Bernie's concerns about overstaffing, we had left the event understaffed. A close family member of mine passed away and I spent that week in Omaha, Nebraska, for the funeral, so I was unable to supervise the event, which ended up experiencing a number of problems due to the small staff presence, most notably a dispute about the size of the crowd.

Yet despite the botched event, we saw a silver lining. We were solidly in second place. In a twenty-candidate primary field, we firmly believed we had an unmovable base of 15 percent. Ideally, we could hold these voters throughout the summer and then rise in the late fall as the campaign reached its climax.

*   *   *   *

IN THE LATE SPRING Bernie was invited to attend the Walmart shareholders meeting on behalf of a coalition of their workers to help demand that the company raise its minimum wage to $15 per hour, and to introduce a shareholder resolution calling for a worker to be placed on the board of the company. Bernie jumped at the opportunity. We would journey to Bentonville, Arkansas, and make the case directly. The Walmart executives in attendance were of course not fans of Bernie, but they rolled out the red carpet in the politest way possible, greeting us and giving us a private hold room.

Bernie even engaged in a firm but polite conversation with one of their executives, asking why it was impossible to raise their minimum wage to $15 per hour. During the shareholders meeting, he would have only two minutes to make his presentation before the vote on his shareholder resolution. We planned to go into the meeting and then rally workers in the parking lot. Obviously, the campaign would not secure permits to build a stage. We would have to go wildcat.

When Bernie emerged from the shareholders meeting, he made his way to a pickup truck sitting in the parking lot. With network cameras in tow, Bernie clambered up onto the truck bed and began speaking to the assembled hundreds of workers and supporters on a megaphone. The campaign would be a megaphone not only for his voice but for the working class overall.

This theme was again evident a few days later at the Iowa Democratic Party Hall of Fame dinner in Cedar Rapids. This is one of the fundraising events for the Iowa Democratic Party that every candidate attends. Campaigns spend tens if not hundreds of thousands of dollars buying seats in the room, creating their own artificial cheering sections. Other seats are filled by lobbyists and other major state party donors. Laughably, reporters gauge the reaction of the crowd to candidates, to decide who has momentum and who doesn't. This was exactly the kind of show that Bernie would not play a part in.

The morning of the event, other campaigns began staking out the streets for blocks around the Cedar Rapids Convention Center. We had made the mistake of staying in the Doubletree Hotel, which was attached to the venue, and woke up to a ruckus. Sign twirlers from Maryland, flown in by Congressman John Delaney, were dancing in the street. His and other campaigns, which had no meaningful grassroots presence in Iowa as far as we saw, moved their staff to the street to demonstrate their nonexistent momentum.

Bernie supporters were nowhere in sight because we had asked them not to show up. Instead, we directed them to a McDonald's about a mile away, where workers were picketing for a $15 per hour minimum wage. We then marched with the workers to the Democratic Party event. Instead of our supporters standing on a street corner cheering, Bernie led them on a blocks-long procession through the streets of Cedar Rapids into the convention center all chanting, not for Bernie, but for $15 per hour and a union. Our message was clear: Bernie was not there to fight for the lobbyists and party donors; he was there for the workers.

In his speech, Bernie decided to take on the establishment interests in the party directly. A week earlier, a Biden advisor declared that his candidate would take a "middle-ground," or more moderate, approach. Bernie had opened his speech at the California Democratic Party Convention earlier that week with a refrain written by speechwriter David Sirota, declaring there was "no middle ground." He pressed that idea in Iowa: "I understand that there are some well-intentioned Democrats and candidates who believe that the best way forward is a 'middle ground' strategy that antagonizes no one, that stands up to nobody, and that changes nothing. In my view, that approach is not just bad public policy, but it is a failed political strategy that I fear could end up with the reelection of Donald Trump. The American people want change, real change, and we have got to provide that change."

With this shot at Biden, the race had truly begun.

* * * *

THE HALL OF FAME DINNER was one of many obligatory events for Democratic candidates in Iowa. Throughout the campaign season there are a series of local fundraisers in the state that are essentially flexes by local politicos, exploiting Iowa's poll position in the primary season to force Democratic presidential campaigns to contribute to their coffers.

For reporters, these events become a cheap and easy way to cover presidential politics. There are many incredibly hardworking journalists who cover political campaigns. In truth, far from the romance of *The Boys on the Bus*, the classic account of the

1972 presidential campaign, the coverage of early primary campaigns in Iowa is a slog of rental cars and lunches of Casey's General Store pizza (which, despite the protestations of Iowans, is terrible). Reporters dash from small event to small event, sometimes in hundred-degree heat, other times in freezing snow.

Then there are those reporters, primarily more prominent names with larger expense accounts, who barely leave the bar at the Marriott in downtown Des Moines. They love the cattle-call events, where all the candidates appear in the same room over a span of several hours. It lets reporters claim they have been on the road with campaigns, without having to miss drinking time with their buddies. Instead of talking to voters, they can drive coverage solely by gossiping with other insiders.

For campaigns without large followings, the cattle calls can be some of the largest crowds candidates will see all cycle. But these events are not actually useful if your campaign has a following. Ailes's maxim that the media only covers pictures, mistakes, and attacks means you are more likely to get coverage for a major blunder than for a great performance. Nearly everyone in attendance is a local political leader with their mind made up on who they will support. There are smaller groups from out of state or even abroad who purchase tickets to the events as a form of weird political tourism. In fact, in Iowa in the weeks leading up to the caucus in early 2020, we would start noticing more and more out-of-state people showing up at town halls and asking questions. We would soon discover there were tour companies selling packages for sightseeing at political events. Imagine an African safari, but on the plains of Iowa.

For Bernie, the cattle calls were an all-around terrible experience. Not only had the audiences mostly made up their minds, but they had made up their minds against us. Even if they had been undecideds, political insiders and those who could afford tickets to these events were not our natural supporters.

The events also provoked Bernie's natural impatience. He prefers to arrive at events precisely on time. Unlike other politicians, he is aware of other people's time and doesn't want to keep them waiting. If he was late to an event, even by a few minutes, he would grumble to me, "No good." More often, we were early, in which case he was just as upset. He hated hanging out in hold rooms and, in his mind, wasting time. The cattle calls were always a scheduling nightmare, especially when the lineups included twenty candidates plus other special guests speaking. They would always run late, making Bernie uncomfortable.

The next big cattle-call event of the cycle, after the Hall of Fame dinner, was Jim Clyburn's World Famous Fish Fry in South Carolina. When asked in 2019 if the event was actually world famous, Clyburn replied, "Well, it's my world. . . . And anybody else who would like to claim space in it."[9] Hosted by the state's most powerful Democratic politician, thousands of people gather outdoors in Columbia, eat fried fish, and hear politicians come and praise Jim Clyburn.

This was also one of the first moments in the 2020 campaign when every candidate was forced to be in the same room. While the audience perspired outside, the nearly two dozen candidates were stuffed together into a single hold room, with a handful of staff. It was interesting to watch how different candidates engaged with each other. Some, like Cory Booker, actively worked the room, smiling and talking to everyone. Bernie remained on the perimeter, having friendly conversations with Kirsten Gillibrand and Amy Klobuchar. The most interesting interaction was the one that took place between Bernie and Biden. They had not seen each other in person since the beginning of the campaign, and it was immediately clear there was a sense of warmth between them that did not exist among other candidates.

The time came to line up for their speeches. Staffers handed out Jim Clyburn T-shirts that every candidate was supposed to wear.

The rest dutifully put theirs on. I handed Bernie his. He looked at me like I was an alien. "What's this?"

"A T-shirt," I replied. "Everyone is wearing them."

"Do I have to?"

"Yes."

Bernie put on the T-shirt as the candidates were getting in line. Then, in a moment of defiance, he took his off, handing it to me and saying, "I'm not going to wear this."

He then marched out into the holding area next to the stage with the other candidates. Bernie's speech was slated for late in the program. As he stood there without the T-shirt on, multiple Clyburn staffers, with increasing irritation, asked me why Bernie wasn't wearing the shirt. I gave them the same truthful explanation: because he was uncomfortable doing so. They replied that he had to put it on before going onstage. I gave them a "what do you expect me to do about it?" look.

In fact, I had debated with my candidate the issue and lost. Bernie stood to the side of the stage joking around with Booker. Finally, when it was his turn to speak, he walked onstage without the shirt on. Joe Biden was standing by the steps of the stage. He grasped Bernie's hand and patted him on the back as Bernie went up and said, "You go knock 'em dead."

Twitter lit up over Bernie's appearance. Why wasn't Bernie wearing the shirt? Was he insulting Jim Clyburn? People were reading all sorts of theories into the moment that just weren't true.

Though I had argued with him, I think Bernie was philosophically right even if politically wrong. Here they were, a group of twenty-plus men and women, competing to be the leader of the free world, and they were forced to wear an ill-fitting T-shirt. Why not put them in clown costumes and have them dance? It was one of those moments where I, as a staffer, both was supremely annoyed with Bernie and loved him. Why couldn't he be the easy candidate who just dressed like he was told to and read off the teleprompter?

But Bernie's stubbornness and difficultness were the exact quali-
ties that allowed him to buck the political establishment on important issues. Shirt or no shirt, his remarks went fine, and when all
the candidates had to go up on stage again after the speeches for a
group picture, he put the T-shirt on, and left it on this time.

The campaign had a complex view of South Carolina's importance for us. From the start, we knew it was the only early primary
state we were unlikely to win. Many outside the campaign, including in the press, would credit that to a lack of support among African American voters. We saw it as a different kind of demographic
problem: the state's Democratic electorate was too old and too
conservative for us to win much more than 20 percent of the vote.
Furthermore, Biden had an enduring popularity among the state's
African American voters that would be hard for any candidate to
break. Our hopes, though small, rested on Cory Booker or Kamala
Harris chipping into Biden's significant support, as Barack Obama
had done to Hillary Clinton in 2008.

Bernie, however, loved South Carolina. Our campaign co-chair,
former Ohio state senator Nina Turner, or SNT as she was referred
to, had adopted our operation in the state as her own. From top
to bottom, she was running the program and outworking nearly
everyone else on the campaign. Bernie enjoyed his events in the
state as well as his travels with the surrogates SNT had recruited,
including actor Danny Glover, intellectual Cornel West, and activist Phillip Agnew.

Throughout the entire campaign, SNT's work in South Carolina was perhaps the most impressive, despite our eventual
performance there. Nine members of the South Carolina Legislative Black Caucus, a significant percentage of the organization,
endorsed Bernie. This was a real political risk for them, given
that Bernie was not as well known or liked as he was in Iowa and
New Hampshire. Our support from local Democratic officials was
actually much more extensive in South Carolina than that for any

other candidates. Bernie would often remark about the sheer guts of those in South Carolina who had come forward to endorse his campaign.

Bernie was also struck by the poverty he saw in the state. "Ari, I wish I had the time to come back here," he said to me more than once. He also was eager to take in the history of the South Carolina civil rights movement. Two days after the Fish Fry, he was scheduled to hold a rally at Clinton College, a historically Black college in Rock Hill.

Rock Hill was the site of the Friendship Nine sit-in. In 1961, after refusing to leave the segregated lunch counter at McCrory's Five & Dime, ten Black students from a local community college were arrested; nine did not pay the fine, becoming the first people to serve jail time for holding a sit-in during the civil rights era. Along with Nina Turner and Danny Glover, Bernie toured the area before the rally. Walking past a mural and sitting at the lunch counter, Bernie was absorbed in the history and the legacy of that moment, and the brave young people involved in it. Before the rally, Bernie had the opportunity to meet with one of the Freedom Nine protesters, one of the highlights of this particular trip to the state.

Bernie often downplayed his own activism in the civil rights movement. As a student at the University of Chicago from 1961 to 1964, Bernie acknowledges he was less focused on learning in the classroom than learning outside it. He explained to campaign press secretary Briahna Joy Gray, on her campaign podcast, that he "spent a whole lot of time in the stacks, . . . buried eighteen miles down in the University of Chicago Harper Library, where I was reading everything except the books I was supposed to be reading. Didn't do particularly well in school but learned a whole lot about history and sociology and politics." As he put it: "What I was exposed to for the first time in my life was the civil rights movement. Became involved in that in a little way. Exposed to the labor movement. Got involved in that in a little way. Exposed to the peace movement. Got involved in that in a little way."[10]

Bernie became the chairman of the campus chapter of the Congress of Racial Equality. In that role he led the first sit-in at the university, in the president's office, to protest the university's segregated housing. This came after the students sent a Black couple to look for housing, only to be denied, followed by a white couple, who were offered an apartment.

His activism did not stop there. Bernie talked about his actions on campus in a profile in the *Atlantic*.

One time there was an incident on the streets that resulted in a picture in The Chicago Defender, *the black newspaper, of a police officer twisting a young black woman's arm, and we made a poster with it, and I was working near the university pasting up these things to announce a demonstration against police brutality. Unbeknownst to me, a cop car was following along behind me, and as fast as I put the posters up, the cops were pulling them down. Finally, the cop car pulls up to me, and they get out and accost me. Needless to say, I'm terrified. One of the cops puts his finger in my face and says, "It's outside agitators like you who're screwing this city up. The races got along fine before you people came here!" Like this is Alabama or someplace. Anyhow, I was late for my class, a political science class, and I remember the teacher was talking about local government, and when I walked in and sat down, I saw right then and there the difference between real life and the official version of life. And I knew I believed in one and didn't believe any more in the other.*[11]

At the time, Chicago's primary and secondary school classrooms were effectively segregated, as African American children were educated in dilapidated trailers. Mayor Richard Daley and School Superintendent Benjamin Willis were complicit in this racist system. Bernie joined a group blocking the installation of new trailers and was arrested and dragged off by the police. He was a white Jewish kid from Brooklyn, but the struggles of the African American community were central to his political philosophy.

CHAPTER 4

"Want to do something crazy?"

"YOU GUYS CARE TOO MUCH ABOUT THESE DEBATES," Bernie said to Jeff and me as we tried to get him to focus on preparation for the first round of presidential debates, which would take place in Miami on June 26–27. Because there were so many Democrats running for president, the event was split into two nights, with candidates assigned by a random draw. Bernie would share the stage with Joe Biden the second night. To the political world, this was a huge moment in the campaign cycle. To Bernie, it was yet another example of candidates for president being treated like contestants on a reality TV show.

Campaign reporters were excited. For many in the media this would mark the beginning of the presidential race, even though for some campaigns it had already been going on for more than six months. For our senior staff, it represented a potentially determinative moment. With Biden's entry into the race, Bernie had fallen in the polls, and while our floor of 15 percent had remained intact, as we believed it would, other candidates were now on the rise—most notably, Elizabeth Warren.

Warren's team put policy at the center of their campaign's strategy. Release a detailed hundred-page piece of legislation in the Senate, and no reporter would pay attention. Put out a short, generic white paper making bold policy points, and you could drive news coverage. Suddenly every other campaign was being asked whether they supported or opposed the positions Warren was staking out. It was a brilliant move, as her campaign was now driving the narrative of the Democratic primary.

This reality did not, to us, diminish her actual policies in any way. In truth, Warren was probably the smartest candidate in the race—a notion Bernie would likely have agreed with; he regularly talked about her sheer intelligence. She had a deep understanding of the need for structural change and was a hugely knowledgeable policy wonk.

The slogan that emerged from her policies, "Elizabeth Warren has a plan for that," was clearly appealing to a particular segment of the Democratic electorate, but not to Bernie's voters. It was a play for the wine track, while Bernie kept his focus on the beer track. Even though her voters and ours came from different ends of the party, we were concerned about a narrative problem if Warren passed us in the polls. Among professional-class progressives in Washington, DC, Warren was the preferred candidate. They and the organizations they worked for had not come out in support of Warren yet because they didn't want to risk alienating a portion of their memberships. If Warren overtook us, we worried there would be calls for Bernie to drop out from the commentariat. Under this logic, which we obviously believed was flawed, we should cede the progressive lane to Warren, allowing her to win the nomination.

Although many commentators saw more similarity than difference, to the Bernie staff a vast ideological gulf existed between Bernie Sanders and Elizabeth Warren. Warren wanted structural change, achieved through technocratic means. Bernie wanted a political revolution led by ordinary people. Warren had a plan for that. Our campaign subscribed to the words of Mike Tyson when he was asked if he was worried about Evander Holyfield's plan before a fight: "Everybody has a plan until they get punched in the mouth." While Warren and Bernie would not be onstage together at this first debate, our staff viewed it as an opportunity to regain the momentum.

Bernie did not believe the upcoming debate mattered as much as we thought it did, a belief that was manifest in his resistance to prep. Yet the details of these sessions seemed to be all the media could focus on, for us and for the other top candidates. My phone did not stop ringing with reporters requesting color from Bernie's debate prep sessions for their stories. But the "color" was, in fact, boring. We would sit in a room with Bernie, and we would go over possible questions that could be asked. We didn't do mock debates ahead of Miami, as we felt that wouldn't make sense. With ten candidates onstage, it would be a free-for-all. It wasn't a one-on-one debate in which Bernie would be forced to respond on every issue. While this could help him avoid some sticky situations, it also meant that every candidate was at risk of fading into the background.

The biggest problem for us was that due to the overstuffed format, the perception of the debate would come down even more than usual to its big moments, but Bernie would not allow himself to be scripted. It always made him deeply uncomfortable. He had spent his career participating in political debates and thinking on his feet. It just didn't feel natural for him to deliver a canned line. He would repeatedly cut off debate prep sessions to spend time with his grandchildren, who had flown to Miami. While irritating to staff, this seemed like Bernie's way of getting comfortable with what he needed to do on the night of the debate, perhaps especially because of all the hoopla that surrounded the proceedings.

That day was oddly eventful. Nearly every candidate visited the Homestead Temporary Shelter for Unaccompanied Children, where minors, primarily from Central America, were detained. While Bernie and Jane stood on ladders to look across the fence and into the yard of the facility, dozens of reporters and photographers fought to get into the scrum around them. It was a dangerous situation. At one point a photographer moved in to get a picture of Bernie and came within inches of knocking Jane over. I put my hand out to prevent them from making contact. He screamed "fuck you" and proceeded to smack me in the face with his elbow.

Later that day, Bernie, on a laptop set up in the debate prep room, Facetimed with Cardi B. She had endorsed him in 2016 with an Instagram video in which she instructed her followers to "Vote for daddy Bernie bitch," and in 2018 they had exchanged social media pleasantries after she had discussed the importance of Franklin Roosevelt and Social Security during an interview.

We all saw the conversation with Cardi B as an opportunity to speak with a largely new audience and bring people into the campaign. Dispensing quickly with pleasantries, Bernie and Cardi B went back and forth discussing policies surrounding health care and college for all—Bernie wearing a blue collared shirt and Cardi in a white bathrobe. I don't think either of them knew what to expect beforehand. But Bernie's focus never wavers, and Cardi B was clearly knowledgeable and passionate about the same issues that animated Bernie.

Finally, we were ready to head over to the debate venue. When we arrived and entered our tiny greenroom, Bernie as always insisted on disconnecting the TV. He didn't want to hear the inane droning of cable news commentators, which was often disconnected even from the reality of the debate itself. Bernie was soon called into the hallway where the candidates lined up in the order they would walk onstage. Candidates were on one side of the hall, staff on the other. Makeup artists walked up and down, applying some last-minute touch-ups. Joe Biden stood right behind Bernie. As they were about to go onstage, Biden rubbed Bernie down the full length of his back with his hands. Barely paying attention, Bernie used his right hand to swat Biden away. Pete Buttigieg, who was standing behind Biden, turned around, smiling at the unusual moment. Then they all began walking. If I hadn't caught the moment on video, I would never have believed it happened.

For Bernie, the debate was inconsequential. He managed to avoid any significant controversy but was not an important part of the conversation, as he admitted in the aftermath, expressing some frustration that the media coverage focused most on personal confrontations between the candidates. The night's pivotal moment was Kamala Harris's attack on Biden for his dalliances with segregationists in the 1970s. "That little girl was me," she said, referring to children who were bused to desegregated schools, a policy Biden had opposed in the 1970s. It was clearly the kind of prepped, canned line that Bernie refused to work on himself, but it was an indelible moment, and it was clear she had won the debate, across both nights.

Walking toward the spin room, I ran into Jim Margolis, one of Kamala's top strategists. We had both worked for Harry Reid a decade and a half earlier. He had a smile across his face. I congratulated him on the big win, and he patted me on the back, saying my guy did good as well. "Not as good as yours," I said. Jim would strike a completely different tone a few months later, after the debate in Atlanta, when he came up to me and joked that since I was a socialist, maybe our campaign could "share the wealth" with Kamala's, which was by that point struggling financially.

But after the first debate, Kamala saw a deluge of money come in, and she sharply rose in the polls, creating, essentially, a three-way tie for second between her, Warren, and Bernie.

The following weeks would test two of our theories about the race. The first had to do with a technical detail of overwhelming importance. Using a commercial service, our online team monitored our competitors' email practices and success rates. We noticed Gmail and other email providers were far more likely to send Kamala's emails into spam folders or just not deliver them at all, as compared to email from other presidential campaigns.

This was deadly for a campaign reliant on online contributions. When it comes to small donors, the first donation from a voter is important, not for the money itself, but because it brings that person in the door. Subsequent contributions are where a campaign raises the bulk of its small-dollar contributions. For example, the average donor to the Bernie campaign made five contributions over thirteen months. If Harris's emails were not even being delivered in many cases, it would substantially reduce the number of people donating for a second time, limiting the fundraising advantage she had won from her debate performance. The week after the debate would mark the end of the second quarter, and each campaign's reported haul would set the tone for the rest of the summer. This was the moment her campaign should have been prepared to take advantage of. Her campaign might appear to be soaring, but it would quickly crash back down.

The second theory was that inauthenticity was more deadly than anything else, even problems with her online fundraising. Medicare for All was highly popular among the base of the Democratic Party. Harris rightfully received a lot of credit being the first candidate to sign on in support of Bernie's legislation in 2017. After the first debate, she appeared to back away from the position.

During our night of the debate, moderator Lester Holt had asked, "Many people watching at home have health insurance coverage through their employer. Who here would abolish their private health insurance in favor of a government-run plan?" Bernie and Harris were the only two candidates on the stage to raise their hands. There were, and remain, two immovable facts about health care policy in the United States. First, Americans undoubtedly are fearful about changes to the health care system. People with even basic coverage are scared of losing what they have, and health care industry lobbyists have used this fear for decades to campaign against any legislation that will change—fix—health care. At the same time, Americans hate private insurance companies. Nearly everyone has had an experience struggling to get a bill paid or feeling like they or their family's well-being was in the hands of an uncaring bureaucrat.

Harris's campaign feared the critique from mainstream media surrounding Medicare for All—seen as too expensive, or simply as too radical and therefore politically unwise—and felt the need to move away from her previous position. This led to a flood of headlines such as "Kamala Harris Walks Back Her Hand-Up Moment on Health Insurance in Democratic Debate,"[12] from NBC. Of course, this led some voters to question not only her position on health care, but her position, her authenticity, on any issue.

Most voters ignore the specifics of policy. Democratic voters do care that candidates mean what they say. A month after the first debate, Kamala released her health insurance plan, which moved even further away from Medicare for All. By the end of the summer, she had lost half of her post-debate bump, and was passed by Pete Buttigieg a month later. While there might only effectively be three stories told about campaigns, there are countless reasons why candidates gain and lose support. Oddly, the media commentary on Harris pointed to her brief support for Medicare for All as a reason she lost support. Yet she rose to second in the polls following a debate where she clearly stood alone with Bernie Sanders on the issue, then fell in the polls as she backed away from that position. I believe her drop-off had less to do her particular policy preferences and more to do with the fact that voters wanted candidates who stood by their principles. Once this perception of Harris was broken, it was impossible for her to regain during the primary race.

* * * *

AS THE PACE of campaigning increased, I was in awe of Bernie's energy. I had worked for him for two years by this point and had spent much of that time on the road alongside him, but even though he was almost twice my age, I was now finding it hard to keep up. Fourth of July weekend would add an exclamation point to this reality. His schedule for the weekend was complicated. On Independence Day, there are parades and celebrations across the country, of course. And Bernie Sanders loves a parade.

For Bernie, politics is a tactile experience. Too much that goes into campaigning, especially for the presidency, is staged and con- trived. Questions at town halls are screened in advance, rallies are scripted, and nothing is left to chance. One of Bernie's biggest fears was that he was living inside a bubble. Parades allowed him to escape. He would walk down the street and people would react. They could wave and smile, or cheer you on; they could boo or, in the worst case, yell four-letter words.

Bernie wanted to maximize the number of parades we would march in on the Fourth of July, which we would spend in Iowa. But the National Education Association, the country's largest union, with more than 3 million members, had a different plan for presidential candidates. They had scheduled their forum for July 5 in Houston, a city without a convenient direct flight to Iowa. In fact, there were no easy flights to Houston from anywhere in the country it would be worth campaigning in on the Fourth. Due to their cost, Bernie had resisted using charter planes thus far, but now there would be no choice. Houston in July was sure to be a miserable experience, but one we would have to endure.

Bernie would march in five parades in under twenty-four hours, then board a charter to speak with the teachers the next morn- ing. His schedule began with an evening parade on July 3 in West Des Moines. When he hit the parade route, Bernie's face lit up. He dashed back and forth across the street, shaking hands and greeting people. At the end of the several-mile stretch, I was beat and sore. Our embedded reporters, Annie Grayer from CNN and Gary Grumbach from NBC, both of whom were in their early twenties, looked exhausted, their clothing soaked through with sweat. Bernie, however, looked only more energized after walking in the heat. The next day we marched in parades in Slater, Ames, Windsor Heights, and Pella. On the drives between the cities, Bernie would stop for events to open local campaign offices. Eight miles of parades and four speeches later, we would finally conclude our Fourth of July. When we left Pella for the airfield in Newton, Iowa, I had the motorcade pull over at a Culver's Restaurant. Bernie might be ready to go, but I was sunstroked and sick. I threw up in the bathroom and barely made it back to the car.

I looked back to moments like these a few months later when people would ask me if I saw Bernie's heart attack coming. The truthful answer was no. At the close of July 4, 2019, if someone had told me that three months later Bernie would have a heart attack, I would have laughed at the ridiculous notion.

In Houston, before taking the stage in the main forum, Bernie met with the Bad Ass Teacher Caucus, a group of progressives within the union. Walking out of that raucous meeting, where teachers spoke with us about the economic struggles they were facing, Bernie said—as I had heard many times, though the effect never wore off—"Those are our people, Ari. They are who our campaign is about."

After Houston, Bernie's energy did not abate. We flew to Las Vegas for a series of local and community events with Dr. Cornel West.

Dinners with Dr. West were one of my greatest pleasures during the campaign. Each was like a seminar in history, culture, and politics. I would always come away with an extensive list of books to read afterward. That night's dinner was no different. You could tell Bernie was enjoying himself with Dr. West because unlike the rushed nature of nearly every other meal Bernie had, with his usual impatience to get to the next thing, this one could have gone on for hours. When we finally left that night, a band was playing a mix of hip-hop and 1990s covers outside on Fremont Street a few blocks down from the restaurant. Dr. West started dancing in the street to the music.

"Want to do something crazy?" Bernie asked.

"What do you have in mind?" I replied.

With that Bernie began walking down the street toward the old Vegas. We reached the crowd at the edge of Fremont Street. There were four of us: me, one other staff member, one of the most famous politicians in the world, and one of the most prominent public intellectuals in America. We stood outside the Four Queens Casino and listened to the band. All the while people stared. A conversation started around us. People were trying to figure out whether it was really Bernie Sanders or an impressionist selling selfies to tourists. Finally, a member of the crowd worked up the courage to come up to Bernie and ask how much it cost to take a picture with him. "Nothing," Bernie said. Others realized it was really him and started to line up for photos. Bernie loved it. These were mostly working-class people enjoying a night out and a free concert in Las Vegas. He even took pictures with a few showgirls in full costume. Cornel West stood nearby, also taking pictures, smiling and laughing.

*   *   *   *

DESPITE OUR FUN in Las Vegas, we could sense the campaign had stalled. For months, Bernie and I had been traveling every weekend to somewhere—and often multiple places—around the country. During the week, he was still focused on Senate work in DC. The pace was becoming extreme, even for Bernie. In mid-July, we decided it was worthwhile to pause for a weekend. A number of senior staff members gathered in Burlington to discuss a road map for the campaign moving forward. That same weekend the Netroots Nation conference was taking place in Philadelphia. While many of Bernie's supporters were savvy internet users, we recognized that attendees of that conference were not our target audience. With no media partner and a relatively small audience, primarily composed of people who worked in the political space, the conference wasn't worth traveling to Philadelphia for. But something else, we decided, was.

We made a considerable amount of progress that weekend in Burlington, getting Bernie to finally agree to build out the campaign's policy shop. We also created a new scheduling system and restructured parts of the campaign. We also were the first people treated to the latest Ben Cohen ice cream creation: "Bernie's Back." It tasted like a Fireball candy. Down the side was a molded chocolate-toffee spine, and there was a disc of chocolate on top—a one-percent layer that you had to break through.

That same weekend, two blocks away from the Netroots Nation conference, Hahnemann Hospital was the site of several rallies trying to prevent its closure. It had been open for nearly 170 years, serving local at-risk populations. The hedge fund that owned the institution had decided it was no longer worth operating and announced it was being shuttered. Thousands of staff members would lose their jobs, and a significant source of medical care in the city would vanish.

Nina Turner had made contact with some of the people organizing protests against the closure. She pushed the campaign to do a rally on Monday. Working with organizers on the ground and elected officials in the city who wanted to turn a national spotlight on the closure, we had the necessary permits in twenty-four hours. The city would shut down North Broad Street, allowing us to rally right in front of the hospital.

That day several thousand people crowded outside the hospital—far more than would have heard Bernie speak at the Netroots conference. It might have come together in forty-eight hours, but it was one of the best moments of the entire campaign, revealing Bernie's most authentic values, as well as his boundless energy, even on a weekend when he was supposed to be "off."

Our rally site was catty-corner to the convention center where Netroots Nation had been held. The two locations were so close that we used a room in the convention center as a hold room for Bernie. Other candidates, political organizers, and progressive activists had gathered for the forum. Elizabeth Warren, Julián Castro, Jay Inslee, and Kirsten Gillibrand along with progressive senators including Sherrod Brown had been in attendance at Netroots Nation. Each of these prominent progressives could have held events similar to ours outside the hospital, using their platforms to fight against an unjust outcome. But only Bernie did.

* * * *

WE HAD TWO WEEKS before the next presidential debate, on July 30 and 31 in Detroit. In Washington, DC, Bernie delivered a major speech on Medicare for All, meant to convey the program's popularity and to continue to put pressure on other candidates—Harris, Booker, and Warren—who might try to step away from the bill. The speech was not only a reminder about the specifics of the policy, but an attack on the outsized influence of the health care industry in American politics. It followed naturally from the speech Bernie had delivered a month earlier at George Washington University, in which he outlined his vision for democratic socialism.

That earlier speech was a monthslong project. Drafts were written by speechwriter David Sirota, Jeff Weaver, and me. Bernie worked on it until the last minute. We were all extremely proud of the final version. One section was particularly ideologically important to me:

What I believe is that the American people deserve freedom—true freedom. Freedom is an often-used word but it's time we took a hard look at what that word actually means. Ask yourself: what does it actually mean to be free?

Are you truly free if you are unable to go to a doctor when you are sick, or face financial bankruptcy when you leave the hospital?

Are you truly free if you cannot afford the prescription drug you need to stay alive?

Are you truly free when you spend half of your limited income on housing, and are forced to borrow money from a payday lender at 200 percent interest rates?

Are you truly free if you are seventy years old and forced to work because you lack a pension or enough money to retire?

Are you truly free if you are unable to go to attend college or a trade school because your family lacks the income?

Are you truly free if you are forced to work sixty or eighty hours a week because you can't find a job that pays a living wage?

Are you truly free if you are a mother or father with a newborn baby but you are forced to go back to work immediately after the birth because you lack paid family leave?

Are you truly free if you are a small business owner or family farmer who is driven out by the monopolistic practices of big business?

Are you truly free if you are a veteran, who put your life on the line to defend this country, and now sleep out on the streets?

To me, the answer to those questions, in the wealthiest na-
tion on earth, is no, you are not free.

While the Bill of Rights protects us from the tyranny of an
oppressive government, many in the establishment would
like the American people to submit to the tyranny of oli-
garchs, multinational corporations, Wall Street banks, and
billionaires.

It is time for the American people to stand up and fight for
their right to freedom, human dignity, and security.

To me, this was the core of what we were fighting for. Conservatives had spent decades creating and entrenching a perverse
definition of freedom centered on lower taxes and a lack of government intervention or assistance in any aspect of people's lives.
This has become accepted as the only one by the media and political elites along with far too many Americans. Our campaign was
trying to present a more authentic, meaningful vision of freedom
that would serve all of society. Our goal was to allow everyday
Americans to experience freedom from the economic shackles that
were holding them down.

After his Medicare for All speech, Bernie joined other members of the Congressional Progressive Caucus for dinner at a Chinese restaurant two blocks from the Capitol. Dozens of pictures of
political leaders adorned the walls, including Bernie's, taken when
he was a House member.

We held these dinners relatively frequently. Though accused
of not doing the day-to-day schmoozing that is seen as a necessary part of running for president, Bernie convened many of these
dinners in 2018 and 2019, creating informal get-togethers that
allowed for casual but important conversations with other progressive politicians. That day Donald Trump had directed a par-

ticularly vicious and racist attack at one member of the House of Representatives, Ilhan Omar, a Somali refugee. At a rally in North Carolina, the president of the United States had led the crowd in chants of "send her back."

Ilhan came to the dinner late that evening, walking into the room with her daughter, still in high school but herself a notable climate activist. Bernie and Ilhan sat at a table together and spoke about Trump's rally. Leaving the restaurant, Bernie turned to me and said, "She is so incredibly strong. I don't know if I would be able to withstand what she has." It was a powerful moment. One of the most famous Jewish politicians in the world forged a bond with a Muslim member of Congress who had been attacked by the president of the United States. Bernie had known Omar but had never had a heart-to-heart with her before this moment. He gave us instructions. He didn't care about the political impact on our campaign; we should do whatever it took to help defend Ilhan. The next day we would use our campaign email list to raise money for her and to defend her from further attacks by the president.

We were soon back in Iowa for an uneventful weekend of forums across the state. Returning to Washington, though, we found ourselves in a crisis. Just as DC's oppressive summer heat set in, the air-conditioning unit in Bernie's Capitol Hill home broke.

Like most old properties in DC, it was not unusual for Bernie's townhouse to be in need of repair. He once called me in the middle of a particularly stormy day in Washington, saying, "Ari, do you have time to go on a secret mission?"

"Sure, Senator. What do you have in mind?"

"Come down to the office."

It turned out Bernie's roof was leaking, badly. After meeting him in his office, we walked the several blocks to his townhouse. The house, which I rarely entered, itself was smaller than my apartment. One small room downstairs had an old cathode ray TV/DVD/VCR combo and a small DVD collection that included several *Star Wars* and *Lord of the Rings* movies. It was unclear if Bernie had ever watched them. Behind the room, there was a tiny kitchen. There was a bathroom in a closet with a small toilet and sink. Upstairs there was a small bedroom, and an alcove area with a bed. Toward the back of the house was another tiny bathroom, this one containing a tub. This was far from the image of Bernie as a secret millionaire with three houses some of our opponents were putting forward.

It was clear immediately upon entering the house that there was water damage. The ceiling of the kitchen was punctured, and water was running down the inside of the window. Bernie had rigged a contraption out of a broken umbrella to try and keep the water from pouring into the house.

He asked me what I thought we should do. I suggested calling a contractor to look at his roof. Bernie, who never would ask a staff member to perform personal or physical labor for him, decided he was going to climb onto the roof through a small crawl space located in the alcove above the staircase. His first idea was to stack chairs on top of a plastic folding table that clearly would not hold his weight. I managed to talk him out of this and instead got a small ladder a friend who lived nearby. Attempting to convince him that it was a terrible idea for him to go on the roof, I demonstrated that the ladder only allowed me to look around the crawl space. Bernie then decided he would rent a taller ladder at a local hardware store. My attempt to convince him how terrible the roof plan was was failing.

The trip to the hardware store was amusing in itself. While we were there, a clerk asked Bernie "if any senator ever went so crazy, they had to be dragged off the floor." Another clerk processing the ladder rental, an elderly man with a long gray beard, had no idea who Bernie was.

"What's your last name?"

"Sanders."

"First name?"

"Bernard."

Returning to his townhouse, we argued over who would go up on the roof. Thankfully he allowed me to take the first look. It was still pouring, and all I could think was that he was going to go up on the roof, fall, and die. This would be terrible for the country—and I would be forever known as the staffer who let Bernie Sanders tumble off a roof. Later that day, I told Jeff Weaver that my fear was that if he fell, the internet would explode: a former employee of David Brock, who ran the principal pro-Clinton super PAC targeting Bernie in 2016, had killed Bernie. He laughed and acknowledged I probably would have needed to go into hiding.

In the end, once I showed him that his roof was on a slant and slippery in the rain, Bernie called a contractor who fixed the problem a few hours later.

Now, in the July heat, Bernie's home needed a new window unit air conditioner. I remarked that perhaps it would just be better if we got him a hotel room, since it would be his last night in DC that summer, as the campaign schedule would no longer allow for time in the city. Bernie looked at me like I was out of my mind.

"What are you talking about?"

"Senator, we laid out your schedule through October last week. I don't see how you are getting back to Washington unless there is a critical vote."

"Ari, you are crazy. I'm a senator."

I was right, as it turned out. It was months before Bernie would be back in DC.

That week, despite his home improvement issues, Bernie again took time out of his schedule to stand with workers, walking a picket line with flight attendants at National Airport.

* * * *

ON JULY 24, the day after Bernie walked the picket line, we flew to Los Angeles for political meetings in advance of the next debate, in Detroit. Bernie would also appear on *Jimmy Kimmel Live!*, meet with the United Teachers of Los Angeles, and hold a large rally in Santa Monica. This trip brought back memories of a trip to California more than a year before, which was critical to our campaign, in that it showed that there was still a fervor surrounding Bernie, and that we could put on big events under the crushing pressure of deadlines and things going wrong.

Our first afternoon in LA, Bernie joined a number of creative types for a lunch to discuss ideas on how they could help the campaign. Health care activist Ady Barkan would then interview Bernie for a video series he was producing. The interview was a few blocks from the lunch, and Bernie decided he would enjoy the walk between the two venues. On our way, a man dressed in spandex running clothes stopped Bernie in the street. "Senator Sanders, Jeff Katzenberg, nice to meet you."

"Good to meet you too."

Bernie just strolled on. Katzenberg, the former Disney chairman and DreamWorks CEO, looked stunned. As we continued up the block, I turned to Bernie and said, "Do you know who that was?"

"He said his name was Jeff, right?"

"Senator, that was Jeff Katzenberg, one of the most powerful media executives in the world and one of the biggest Democratic Party donors."

Bernie didn't even bother with a response. Most Democratic politicians are desperate to secure meetings with people like Jeff Katzenberg. For Bernie, Katzenberg didn't matter—it was as though his mind couldn't process the idea of his supposed importance or relevance. Bernie would have been more likely to stop for a teacher, a nurse, or a mechanic. We just kept moving toward our interview with Ady.

During our hour with Ady, it would become clear to me how many of Bernie's political beliefs were formed in his relationships with his parents. It is a subject he still will not discuss in depth with me. The early deaths of his parents clearly still shape him. Bernie's mother fell ill and died when he was eighteen. She had rheumatic fever as a child, leaving her with permanent heart damage. Before her death, she had been sick for some time, which led to two heart surgeries and hospitalization in New Jersey. Bernie was deeply impacted by his mother's illness. Prior to it, while clouded by his parents' financial difficulties, Bernie's childhood did have some idyllic elements. He talks fondly about his time on the streets in Midwood, near Kings Highway, playing punchball, stickball, and other games with his brother and neighborhood kids. He went to James Madison High School, whose graduates also include Supreme Court Justice Ruth Bader Ginsburg and Senator Chuck Schumer. Bernie was co-captain of the track team, lettering in his sophomore year after running a 4:37 mile. He ran for student body president, promising to fundraise for a student at the school whose parents were killed in the Korean War. He lost the race but did organize a fundraiser, which featured a basketball game between students and alumni. The student newspaper wrote that Bernie "made a campaign promise to bring back the stars, and that's exactly what he is doing." He wrote in a friend's yearbook that the game was "the most gratifying" part of his high school career.[13]

But when his mother got sick, things changed. Bernie began missing track practices and decided not to leave the city to attend college. While he never speaks about the experience, over the years it has become clear to me that he believes his mother never received adequate health care because of his parents' lack of money. His mother's illness had kept him in New York, and her passing prompted him, in the end, to leave in 1961. As he told the Associated Press in 2019, "Losing one's mother at the age of, I believe,

18 . . . was very, very, difficult." He continued, "In fact, I graduated Madison High School and went to Brooklyn College for one year, and I decided to leave Brooklyn because I kind of wanted to get away from the community I'd grown up in."[14] Bernie's father died three years after his mother.

That his memories of his parents are still very present, decades later, became evident during the interview with Barkan, a progressive activist who has ALS and who has helped lead the fight against Republican attempts to destroy the Affordable Care Act. Before his diagnosis, Barkan was an unstoppable organizing force focusing his considerable energies to press the Federal Reserve to enact pro-worker policies. Most people would at least slow down when faced with a death sentence. But not Ady. He continues to use his platform to push progressive priorities. In the summer of 2018, Bernie and Ady held rallies in Minnesota for Keith Ellison, who was running for attorney general of the state, and in Vermont in support of a progressive organization called Rights and Democracy. This was despite the progression of the illness and the fact that Ady was in a wheelchair.

In the summer of 2019, Ady produced a series of videos in which he interviewed every presidential candidate about Medicare for All—every candidate except Joe Biden, who at the time declined to participate. Bernie and I arrived in the studio to record the interview. At the start the conversation was jovial; it began with them laughing as they talked basketball. By that point Ady's ALS had left him unable to speak, and he could only communicate through a keyboard that tracked his eye movements. I snapped a picture of the two of them smiling as they chatted. Then the mood turned.

Ady asked about Bernie's mother's death in the context of his own mortality. When Bernie dodged the question, Ady pressed. You could see Bernie's shift from affable to sullen, and he cut the interview off. In the car, Jane and I pushed Bernie to talk about what had happened. "Ari, you told me that this was about Medicare for All. Now he is asking about my mom. I don't want to talk about my mom. We shouldn't have done that."

When Jane asked him again, Bernie said, "Look, I just never want to talk about that." It was clear that nearly sixty years after his mother's death, the pain was still visceral.

From my time at Bernie's side, I came to understand him as someone who was confident onstage in front of tens of thousands of people but uncomfortable in situations that would be standard for most politicians. Seeing his reaction to a question about his parents brought this home. He didn't just find the personalization of politics distasteful. He found it personally painful.

* * * *

FROM CALIFORNIA, we flew directly to Detroit for the second presidential debate. Bernie's focus, however, was on another part of our trip. In 1999 Bernie got on a bus in Burlington with breast cancer patients. He drove them across the Canadian border fifty miles away so that they could get a medication called tamoxifen, whose price was ten times higher in the United States. While at least half a dozen other members of Congress re-created the ride in the years that followed, drug prices in the United States have only continued to skyrocket.

In 2017, Bernie spoke to me about wanting to repeat the trip, this time with some of his Senate colleagues. We began to plan trips on several occasions, but something always came up, getting in the way. Windsor, Ontario, is right across the river from Detroit, and we saw that we could use the opportunity the debate presented to make the trip happen. This time, however, it would be with young people with diabetes and their parents, who were confronting the outrageously high price of insulin.

Like tamoxifen in 1999, insulin in the United States costs ten times as much as it does in Canada. Furthermore, people with type 1 diabetes must take insulin for their entire lives. The man who first refined it for use as a medication, Sir Frederick Banting, sold the patent to the University of Toronto for $1 so it could be widely produced. He famously said, "Insulin does not belong to me, it belongs to the world." Yet that idea remained a dream.

Today in the United States, a single vial of insulin can cost over $300. The people who boarded our bus in Detroit had harrowing stories to relate. One was a college football player who nearly died because he didn't want his mom to face the financial burden of paying for the drug. This was not uncommon; people with diabetes will often ration their insulin, leading to hospitalizations and even death.

Other campaigns claimed what we were doing was a cheap stunt. But one of the people we brought across the border had a response to that. "I've seen the criticism from people (on social media), saying this is a publicity stunt," said Quinn Nystrom, a type 1 diabetic. "But I really don't give a s**t. Because for the Type I diabetes community and for the 7.5 million Americans who depend on insulin, this is the biggest thing, today, that has happened to the insulin crisis, by shining a light on this topic."[15]

That was the point of the "stunt." Beyond its larger implications, the trip would make a real difference in the lives of those people on the bus: they needed insulin and our campaign was helping them get it. The trip itself was remarkable, featuring testimonies from diabetics and their families. Everyone who was on the bus appeared to be genuinely moved by what they had experienced. For Bernie, this was yet another example of how our campaign could be a platform for others to share their stories of struggle, in a nation that seems at times not to care for most of its citizens.

When we returned to Detroit, we did have a real stunt to prepare for. Cardi B had flown in, and that evening she and Bernie would meet in person for the first time. Then the next day, they would film a video in a beauty salon together. As we waited for Cardi B, we held an extended debate prep session. The appointed time for the meeting with her came and went, and she hadn't shown. Bernie grew frustrated. He didn't like debate prep, and he certainly didn't like to wait for anybody.

Eventually, Cardi walked in. After brief introductions, the staff exited the room to allow the two of them to speak in private. When I asked Bernie, afterward, what the conversation had been about, he told me, "Ari, she is so smart. She just understands how to reach out and talk to people. We might understand issues, but she understands communications better than any of us."

The next day, in their more formal, filmed conversation, Bernie and Cardi B, despite their different backgrounds, both came off as authentic and unpretentious. Bernie did not do what most politicians do in these situations: he did not fake being hip. At the same time, Cardi did not attempt to be a political commentator. They were two people sharing their messages for their fellow citizens. A few weeks later, when the video came out, it became one of the most viewed products of the campaign.

That night, after the interview, one of the most remarkable gatherings of the campaign took place. By chance, a number of senior staff from the top presidential campaigns all descended on the MGM Grand Detroit. We ended up around a craps table. The game that ensued told the story of the entire campaign.

A top Harris aide rolled first. They immediately went on a huge run but crapped out spectacularly. When the Harris campaign itself ended, this staffer ended up joining Biden's team during the primary. Next, a top staffer on Cory Booker's campaign rolled and crapped out immediately. At the time, two Elizabeth Warren staffers were circling the table discussing their plans to play, but they never put their chips down. Finally, a reporter at the table rolled. Jeff Weaver and I bet the "Do Not Pass" line against her. Craps is a game where the entire table plays against the house; Jeff and I were taking the house's side against the reporter. And we won. The whole group went to the bar together. The reporter snapped a picture of the motley group, telling us to say "Hillary."

The debate was the next day. Bernie's greenroom was a tiny space upstairs from the stage. Faiz, Bernie, and I sat there in total silence. Bernie did not seem to be in a good place. He closed his eyes and leaned back in his chair. The silence was nerve-racking. Then we received a press release from Congressman John Delaney's campaign. It was clear he was going to use that evening to go on the attack against Bernie. His opening statement would point to "bad policies like Medicare-for-all, free everything, and impossible promises, that will turn off independent voters and get Trump re-elected."

Suddenly Faiz and I received a text from Jeff Weaver: "Read him the statement." We looked at each other. With a relationship dating back more than thirty years, Jeff knew Bernie better than any of us. He understood his moods, and both how to calm him down and how to rile him up. He often joked that he had "healing hands."

Faiz turned to Bernie and said, "Senator, can I read you something?"

"What is it?"

"Congressman Delaney is going to attack you tonight. Here is what his campaign is saying he will say."

Faiz read the statement.

Bernie looked down for a second, and then he looked at us and said, "You guys know the Charlie Brown song?" Then, in a near-perfect imitation of the 1959 hit by the Coasters, he sang, "Why is everybody always picking on me?"

Faiz immediately pulled the song up on his phone. It filled the small room. "Fee fee fi fi fo fo fum, I smell smoke in the auditorium. Charlie Brown, Charlie Brown, he's a clown, that Charlie Brown. He's gonna get caught, just you wait and see. Why is everybody always picking on me?"

With that, Bernie rose to his feet and started dancing, air-boxing and psyching himself up for the debate. I filmed him, knowing Jane would love to see it later. It was a sweet, endearing, remarkable moment. After several minutes of awkward movements—Bernie is a committed dancer, but not a natural one—he was ready. The Delaney release had completely changed the tone of the evening for Bernie. He went from sullen to ready-to-fight in an instant. This attitude carried through, leading to his best debate performance of the campaign and his most memorable line. "I wrote the damn bill," he said in response to an attack from Tim Ryan, who claimed Bernie didn't know if Medicare for All would cover dental care, hearing, and vision for seniors.

The media was preparing for the top two candidates onstage that night, Elizabeth Warren and Bernie Sanders, to argue with each other about policy. Instead, they formed a united front, parrying attacks from the moderates. Bernie was feisty. While not a strong puncher, Bernie is among the best counterpunchers in politics. We left Detroit feeling pretty good.

Unfortunately, the next day we received discouraging internal polling. Running our first poll in Iowa, we were in a dead heat with Elizabeth Warren for second, but we were below 20 percent, with Joe Biden leading both of us by double digits. If Biden could maintain this lead, the election would end in a Des Moines hotel room.

CHAPTER 5

"I made it to spring training."

AN ARCADE IN SAN DIEGO AT 10 PM ON A SUNDAY NIGHT IS not where you would expect to find a seventy-eight-year-old. But that's exactly where Bernie Sanders was one evening in early August 2019.

We were in California for the annual convention of UnidosUSA, one of the country's largest Latino advocacy groups. We could not miss the event. Latino voters were not simply crucial to our campaign; they were our base.

That night we stayed in the city's Gaslamp Quarter and Bernie took the opportunity to stroll around the area. We stopped for ice cream at a Häagen-Dazs, where a selfie line ensued. A few blocks later, our campaign photographer, Bryan Giardinelli, who knew the area, pointed out a small arcade. Bernie didn't hesitate. In the middle of a group of drunken twenty-somethings, he started playing on a basketball machine, with people around him cheering as he sank shot after shot. Bernie then turned his attention to the Skee-Ball machines and had more trouble. He said he was out of practice, decades removed from the Brooklyn arcades of his youth. The moment was again evidence of Bernie's extremely competitive nature, not just in politics, but in any athletic competition. Put a ball in his hands and he has an intense desire to defy his age.

Our visit to the arcade also showed the side of Bernie that loved being out among young people. While Bryan and I had our cameras, there was no press around. Bernie wasn't performing. He was having a good time in a bar packed with college-age kids. He felt more comfortable there than he did at political events with senators of his vintage.

That first night set the tone for the trip. The next day as we drove up the coast, we were supposed to do a small town hall in Vista. On the way there, we stopped at an outlet mall to have lunch at a Johnny Rockets. After we finished our burgers, Bernie chatted with the restaurant staff, answering questions and taking selfies. He then wanted to take a walk around the mall to get some exercise. For a few minutes we went unnoticed, people eventually started asking him for selfies. But a standard selfie line did not form. Standing outside the mall, he engaged with a crowd of around a hundred people, who happened to be shopping that day, in an impromptu town hall, talking about the cost of college and health care. He quizzed his audience: "Do you think it's right that Americans pay more than four times more for prescription drugs than every other major country?" "Are you planning on going to college? Tell me, do you think it is fair that you will end up in debt?" "Talk to me about your family's health care." People answered honestly, and Bernie engaged them with respect, regardless of their response.

As usual for these casual encounters, some of the people recorded videos on their cell phones, but none of the resulting videos ever made news. And there was little newsworthy about them, at least by the standards of the news media and social media: Bernie was being Bernie—he was always on message.

Our stop in Vista was one of the most indelible of the campaign. We had planned to hold a town hall on immigration for a few hundred people. We set the room up for around 1,000 people to be safe, but nearly double that number ended up crowding inside. Bernie was visibly moved by the stories he heard about family separations during the Trump era and the struggles people went through to get to, and survive in, this country. The room became sweltering as the air conditioning failed. But Bernie didn't want to leave the stage. He stood there, listening to people who needed help from the government. He heard their pain, and in those moments, you knew that Bernie Sanders desperately wanted his White House to be the solution.

* * * *

IN AUGUST, OUR SUPPORTERS started to talk about what they called the "Bernie Blackout," the notion—the reality—that the mainstream press was ignoring Bernie. While staying slightly below the radar, and not being attached as the frontrunner, was to our campaign's advantage, we were now in a place where it felt nearly impossible to get any coverage at all. There were a number of journalists assigned to cover our campaign, but we would often find ourselves fighting with editors and executives at news outlets trying to convince them to send their staff on the road with us. Several reporters expressed to me that their media companies didn't believe covering our campaign was a worthwhile expense.

There was a natural tension between Bernie and the press. He believed they were obsessed with gossip, and often ignored substantive issues as a result. At the same time, he was acutely aware that the president of the United States was using rhetoric that put many members of the media in grave danger. Bernie's view of the media was obviously not Donald Trump's. He wasn't demanding fawning coverage or obedience. Bernie looked at the fourth estate as an essential part of American society and politics. He simply wanted its members to do their jobs better.

The coverage our campaign did get was also becoming problematic, a trend best exemplified by the press we got for Bernie's trip to the Iowa State Fair on August 11. The event is a mecca of fried foods, butter cows, and politics. And every four years the

Des Moines Register hosts a "Political Soapbox" inviting presidential candidates to speak at the state fair.

As soon as we arrived, Bernie was mobbed. Hundreds of people came up to him, taking selfies and greeting him. We reached the stage, where he gave a speech, followed by a press conference in a tent next door, and then proceeded to traditional fair activities. Bernie played along: he went to see the butter cow and eat a corn dog.

The *New York Times* piece on the state fair began with the subheadline "Most candidates go to the fair to establish human connections with voters. Mr. Sanders's approach underscored how his campaign is focused primarily on championing ideas." The article went on to say, "Bernie Sanders examined the butter cow. He power-walked by the Ferris wheel. He gobbled a corn dog. He spoke to almost no one." As the article explained, with the casual authority of the *Times*: "Mr. Sanders's approach to the event on Sunday—stride briskly, wave occasionally, converse infrequently—underscored how he has grounded his campaign in championing ideas rather than establishing human connections."[16]

The article then offered the common criticism of our campaign's operation in Iowa at this point, namely that we were "struggling to gain traction." It quoted a number of Iowa politicos claiming we could not win Iowa, featuring a photograph of an anonymous person looking down at Bernie from a window giving a thumbs down. Bernie would go on to win the plurality of the vote in Iowa, something that would have been unthinkable if one's context for the race came from stories like this.

Here is what took place at the fair from our perspective. The press corps, in particular photographers, became physically aggressive as they jockeyed for position to get the best pictures of Bernie during his walk through the fair. Our campaign photographer, Bryan, was thrown into a pole, slamming his head and breaking a camera. A news videographer walking backward knocked over a baby carriage. The security at the fair could not handle the crowd of reporters and onlookers. A staff member asked me if we could exit as quickly as possible because they were worried about people getting hurt, primarily by the pack of news photographers and videographers covering the event who were invading others' physical space. We followed the instruction, and this was why Bernie had largely avoided talking with fairgoers. But even so, the accusation that Bernie didn't greet anybody was false. The campaign had scores of pictures of Bernie taking selfies, shaking hands, and saying hello to the people gathered at the fair.

In truth, the tensions between our campaign and the press were boiling over. Ryan Nobles, the reporter CNN assigned to our campaign, and I began talking about a friendly game of softball to smooth things over. We had a few ringers on our team: Faiz had played baseball at Harvard, and our Iowa press secretary also played in college. I joked that we should play the game at the Field of Dreams in Iowa, where Kevin Costner filmed the classic movie. Ryan told me if I could get that done, they were in.

The next day we received confirmation from the people who ran the Field of Dreams. We rented the field, and the game was set for the end of August. The campaign did not lack for would-be players, nor did the reporters on our campaign have much trouble fielding a team.

Bernie himself was excited about the game—the idea of it, and to play in it himself along with one of his grandchildren, who had accompanied us on the trip. Baseball played a foundational role in his life, and even in his political views. Back in 2018, before a trip to Arizona, I had gotten in touch with Olivia Garvey, the sister of a friend and the daughter of baseball great Steve Garvey, to ask if Bernie could visit the Los Angeles Dodgers' spring training. Olivia, now a local sportscaster in Washington, DC, was working for the team's PR department. When we pitched Bernie the idea of going to spring training, he didn't need convincing.

On the way to the training facility, a staff member gave Bernie a gift: a vintage Brooklyn Dodgers cap that he immediately put on. Bernie was transported back to his days as a young fan. While meeting with manager Dave Roberts, he jokingly asked for a try-out. As we waited for the players to appear, a crowd of Dodgers fans lined up to get autographs. Many were shocked to see Bernie and exploded in cheers. Bernie went down the line of fans, signing balls and shaking hands. "Well, Ari, I made it to spring training," he said to me. At the batting cages, he spoke with outfielder Yasiel Puig about his hitting, and also took time to watch the pitchers and catchers throw to each other. "Look at that control, Ari, it's remarkable," he said, reacting to the gunshot-like sound of a fastball hitting the catcher's mitt at nearly 100 miles per hour.

In the team's locker room, while Bernie was admiring a portrait of Jackie Robinson, a Dodgers staffer asked him to switch his old Brooklyn Dodgers hat for an LA one. He politely refused and was soon reciting Brooklyn Dodgers lineups from the 1950s from memory. The Dodgers were his childhood. The players from that era were still his heroes—the guys he had tried to emulate playing stickball on the streets near Kings Highway in Brooklyn. Before Bernie was obsessed with politics, Bernie was obsessed with baseball. In fact, baseball helped form his ideology.

Jeff Bezos, the Walton family, even the Koch brothers—Bernie may oppose and even detest them; but nothing compares to the raw hatred he feels for Walter O'Malley over his decision in 1957 to move the Dodgers from Brooklyn to LA. Bernie had been sixteen years old at the time, in his prime as a baseball fanatic. That day in 2018 at Dodgers spring training, Bernie told an old Brooklyn joke: "The three worst people in modern history were Adolf Hitler, Joseph Stalin, and Walter O'Malley, but not necessarily in that order." He explained to a reporter that to his teenage self, the Dodgers were as much a part of Brooklyn as Prospect Park or Coney Island. O'Malley could just as well have moved the Brooklyn Bridge to California. It was incomprehensible that a wealthy person could simply take the team and move it across the country, with only profit in mind. His heroes were gone because, as Bernie saw it, in the United States of America profit is more important than community.

Baseball also played a significant part in Bernie's legacy as mayor of Burlington, as he brought a minor league team, the Vermont Reds, to the city in 1984. The city's current minor league team, the Burlington Lake Monsters, and their mascot, Champ—named for the large mythical lizard sea monster who makes his home in Lake Champlain—have become an important part of city life. While the city of Burlington has a population of just over 42,000 people, and more than 80,000 people in total attended Lake Monsters games every season. Bernie viewed their games as true civic events, where for a few dollars parents could bring their kids out for the afternoon, and even possibly get autographs from the players.

In the fall of 2019 Major League Baseball announced it would be contracting the minor leagues, and the Lake Monsters were disbanded. To Bernie, it was almost like the Dodgers all over again. We were in New York for an interview with the *New York Times* in the lead-up to their endorsement of a candidate, which Bernie viewed as a waste of time—and fairly, because everyone knew the *Times* would not choose him. Faiz, Bernie, and I ended up at MLB headquarters for a meeting with commissioner Rob Manfred. Bernie had asked for the meeting, and the commissioner seemed eager. It therefore was surprising that it was, from the start, one of the most hostile meetings I have ever attended.

Manfred came in hot and immediately raised his voice, screaming at Bernie that he knew the business of baseball. Bernie yelled right back. After a few minutes the room cooled down and they discussed their disagreement over the elimination of minor league teams, with no real solution. Bernie's passions ran high throughout. Baseball was, to him, a core part of the American experience, and minor league baseball was important to rural Americans in particular. "This seems small, Ari, but to rural towns across America, their teams matter," he told me. The campaign focused on the issue, holding an event in Iowa with representatives from three local teams that were slated to lose their minor league affiliation; giving interviews on the subject with major publications; and discussing the issue every chance we had.

As for our softball game with the press: it blew up a few hours before it was supposed to start. Beforehand, our online team had made baseball cards featuring a picture of Bernie that we offered to our fundraising email list as commemorative items to low-dollar donors. The reporters we were slated to play felt it was inappropriate to use a game with the media to fundraise for the campaign. We hadn't even considered their reaction before we sent the email. So, with a few hours before the first pitch—and with thousands of people coming out to watch—we were left without an opponent.

We ended up recruiting a team of local high school kids to play—and they annihilated us. Our MVP was Bernie's grandson Dylan, who scored two runs. The important thing, at that point in the campaign, was that we could all cut loose.

* * * *

THE SECOND HALF OF AUGUST was a whirlwind of travel. The most notable trip was a visit to Paradise, California, the community that was almost completely destroyed by a forest fire whose intensity was magnified by the effects of climate change. We walked through the remains of the town, past burned-out cars, trees turned to charcoal, and the melted knickknacks that used to sit on residents' mantels. It had been a year since the fire, and Paradise was still a moonscape.

On the way to Paradise, our connecting flight was canceled, causing us to have to rebook tickets while running through the Denver airport. We quickly found another flight, but Bernie was done with the logistical nightmare of commercial air travel. Our schedule was being held hostage by United and American Airlines. Every time a flight was canceled, a series of audibles ensued—quick flight changes, rented cars to drive between airports (somehow this always seemed to work)—but these extra steps had taken a physical toll on all of us. We were in the Denver airport, and Bernie said to me, "It's time to get a plane."

The other memorable stop that August was Louisville, Kentucky. Bernie wanted to make sure we weren't leaving red states out of the mix, believing they should be an important part of our campaign. In Bernie's mind, it would be possible to unite people regardless of the political makeup and history of their state. In Louisville, we heard that a local CWA union was on strike against AT&T Southeast. As always, we put our comfortable walking shoes on and headed over to march with the workers.

We had rented the plaza outside the Muhammad Ali Center for a rally. I had visited the museum briefly when Bernie and I traveled to Louisville in 2017. Now, because of the proximity of our event, Bernie would get a private tour.

Boxing is another passion of Bernie's, though below baseball. He often unwinds by watching a YouTube video of an old fight on his iPad. Naturally, he is also an admirer of Muhammad Ali's personal and political courage. At the museum, in addition to taking in the history of Ali's boxing career and his struggles as an activist for justice and against the Vietnam War, Bernie hit a speed bag, and jokingly dodged its imagined punch back.

* * * *

EARLIER IN AUGUST, Jeff Weaver had called me. "Ari, you are going to have to eat your vegetables," he said, and I readied myself for what was coming. Throughout the campaign, we had been interviewing media firms. We spoke with traditional political operatives as well as firms that primarily worked in the commercial space. Nothing felt right.

For several months, Faiz and I had discussed the idea of moving television production in-house. We already had a media buyer whose rates would save the campaign a tremendous amount of money. Media firms, which often demand millions of dollars for their expertise, charge a percentage of the overall ad buy and also need to be paid for production. Faiz and I calculated that we could hire the necessary staff for less than half of the production costs of a traditional firm—not to mention the savings from not paying large commission checks.

But Jeff was calling to say we needed to bring the DML team back into the process. I allowed that if we were going to hire an outside media firm, they would make sense. They knew Bernie, knew the campaign, and could get to work quickly. My only reservation was that they had to bring a bit more humility than they had demonstrated to that point.

In an interview with the *New York Times*, when they left the campaign in February, Mark Longabaugh had specifically cited strategic differences with Jane Sanders as one reason for their departure.[17] I suggested they needed to make that relationship right. The critical thing about Jane—in addition to her centrality in Bernie's world and her talents and skills—was that she listened. You could always disagree with her suggestions and offer alternative plans; she was not difficult to speak with. But she did want to be respected by people on our team.

On a call with Bernie a few days later, Jeff raised the idea of DML's return. There was some grumbling, but Bernie agreed to hear them out. When we spoke with DML, he made a simple proposal. They would pitch and produce two ads. The first would reintroduce Bernie to Iowa voters. The second would focus on the high cost of prescription drug prices. When the scripts arrived a few days later, we all agreed they were OK—nothing spectacular, but serviceable work from a professional firm. On a follow-up call with DML, Bernie asked that they produce the ads. He would pay for the production, and the relationship would progress from there. I thought this was an excellent idea, believing they could seamlessly reintegrate themselves into the team. When past issues with Jane were raised, DML brushed them aside too quickly, failing to take responsibility for what they had said to the press in February—a warning sign.

We then waited for a proposal from DML that would lay out the production costs. More than once Bernie asked for this document. Finally, we got it: instead of a budget for two ads, as Bernie instructed, it was a pitch for the entire campaign, with a payment structure based on commissions.

"He's never going to bite on this," I told Jeff. Nearly every other consultant with a strategic role in the campaign had forgone a commission, instead being paid by retainer. This was by design: our strategies would never be driven by their potential for staff to profit financially.

When we finally told Bernie what DML had proposed, he was apoplectic. He had felt taken advantage of during the 2016 campaign, with consultants making millions of dollars on his back, and he was determined not to allow that to happen again.

Bernie decided we would bring the paid media operation in-house. After the call on which the decision was made, he said to me, "Ari, this campaign is revolutionary. Not just because of our policies, but because we should change the way campaigns run. These consultants who want to make millions of dollars. Fuck 'em."

* * * *

I LOOK AT SEPTEMBER 2019 as a month where I missed something. We began with a trip to New York to do Seth Meyers's and Dr. Oz's shows. Why would we go on *The Dr. Oz Show*? For the same reason we had gone on Joe Rogan's podcast in August: we could reach a vast audience that wasn't paying attention to the standard political media. On *Dr. Oz*, Bernie could talk about Medicare for All and his own physical fitness. While at the time we believed Bernie was uncommonly healthy for his age, he was still seventy-eight. Questions would be raised related to his age, and we needed to begin building up the case that he was completely healthy and fit. It turned out to be a spectacular interview, ending with the two of them playing basketball on a makeshift court in the studio. Bernie appeared to be on top of the world.

Yet in retrospect, I should have seen Bernie growing more fatigued. After New York, with the school year starting, we did a series of rallies at colleges and universities in Iowa; this was the kickoff of our campus organizing program in the state. We would then fly to Colorado for a large rally in Denver before heading to Boulder to prep for the third debate, to take place in Houston on September 12. In Iowa, Bernie's voice was a little hoarse. After the rally in Denver, he had completely blown it out. He sounded terrible.

One of Bernie's few previous health problems had been a cyst on his vocal cords years before his first run for president. Now he was again experiencing problems with his voice at the worst possible moment. Elizabeth Warren had moved into second place in the polls. She, Joe Biden, and Bernie would all be on the stage together for the first time at the debate in Houston. Not only was his voice a problem, but he seemed to be getting progressively more tired.

During debate prep, the staff had a mission. Because Warren and Biden were polling at one and two, respectively, they would be at the center of the stage. Bernie would be shuffled to the side, an unusual place for him. He needed to put himself at the center of the action. If you want a crowd, pick a fight. There was general agreement among the staff that he should begin the debate with an attack on Biden. He should go after him on an assortment of issues, from his previous advocacy for Social Security cuts, to his vote for the Iraq War, to trade treaties he had backed that had cost our country millions of jobs.

We pitched the strategy to Bernie throughout the day. It was reinforced by two additional staff members who showed up at debate prep to deliver a memo making this point. He seemed to agree with it. Jeff Weaver wrote an opening statement that we all signed onto. Bernie made some alterations and practiced it several times. While he was behind it, he seemed a bit hesitant. Bernie was very particular about one thing: that the attack not be personal. It would be about policy. At the same time, he knew that he needed to do something to take command of the stage.

We arrived in Houston with Bernie still saying he was sticking to the plan, but something was off. With Faiz, myself, and Jane in the greenroom, Bernie practiced his opening, jotting it down on his ever-present yellow legal pad. What we saw as Biden's prior missteps would be framed not just as policy disputes, but as an argument about electability. Bernie would make the case that Biden's repeated errors in judgment over a long career made him a weak candidate to take on Donald Trump in the general election.

In the greenroom, Bernie read the statement with a perfect delivery. Jane listened carefully, clearly sensed his discomfort, and said, "Talk about your issues, don't attack Joe." Jane's words were all he needed. He would not take the road he never wanted to travel down in the first place. This was not a candidate's spouse making a political judgment. It was Jane performing one of her most important duties on the campaign—making sure Bernie stayed true to himself.

After Jane left the greenroom to take her seat in the audience, Faiz and I, committed to the strategy we had agreed to in debate prep, encouraged Bernie to go onstage and deliver the statement as prepared. There was even more discomfort in his voice. We made one last attempt to pump him up. At the prior debate, he had left the greenroom dancing and ready for a brawl. He left the greenroom in Houston with a burden on his shoulders. When it came time for his opening statement, I turned to Faiz and said, "Is he going to do it?"

"I don't know."

Instead of the practiced opening, Bernie delivered his Bernifesto, the list of the policies he supports: Medicare for All, College for All, and a Green New Deal. Faiz and I looked at each other. We didn't need to speak. We could tell what the other was thinking: fuck.

While Bernie performed well enough for the rest of the debate, much of the staff saw it as a wasted opportunity. What made us nervous was that Bernie had seemed to relish counterpunching against John Delaney and other moderate Democrats during the July debate, but he now seemed very hesitant to attack Joe Biden.

* * * *

ON SEPTEMBER 13, at a town hall in Carson City, Nevada, one of the most shocking moments of the campaign took place. A military veteran named John Weigel, suffering from Huntington's disease, had had his government-sponsored health insurance canceled. He was dying and spending his last days fighting hospitals while drowning in $139,000 in medical debt. He told Bernie, "I can't. I can't. I'm gonna kill myself."

Bernie responded, "Hold on, John, stop it, you're not gonna kill yourself." He told him they would speak after the event. Soon enough, Bernie, Jane, and John sat down together. Bernie diligently wrote down all the relevant information from the conversation and handed it to me. He told me to call his Senate office, and have them make contact with the Department of Veterans Affairs. We needed to get John's situation resolved. Bernie called Catherine Cortez Masto, one of Nevada's senators. He asked if their staffs could work together to make sure John got the care he needed.

Every few days he would ask for an update on the case. Finally, after Bernie's and Cortez Masto's offices worked on the case, with a simple payment of a few hundred dollars in back premiums John's health care was restored and his bills were paid. Bernie was elated. I wanted to do some press on it. Bernie said no, it wasn't our place: we did this to help John, not get publicity.

A few months later, at another town hall in northern Nevada, John would again be in attendance. He approached the staff and told us he had something to say to Bernie. I prepped Bernie, telling him John was in the audience and wanted to ask the first question. After Bernie's opening talk, he turned to John, who told the crowd the story of the restoration of his insurance. He wanted to give Bernie his Navy flight jacket. Bernie, clearly touched, said he could not take it. John had earned that, not him. Instead, he would accept a flight patch John had worn while in the military.

When we left the venue, I started to reflect out loud on what we had accomplished. Bernie waved me off. "He never should have had to struggle to get health care in the first place."

* * * *

I DIDN'T NOTICE at the time, but looking back, my photos from the period right after the Houston debate reveal that Bernie was looking more and more tired, his skin becoming gray. And his speeches lost their pep. After taking a few days off to recover his voice, we were back out on the road. This time we were on a tour of colleges and universities in North and South Carolina. Then we would fly to Iowa for another series of effectively mandatory political events and rallies.

We arrived at the Polk County Steak Fry on September 21. Politicians gather at this event to eat steak and give speeches. Again, the media drew conclusions from a crowd whose tickets had been primarily bought by the campaigns. While we would do these events in Iowa out of obligation, that week we also took advantage of our new campaign plane: a Gulfstream IV we leased for the fall whose owner painted the Grateful Dead dancing bears on the wing flaps.

The plane allowed us to leave Iowa between events and fly to Oklahoma. After holding a large rally in Norman, home to the flagship state university campus, we drove to Lawton, where the Comanche Nation has its headquarters for the tribe's fair and powwow, where we met tribal leaders and watched dancers in traditional garb. All of us, from Bernie to the journalists who tagged along, to the staff, were amazed and humbled by the visit.

Bernie has a deep and abiding interest in Native American issues. But the primary encouragement to attend the event came from Jane, who constantly reminded us that while our country had long ignored the plight of Native Americans, our campaign should not. While Vermont is not the home to a large Native population, Bernie and Jane have educated themselves on the injustices Native nations have faced, historically and into the present day. They see the United States' treatment of Indigenous people as a blight on our country that must be rectified. During the event, Bernie's respect for the tribe and its members was apparent. At the end of the ceremony, he was presented with a beautiful Comanche blanket to wear for protection.

As we were departing, the tribe's chairman gave me a blanket as well, telling me he needed me to keep it with us for protection—that it was my job to protect Bernie, and the blanket would help protect me. I didn't really know how to respond, so I awkwardly thanked him. I had never been more convinced of the importance of our campaign.

After another event back in Iowa, we thought our week was done. But on this campaign, standing with labor is what we did, and two strikes were about to take place in the Midwest. Chicago teachers were about to vote to authorize a strike, while the United Auto Workers were walking a picket line outside Detroit. With our plane, we could reach both these strikes. So instead of heading back to Burlington for a few needed days off, we went to Chicago and Detroit.

Walking the picket line in Detroit and meeting with the teachers in Chicago seemed to energize Bernie. For the first time in several weeks, he seemed to perk up and find his usual energy level. Perhaps, I thought, he was also looking forward to a brief break back home.

—

CHAPTER 6

Bernie's Back

ONE CRUCIAL DECISION MADE DIFFERENTLY ON THE NIGHT of October 1, 2019, and everything could have changed, for Bernie, for me, for the campaign, and for the country. What if Jesse Cornett and I had decided not to overrule Bernie and go to the urgent care clinic, and instead continue back to the hotel? I would have had an early night off in Las Vegas. I might have played some poker or enjoyed a nice dinner. Bernie, meanwhile, would have been alone in his hotel room, and he would surely have just gone to sleep.

Instead, the heart attack became a moment of strength and resilience that helped define Bernie Sanders—and also helped turn the campaign around. Bernie would not be stopped; he would keep fighting for what he believed no matter what. At the same time, the event served as a stark reminder not only to us but to his supporters around the world both of his mortality, and of his unique place in politics. If he had not asked for the chair at the grassroots fundraiser in Las Vegas or remarked about the pain in his arm, what would have happened to the movement, and to everything he stood for?

We had arrived in Las Vegas from Burlington with Elizabeth Warren peaking, while our campaign was now at a standstill. Now, cloistered in a suburban hospital, Bernie made clear that we were going to stay in the race. But enormous questions remained.

Could we even run a successful campaign now, given his health issues? Already, reporters were on a campaign "death watch." I was receiving hundreds of text messages: Would Bernie drop out? How far would we fall in the polls at a time when Warren was surging both in Iowa and nationally? Even some inside the campaign, as well as a handful of influential surrogates, believed Bernie should drop out. Faiz and I fielded calls at the hospital, listening to a number of supporters tell us whom Bernie should endorse when he quit.

After Jane and Faiz arrived separately in Las Vegas, I felt as though I needed to escape. Other than a brief trip back to my hotel to shower and grab a change of clothing, I had been in the hospital with Bernie for nearly twenty-four hours. I told Faiz I needed a few hours off and called Bryan, our campaign photographer.

"Figure out how to book a helicopter and make sure there are no doors on it," I told him. He called back a few minutes later and told me the cost of a doorless helicopter charter that would depart North Las Vegas Airport at 7:30 PM. Along with Bryan and the campaign's videographer, Chris Witschy, we would fly up and down the Strip, photographing Las Vegas at night, simply to do something fun and unrelated to the stress of the campaign. I then called Charla Bailey and Jesse and told them to meet me at the restaurant Nobu, where I bought them an outrageously expensive dinner to thank them for their work the night before. It was a momentary act of insanity that cost me several thousand dollars, but one that was sorely needed. Thankfully, a few nights later, I won a poker tournament at the Aria Hotel, which covered the cost of that extravagant evening.

In reality, before Bernie's heart attack, the campaign was already in trouble. We were in fourth place in Iowa, according to a *Des Moines Register* poll. By Tuesday, October 8, exactly one week after Bernie's heart attack, Warren would briefly overtake former vice president Joe Biden in the polls. Now, at a minimum,

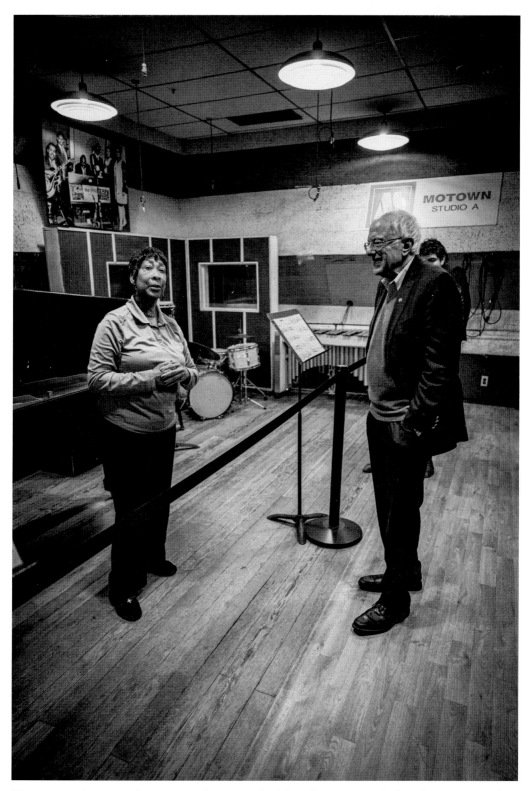

Motown was the music of Bernie's youth. On our final day of campaigning before the COVID-19 shutdown, we spent an hour at the Motown Museum, located in the record company's old Detroit office. Bernie and our tour guide dueted to "My Girl" in the studio where the hit was recorded.

It was hard not to feel the momentum in February 2020 with crowds often exceeding 10,000 people, like at this rally in Richmond, California.

In 1988, as mayor of Burlington, Bernie endorsed Reverend Jesse Jackson for president. In March 2020, Jackson endorsed Bernie in Grand Rapids, Michigan. Bernie was deeply moved and let Jackson know it during a conversation after the rally.

Before going onstage in Grand Rapids, Bernie and Jesse Jackson shared a private moment backstage.

On February 10, 2020, Bernie was joined by Jane, his daughter Carina, son Dave, and their children onstage with Alexandria Ocasio-Cortez, Tim Robbins, Cornel West, Cynthia Nixon, and The Strokes at the University of New Hampshire. Bernie was happiest when his family could join us on the road.

Bernie and I with other staff members in Cedar Rapids, Iowa, in September 2019. Each morning, Bernie would ask me for the latest political gossip. (Photo by Jared Polin FroKnowsPhoto)

Nearly every evening on the campaign trail, Bernie and I would have dinner. Small steak houses like this one in Iowa were among Bernie's favorites. (Photo by Jared Polin FroKnowsPhoto)

Activist Ady Barkan, confined to a wheelchair by ALS, and Bernie discuss basketball before taping an interview in Los Angeles, California, on July 26, 2019.

Joe Biden wishes Bernie luck before he goes on stage at Jim Clyburn's World Famous Fish Fry on June 22, 2019, in Columbia, South Carolina. While other candidates were closer to Bernie ideologically, he and Biden enjoyed a friendly relationship.

Early for a rally, Bernie and I talk on a playground in South Carolina in the spring of 2019. (Photo by Arianna Jones)

In 2018, the crowd expecting their Major League heroes at Dodgers spring training broke into applause as Bernie emerged onto the field to sign baseballs and interact with fans.

Above: Bernie, Jeff Weaver, Congresswoman Pramila Jayapal, and her husband, Steve Williamson, at a coffee shop in Des Moines, Iowa, in January 2020.

Left: We landed in Iowa on February 4, 2020, still not knowing the caucus results due to errors in the Democratic Party's vote counting app. Bernie put his arm around me on the tarmac and gave me a bit of a pep talk. (Photo by Josh Orton)

Bernie, Jane, and their sons, Levi and Dave, walk together into the debate venue in Los Angeles in December 2019.

Bernie and Bernie impersonator James Adomian after taping a Bernie vs. Bernie interview in California on November 16, 2019.

My turn at bat on the Field of Dreams. After the press team backed out, the game went ahead anyway. "Is this heaven? No, it's Iowa." (Photo by Bryan Giardinelli / Breathe New Winds)

Bernie smiles at members of the Sunrise Movement, an organization of young people fighting for action on climate change, in the front row during a rally in Minneapolis on November 3, 2019.

The biggest crowd any Democrat brought out during the 2020 campaign gathered to watch AOC announce her endorsement of Bernie in Queensbridge Park, New York, on October 19, 2020. Only three weeks before, Bernie was in the hospital after the heart attack that should have ended our campaign.

Bernie and AOC in Queensbridge Park before the rally. They have a natural rapport that comes through in joint interviews.

Bernie, Danny Glover, Susan Sarandon, and Nina Turner onstage in South Carolina in February 2020.

It was no surprise that Bernie wanted to go to Chicago in September 2019 in solidarity with the Teachers Union as they negotiated a new contract. If there was a picket line, our campaign was joining it.

Bernie shooting baskets at the Minnesota State Fair on August 27, 2019.

Our campaign bus, which we rented in January 2020, gave us a new way to see Iowa. Here, Bernie and staff members look out of the front cabin as we arrive at an event.

AOC's first trip to Iowa in November 2019 ended any doubts that she was one of the most popular figures in the national Democratic Party.

Bernie and Congresswoman Rashida Talib sit in the rear cabin of the campaign bus as we crisscross Iowa in January 2019.

Fist in the air as Bernie concludes his speech in Fresno, California, on November 15, 2019.

our candidate would be recovering for a few weeks and unable to stay on the campaign trail. Moreover, we knew from polling that one of the top concerns voters expressed about Bernie was his age—and once news of the heart attack got out, that concern would be amplified. In the event, it was worse than that: the media quickly accused the campaign of not being fully transparent about the details of Bernie's condition.

There was one person who knew all the facts—nearly as they were happening. My old boss, former Senate Democratic Leader Harry Reid, had called Faiz on the morning of Thursday, October 3, and announced he would be visiting the hospital that afternoon. No one was supposed to know which hospital Bernie was recuperating in, but Reid not only knew where Bernie was but also his room number; he also knew which doctors had treated him and had a general sense of his condition. Clearly, in Nevada, there is a HIPAA exemption for Harry Reid. Reid showed up a few hours later and, after talking with Bernie, called the *New York Times* to let them know he "looked really good."

Soon after Reid's visit, the campaign took another dramatic turn. Corbin Trent, communications director for New York representative Alexandria Ocasio-Cortez, called me. "Can Bernie pick up his goddamn phone?" he said in his Tennessee drawl. "Trust me, he is going to want to take this fucking call."

I had first heard about AOC when Stephanie Kelton, who served as Bernie's chief economist on the Budget Committee and is a leader of the Modern Monetary Theory movement, phoned in early spring 2018. "Ari, I just met this woman, Alex, who is running for Congress in New York against Joe Crowley. She is amazing."

A few days later, I received a call from my friend Zack Exley. I had known Zack for more than a decade, working out of his apartment in DC on a project for MoveOn in 2003 and with him on John Kerry's presidential campaign in 2004. Zack was always plotting a revolution and looking for candidates to carry it out. "Ari, you don't understand. This woman, Alexandria, who is running against Joe Crowley in New York. She is going to win this primary." This was months before the primary election or any media reporting on the race.

Zack and others were working with a new group called Justice Democrats that had sprung from the Bernie campaign in 2016. They were recruiting challengers to conservative Democrats who had won in safe blue districts for years. AOC was their star. In the weeks after those first two calls about her, friend after friend called to tell me about meeting this compelling young Latina running an improbable race against Joe Crowley in Queens and the Bronx.

Crowley was a giant, not only in his district, but in Washington. In the House of Representatives, he was expected to be one of the Democrats vying to succeed Nancy Pelosi when she left the speakership. He had raised millions of dollars for his fellow House Democrats and was not considered to be in any danger of losing his seat. Back in his district, Crowley ran the local Democratic Party machine. Through these mechanisms, he could ensure that he would face limited challenges.

The problem is, like many who gain power in Washington, he had lost touch with a rapidly changing district, which had become younger and more racially diverse since Crowley had first won his seat in the House, in 1999.

A few weeks before the New York primary on June 26, 2018, Bernie was speaking at a press conference outside the Capitol held by a coalition of progressive organizations. Dozens of members of Congress would attend these events. When we arrived, Crowley, who towered over the crowd, made a beeline toward Bernie, and an uncomfortable conversation ensued.

"Hey Bernie, how are you doing?"

"Good, Joe. You?"

"Good. Can we meet?"

"Sure, just have our staffs set it up."

"OK, thanks."

Crowley walked away and Bernie turned to me and asked, "You think he is nervous about his primary?" Bernie never scheduled that meeting.

Bernie followed the race closely. The night of the primary, Bernie and I were strolling to dinner from his Senate office to a restaurant in Union Station. When Bernie was in DC, the two of us would have dinner together at least once a week. As we crossed the traffic circle in front of Union Station, he asked what I thought of AOC's chances; I said I didn't know—in a low-turnout election, anything could happen. But with New York's draconian voting laws and with corrupt election judges often put in place by party bosses such as Joe Crowley, she was not just the underdog, but faced a series of major obstacles.

When Democrats criticize voter suppression laws, most people—including elected Democrats themselves—assume or act as though these laws only exist in Southern and Republican states. In fact, New York has some of the most rigid voting laws in the country. From long gaps between voter registration deadlines and primary election days intended to reduce turnout, to very tough ballot access laws, New York's electoral system is designed to protect incumbents. AOC was a brilliant candidate, but she would have to overcome an inherently undemocratic system.

A few hours later, after our dinner, I called Bernie and told him AOC was going to win. "Holy shit," Bernie said. "Can you get me her number?"

It took a few days for them to connect, but when they did, they immediately agreed to start working on behalf of other progressive candidates. That is how, only weeks later, AOC, Bernie, Corbin, and I ended up in an SUV driving across Kansas campaigning for two Democrats running for Congress.

Bernie and AOC's bond was immediate and obvious to me. The

first time they met in person was over breakfast at the hotel in Wichita. I could sense they were both extremely excited to meet each other, but also that they both were nervous about the day ahead and wanted to focus on the speeches they would be giving.

This was AOC's first big political event outside her district, and she wasn't in another liberal bastion like San Francisco, Austin, or Chicago. Wichita is a deeply red city in a deeply red state. Conservatives had been trying to spin her win over Crowley, arguing that a socialist could win in New York City, sure, but never in middle America. Well, that day, several thousand people packed into an auditorium in the middle of Kansas, waiting for her to speak. It was perhaps the only time I have ever been with Bernie when he was not the main draw in the room.

Before their rally in Wichita, Bernie and AOC taped a joint appearance on CBS's *Face the Nation*. It would be one of AOC's first big Sunday show interviews, and when we arrived at the site, it was evident she was nervous. Josh Miller-Lewis—Bernie's then-communications director—Bernie, Corbin, and I chatted with AOC while she sat in the makeup chair. What was remarkable to me is that even in this early moment of her career, she had the foresight to anticipate various rhetorical traps, the tenacity to demand we discuss them ahead of time, and the poise to go out and deliver a topflight performance, not only on the Sunday show but also onstage at the rally later that day.

Following the rally, Bernie, AOC, Corbin, and I drove across the state to Kansas City, for an event with another progressive congressional candidate. It was not unusual for Bernie to sit for hours in a car saying only a few words, surfing the internet on his iPad. But on this ride, he and AOC talked without any breaks about life in Congress, how she should set up her office, which committees she should ask to be on, and more generally, about their views of the world.

Every time Bernie spoke with her, he would get off the phone and say, "Ari, she is so smart." He saw her as a politician who intuitively understood how to get her message out, who had the right set of values, and who possessed the instincts to be a true progressive leader in Washington. Reporters often tried to frame their relationship as mentor and mentee, suggesting that there was a torch to be passed. This was not, in fact, accurate. From the start, Bernie always believed he had as much to learn from AOC as she did from him.

A few minutes after Corbin's call to me at the hospital in October 2019, AOC rang Faiz. He immediately handed his cell phone to Bernie, whose smile grew wider and wider as he listened. He hung up and said, "Well, she's going to support us. You two figure it out." I later asked a member of her staff what the deciding factor or moment was. This person didn't know, but said that when she heard Bernie had a heart attack, it was like a light switch flicked on.

Faiz and I immediately got on the phone with Corbin and Rebecca Rodriguez, AOC's campaign manager and closest advisor. We began planning what we all understood would be the most important moment of our campaign: a rally in Queensbridge Park three weeks later at which AOC would make her first appearance with Bernie after endorsing his candidacy.

*   *   *   *

ON OCTOBER 5, we flew back to Vermont for two days off, before starting to prepare for the next debate, in Westerville, Ohio. Though Bernie had already decided to continue the campaign, we still had to determine if he was, in fact, healthy enough to do so. In Burlington, Bernie met with cardiologists, who gave the all clear.

*   *   *   *

BUT THE OHIO DEBATE WAS LESS THAN TWO WEEKS AWAY. Bernie was seventy-eight years old and had just suffered a heart attack. Would he be able to stand on his feet and debate for three hours?

We also had to decide how to publicly relaunch the campaign. Bernie's Burlington home was being staked out by our embedded reporters, young beat reporters from networks assigned to travel with the campaign full-time, and other journalists, eager for information on a major public figure laid low. We needed to show the world that he was not just OK, but better than OK. So far, since the heart attack, there had been video of him leaving the hospital, a photo posted on my Instagram account of Jane and Bernie walking through a park in Las Vegas, hand in hand, and a long-lens paparazzi picture of us boarding the campaign plane for Vermont.

We developed a strategy in which we would let Bernie be interviewed by a national media figure nearly every day in Burlington. These included CNN's Dr. Sanjay Gupta, who had a sample version of the stent placed in Bernie's heart delivered to the house in Burlington, where his interview would take place, so that he could show it on TV. Every day Bernie would go for a walk, as prescribed by his doctor. The TV cameras would show him entering and exiting his house.

We made nice with the press surrounding Bernie's home. We would broadcast his movements and call a "lid" as early as possible, often by the early afternoon. They were then set free for drives around the state, hikes, and winery tours.

In short: we were projecting confidence. And the AOC endorsement, which would only further boost us, remained a secret. Now we had to strategize that rollout. The decision was made to do it around the next debate on October 15. AOC had by this point been joined by two other members of the Squad, Minnesota congresswoman Ilhan Omar and Michigan congresswoman Rashida Tlaib.

If Bernie had a good debate, it would only add to our momentum. If he had a bad debate, it would immediately create an alternative media narrative. There were several ideas floated about how exactly to present the endorsement, including quietly flying the congresswomen out to Ohio and having them walk into the spin room to make the announcement, or doing it at a press conference early the next morning. However, all three said they wanted to have large in-person rallies to put as much energy as possible behind their endorsements.

Jean-Michel Picher, the campaign's advance director, and I had already begun planning the Queens rally. Because of the complications involved in permitting and other processes in New York City, JMP flew to New York to choose the site and file the initial applications. I suggested to him a small park under the 59th Street Bridge. Queensbridge Park was right beyond the border of AOC's district but would offer a spectacular scene, along with a great message. Along the side of the park was the country's largest public housing project, while across the river in Manhattan, visible from the park, sit some of the world's most expensive condo units, in Steinway Tower. On the south side of the park is the 59th Street Bridge, a symbol of American industry, which members of Jane's own family had helped build. On the north side sits one of the dirtiest coal-fired power plants in the United States.

Other staff were insistent that we use Corona Park, which, as the site of the 1939 and 1964 World's Fairs, is home to the iconic Unisphere. It was also located in AOC's district. JMP called me from Corona Park as I was sitting in Bernie's backyard, where we did most of our prep sessions for the Ohio debate.

"This isn't going to work. Listen . . ." as a loud rumbling filled my phone. Every ninety seconds or so a plane from LaGuardia Airport ascended over the park.

"Go check out Queensbridge Park."

"I'm in Queensbridge Park, Ari."

"No, you are in Corona Park." I gave him directions to Queensbridge.

About forty-five minutes later, he called me again.

"Oh fuck."

He got it. The problem was, no one had ever booked the park for an event as big as the one we were planning. We were trying to get a permit for 20,000 people. JMP noted that on the day of our rally, the park was scheduled to play host to a few softball games and family barbecues. Our event was on an entirely different scale. Fortunately, the plan started to come together, and we decided to announce the rally before the debate, to build excitement.

Now the focus was purely on debate prep. Even Bernie agreed this debate would be different, given his health scare. Instead of resisting prep, as he always had, Bernie seemed to relish the opportunity to show us how ready he was for the debate and for the campaign. In his backyard and living room, we created mock debate spaces. Bernie would stand behind a chair we used as a podium and answer questions for three straight hours, the amount of time he would need to be on his feet during the actual debate. Warren Gunnels played the moderator, and I and other staff played his opponents, firing attacks at him. Before the first run-through we were nervous, though of course we didn't tell Bernie. He had just had a heart attack and had been in the hospital for several days. Would he even make it through the test run?

In reality, the heart attack didn't seem to faze Bernie at all. After the incident in South Carolina, I referred to Bernie as Wolverine, a nod to the iconic X-Men character with incredible healing powers, but even I would not have thought he—or anyone—could react in such a way to a near-death experience. Not only was he more than capable of debating, but the energy he seemed to have lost pre–heart attack was back. As we boarded the plane for Ohio only days later, we had an odd confidence about the campaign.

The debate "greenroom" at Otterbein University was a parking lot filled with RVs, with every campaign assigned one. In our trailer, Bernie was focused. In the lead-up to the debate, we had released to the media that there would be a special guest joining us in New York. Reporters were texting me nonstop with guesses. Before Bernie stepped on that stage, we were already in control of the narrative.

When the debate began, Bernie was energetic and feisty. In a back-and-forth over Medicare for All, he told his opponents, "I get a little bit tired—I must say—of people defending a system which is dysfunctional, which is cruel, 87 million uninsured, 30,000 people dying every single year, 500,000 people going bankrupt for one reason, they came down with cancer." He then went on the attack: "I will tell you what the issue is here. The issue is whether the Democratic Party has the guts to stand up to the health care industry, which made $100 billion in profit, whether we have the guts to stand up to the corrupt, price-fixing pharmaceutical industry, which is charging us the highest prices in the world for prescription drugs."

He even directly challenged Joe Biden, as he hadn't in Houston, though his personal affection for Biden still managed to come through. "But you know what you also got done—and I say this as a good friend—you got the disastrous war in Iraq done. You got a bankruptcy bill, which is hurting middle-class families all over this country. You got trade agreements like NAFTA and PNTR with China done, which have cost us four million jobs."

Thirty minutes into the debate, Obama administration alum and Pod Save America host Tommy Vietor tweeted, "Bernie Sanders does not look like a guy who just had a heart attack." He was not alone; this was the general reaction we were getting from reporters covering the debate, and we knew the best was yet to come. The feeling of elation in moments such as this—after facing mortality, both for the campaign and your candidate—is hard to describe. It is something like the sudden sense that you might actually have a path to victory.

When the inevitable question came from one of the moderators, CNN's Erin Burnett, about his heart attack, Bernie interrupted before she could finish, retorting, "I'm feeling good. Can I respond to the last question?" With everyone laughing, he then promoted the upcoming New York City rally and spoke of the "special guest" who would be onstage with him, teasing the announcement without mentioning AOC by name. Most reporters started texting, asking if it was Cardi B who would be joining us.

During the second hour of the debate, the AOC endorsement leaked to the *Washington Post* and reporters started publishing stories on it. In the media filing center, where the press watches the debate, reporters stopped paying attention to what was happening onstage and were frantically calling to confirm the story that the *Washington Post* was running with.[18] AOC and Ilhan Omar would be endorsing the campaign. There was some confusion about Rashida Tlaib in the press; she would wait until Bernie visited Detroit a few weeks later. Other campaigns were still focused on the debate, but we knew we were about to win the spin room—and Bernie wouldn't have to even make an appearance.

When Bernie arrived back in his trailer after the debate, he was his typical dour self. He didn't believe he had performed well, saying, "I could have done better," and registering how much he "hates" the reality show–style formats of presidential debates. Jane was the first to push back, kissing him and saying, "You were brilliant." She was, as always, right.

When I strode into the spin room, reporters began congratulating me as though we had won the election—the general election. By holding back the AOC-Ilhan-Tlaib endorsement announcement until that moment, not only had Bernie dominated debate night, but he had controlled the coverage for perhaps the first time. We were not the front-runner, nor were the media predisposed to like us, or us them. For months, at this point, our campaign had been written off. We were in fourth place in Iowa and third nationally. And at that moment, the Squad came through.

Bernie returned home to Vermont the next morning with the

campaign revived. I headed to New York City. For the Queens-bridge Park rally, I didn't want to simply travel with Bernie to the site, but instead to help build it from the ground up. On October 18, the day before the rally, we worked to set up the park. It occurred to me that I was a bit old to be carrying bike racks around the giant venue. We still didn't know if we would fill it up. Those butterflies from the earliest part of the campaign started to creep in.

The next day Bernie would arrive from Burlington and go directly to the park. He would do national press interviews with AOC before the rally, and after the rally, they would head up to the Bronx together to tour the community and visit a diner before Bernie returned home to Vermont.

That morning the lines formed early. People began to throng into the park. Then admissions stalled. When Bernie and AOC sat for their interviews, only about 6,000 people were in the park. We were growing anxious. Would our momentum from the past few weeks come to an abrupt end? Then, almost as though through mass teleportation, all the surrounding areas of the park were full. I asked Nina Turner, who was opening the rally, to extend her speech—in order to allow the crowd to reach its peak size. Soon, we were told by the police working the event that 20,000 people had entered, and they could not allow any more in. The street outside the park filled up. In total, 26,000 people were with us in person on what was a glorious mid-fall day in New York City.

As AOC finished her introduction of Bernie, the PA system blared AC/DC's "Back in Black," the refrain reverberating around the park: "'Cause I'm back. Yes, I'm back. Well, I'm back. Yes, I'm back." Bernie and AOC embraced onstage as the crowd erupted.

The conclusion of Bernie's speech was a cathartic moment for all of us on staff, hundreds of whom had traveled up from Washington, DC, for this rally. Bernie articulated in the most explicit way the reason we were all working on the campaign: "I want you all to take a look around and find someone you don't know. Maybe somebody who doesn't look kind of like you. Maybe someone who might be of a different religion than you. Maybe they come from a different country. My question now to you is, are you willing to fight for that person who you don't even know as much as you are willing to fight for yourself?"

Less than three weeks earlier our campaign was dead. Bernie was a seventy-eight-year-old Jewish socialist, hated by much of the establishment, and he'd just had a heart attack. We were down in the polls and out of the media narrative.

Bernie's indomitable response to his heart attack and his slipping polls was, strangely enough, the jolt our campaign needed. For many briefly wavering supporters, the heart attack alone, and the glimpse of Bernie's mortality, brought them back to our campaign. The possibility of losing Bernie reminded them of how important he was to the political process. They could not imagine a 2020 campaign without him. The heart attack, of all things, had brought them home.

*　*　*　*

WE HAD BEEN PLANNING on launching our television campaign in Iowa the week of Bernie's heart attack. It was to be a big moment for our campaign, testing our theory that ads produced in-house could perform just as well as those put out by expensive media consulting firms. Our first buy would cost $1 million for ads in Iowa alone. After the heart attack, we made the quick decision to take the buy down. It would have been a waste of money with the media focused on Bernie's health.

A week later, we put it right back up and immediately saw our polling in the state begin to rise. We had fully expected Warren's campaign to match our buys, but the weeks rolled on and still they hadn't. Other than a single ad during a college football game, she stayed off the air. We were mystified. Only our campaign and Pete

Buttigieg's were running ads in Iowa, and we were targeting different sets of voters. Warren was ahead in the polling, but she was giving us a chance to catch up.

On our weekly strategy call, we could not puzzle out what her campaign was thinking. But through November, there was no response. Other campaigns didn't have the resources to compete; Warren's campaign did, yet remained off television.

At the same time, we also heard about odd hirings by the Warren campaign. While we had just begun to hire in Super Tuesday states, they were hiring organizers in Washington State and even Florida, which would not be contested until late in March.

Staffing decisions are among a campaign's most challenging. Media buys could be canceled, and mail budgets could be altered. But staff, especially a unionized staff, is an expense you would have to cover month after month. Try to move, fire, or downsize staff and it would immediately appear in the media. Stories about how you were closing offices would lead to a death spiral of coverage, but at the same time, if you continued spending money you didn't have on staff, it would inevitably choke off your ability to communicate with voters. Warren's campaign had grown about 30 percent bigger than ours, a massive monthly payroll expense. Now they were spending money in states they would not even necessarily be competing in, locking themselves into high costs deep into the winter.

* * * *

THE FINAL STOP on our Bernie's Back media tour took place later that week with an appearance with Jimmy Kimmel, who was doing his show from Brooklyn. It allowed Bernie another homecoming, and a stop at Francesco's Pizzeria, before we flew to Iowa.

The most exciting events of the following weeks were our rallies with Rashida Tlaib and Ilhan Omar. From Iowa we headed to Detroit. Our rally at Cass Technical School with Tlaib also included its most famous alum, Jack White of the White Stripes.

He had demanded that the auditorium be empty during his rehearsal with his band, but Arianna Jones and I snuck under the bleachers to listen to him playing. This was a special moment for me. While my main responsibilities were on the road, Arianna, a fellow deputy campaign manager, kept the entire campaign infrastructure in Washington, DC, running. We were partners, but rarely in the same place. My job would have been impossible without her. This was especially true during Bernie's heart attack, when she, as the most senior person in campaign headquarters, kept the entire staff together and functioning. Arianna doesn't brag. And she doesn't seek publicity—while I was on the road next to Bernie, experiencing the rush of rallies and events, she was doing the behind-the-scenes day-to-day management of the entire operation. More than any other staffer, she exemplified "Not Me, Us." The moment under the bleachers was magnified because we got to experience it together.

At the rally, Jack White ended his set with "Seven Nation Army." The crowd was in a frenzy. Nearly 5,000 people had pushed into the school's gym, about the same number who had attended President Obama's rally in the same location in 2018.

The Detroit rally marked the beginning of a sprint. After a few weeks of relative calm following Bernie's heart attack, we would now be piling on the events through the end of the year. We would combine swings across Iowa with giant rallies signifying our newfound strength. Tlaib's rally, where she officially announced her endorsement, was as exciting in many ways as the Queensbridge event. Glued to his side most of the time, I saw that Bernie could not have been happier. We were engaging in the type of campaigning he lived for.

The next week, in early November, we would rally at the University of Minnesota with Ilhan Omar. But before that, we faced the last of Iowa's major events for the cycle. Formerly the Jefferson-Jackson Dinner, it was now called the Liberty and Justice Celebration, given the recent reckoning over the racial legacies of Thomas Jefferson and Andrew Jackson. Of all the Iowa events, this was the largest and most significant. It was held in a stadium in Des Moines, and over 10,000 people would attend, primarily with tickets paid for by the campaigns or large donations to the state party. Barack Obama's speech at the event in 2008 is widely regarded as the event when his campaign took off. Candidates, in particular Pete Buttigieg, would try to emulate his performance, elevating the importance of this particular cattle call.

Campaigns would spend hundreds of thousands of dollars to line the stands with their supporters, who arrived carrying noisemakers and signboards. A few months beforehand, Misty Rebik, the campaign's Iowa state director, and Pete D'Alessandro, an old political hand who advised the campaign in the state, pitched Bernie on a radical idea. The state party had asked us how many tickets we wanted to buy. Rebik and D'Alessandro were suggesting forgoing the process entirely.

Sitting at a table at an Outback Steakhouse—this was before the heart attack—Bernie pondered the proposal. Iowa's privileged position as the first caucus or primary was a financial windfall for the state. Operatives who work in Iowa are prized on presidential campaigns, local TV and radio stations earned millions from television ad buys, hotels in Des Moines and Cedar Rapids benefited from the throngs of campaign staff and reporters. But no group benefits financially more than the Iowa Democratic Party.

Between the Steak Fry, the Wing Ding, and the Liberty and Justice Celebration, millions pour into the state party and its affiliates' coffers. While most state voter files can be purchased from the Democratic National Committee, Iowa's must be purchased from the state party, costing campaigns hefty sums. Whenever you hear a political operative from Iowa declaring the sanctity of the state's caucus system, know that it is a claim likely made in bad faith. What they care about are the dollars.

Bernie took to the pitch from Misty and Pete. We wouldn't forgo the event entirely. Rather, he would speak at it and make a smaller contribution to the state party. Our supporters would hold a march outside the event and attend a dinner across the street with grassroots leaders, not the usual Iowa politicos. We would use it as an organizing opportunity, rejecting the notion of a fake cheering section. "This is a radical idea," Bernie said approvingly. Misty and Pete went ahead with their plans.

*   *   *   *

WHAT MISTY AND PETE were proposing played into one of Bernie's long-standing biases. For his entire career, he had been a political loner. It was not entirely by choice. When he was elected to Congress in 1990, Democrats did not know what to do with him. The Cold War had just ended, and "socialism" was still a four-letter word. Now the Democratic caucus would have to contend with a socialist within its ranks.

When Bernie describes that period in his life now, I can still sense the combination of irritation and the pain of being an outsider. There were some in the party caucus who wanted nothing to do with him because of his politics and would have preferred Vermont's House seat remain in Republican hands rather than allow him in the Democratic fold. There was a delay in assigning him committee seats and to this day, he speaks with a sense of frustration at how poorly leadership in the House treated him.

He was the first independent elected to Congress in five decades. "He is out there wailing on his own," Massachusetts Democratic congressman Joe Moakley, then chairman of the powerful House Rules Committee, told the *Los Angeles Times*. "He screams and hollers, but he is all alone." In the same article, Democratic representative and future UN ambassador Bill Richardson is quoted as calling him a "homeless waif."

For his part, Bernie responded much as someone would expect him to today. As he told the *LA Times*, "What you see, on major issue after major issue, is that the Congress does not have the courage to stand up to the powerful interests. I have the freedom to speak my mind and, ultimately, right now in American politics, we need to raise the issues these guys don't want to, and I can do that."[19]

Bernie's relationship with fellow members of the House improved over the next decade. Ultimately, he learned how to effectively use the Rules Committee process to pass more amendments on the floor than any other member, earning him the moniker of "Amendment King." His amendments had real effects, from creating a National Cancer Registry to banning the import of goods made with child labor. Regardless of his successes, his remained an uncomfortable existence, and he was never fully able to feel at home in Washington.

His experience in the Senate was just the opposite. Chuck Schumer and Harry Reid, recognizing him as a potential electoral juggernaut in Vermont, recruited him to run in the 2006 Senate race in the state. While today Vermont is viewed as an easy win for Democrats, Patrick Leahy—against whom Bernie ran as a Liberty Union candidate for Senate in 1974—is the only Democrat ever elected to the United States Senate from the state.

Vermont senator Jim Jeffords, a Republican who quit the party and became an independent during George W. Bush's presidency, swinging the Senate for a brief eighteen months into Democratic hands, had announced his retirement. His Senate seat had been won by the Republican Party and its predecessors since the signing of the Constitution. The new Republican candidate, Richard Tarrant, was on paper a formidable opponent. His Vermont-based medical payroll and claims processing company had been purchased that year by General Electric for $1.2 billion, and Tarrant would end up spending $85 per vote, more than any other candidate running for Senate that year.

I remember when Bernie was declared the winner over Tarrant. I was in a suite at the Hilton Hotel next to the US Capitol, with Reid and Schumer, watching Senate returns come in from around the country. Bernie's victory was one of the first races called that night. It was expected, but there was still a great deal of joy in the room. I recall speaking with a fellow Reid (and future Bernie) staffer, Josh Orton, and remarking how amazing it would be to see Bernie Sanders in the Senate, unencumbered by the House's strict floor procedures. In my best Bernie voice I said, "I'm going to filibuster. Yeah, I think I am going to filibuster."

This joke came to seem prescient, because the first event that drew massive national attention to him was a 2010 filibuster on the Senate floor. Bernie was incensed over a deal to extend some of George W. Bush's tax cuts in exchange for extending Obama's 2009 recovery bill. Holding the floor, Bernie spoke for eight and a half hours on income and wealth inequality, oligarchy, and the power of the wealthy over the political process. After years in the House of Representatives, where he was confined to speeches that would last about a minute, Bernie's full-throated articulation of his message became an early viral moment and foretold how compelling his presidential campaign would be.

While Reid and Schumer welcomed Bernie into the Senate, he was still an outsider. I believe he has always suffered from impostor syndrome. Even when entering college, he described himself as a nonconformist, saying, "That was in me before I had politics."[20] The son of lower-middle-class immigrant parents did not believe he belonged in an institution like the Senate. He was never a good student, and before winning the mayor's race in Burlington by ten votes when he was thirty-nine years old, he had done odd jobs such as carpentry and making and selling filmstrips about the history of New England to primary and secondary schools. It was not exactly the resume of a member of an elite body that includes Rhodes Scholars, Ivy League lawyers, successful businesspeople, and overachievers who had been building their political resumes since joining the Young Democrats and Young Republicans.

Bernie's first mayoral win relied on an accidental confluence of several factors. After moving permanently to Vermont in the early 1970s, Bernie became a perennial candidate of the Liberty Union Party. He received the party's nomination for a special Senate election in 1972 after being the only person in a meeting to raise his hand and say he would do it. Bernie won 2 percent of the vote. He also ran for governor that year on a platform that included opposition to the Vietnam War, "a radical revision of the state's regressive tax structure," and abolishing anti-abortion and drug laws in addition to those that discriminated against homosexuality.[21] Only 1 percent of Vermonters voted for him. In 1974 Bernie would receive 4 percent of the vote in the race that sent Pat Leahy to the Senate. He would improve to 6 percent when he ran for governor in 1976.

After that, Bernie declared himself done with politics. He started doing well making historical films, and didn't want to waste time on more fruitless campaigns. But two friends, Huck Gutman and Richard Sugarman, showed him that while he had not performed well around the state in his prior races, he had developed a strong base of support in Burlington. He could win the mayor's race.

With their encouragement, Bernie decided to run one last time. He vigorously campaigned door to door in the city's poorer neighborhoods, talking with voters he believed had been alienated by city politics, which favored wealthy real-estate developers. At the time the Burlington waterfront on Lake Champlain was in decline.

Mayor Gordon Paquette wanted to clean it up by turning to private developers. Bernie campaigned on making it a public waterfront for anyone and everyone to enjoy. But perhaps the two most critical factors in that race were that Bernie opposed a property tax increase proposed by the incumbent mayor, and that he received the endorsement of the city's police union just before voters went to the polls. When Bernie won that night by the slimmest of margins, he was like the dog who caught the car. He didn't even own a suit and tie. The *New York Times* ran a story with the ludicrous headline, "Vermont Socialist Plans Mayoralty with a Bias Toward the Poor."[22]

His first years in office were difficult. The city council refused to work with him or approve the budget to run his office. In response, he set up citizen's councils, and according to his own description, normally boring city meetings became enormous public events. In the next municipal election, numerous members of the city council were swept out and replaced by allies of Bernie's.

Far from a wild-eyed radical, Bernie was a fiscally disciplined politician focused on cutting waste in city budgets—"Ari, you wouldn't believe the stuff we found"—and improving city services. One major step he took was to redirect the city's snow plows to clear the poorer city neighborhoods before heading to wealthier enclaves; for as long as anyone could remember, the plows had taken care of the richer neighborhoods first.

Due to the curiosity of a socialist being elected mayor of Burlington at the height of the Cold War, a series of profiles appeared in national magazines. In its profile, the *New Republic* described his accomplishments: "He replaced the politically well-connected accountants who had run the city treasury with people who were experienced in public finance. He started free health clinics for women and old people. And he created a city arts council that produces free concerts in Burlington's Battery Park." In Bernie's words, "You could say, 'What is Socialist about any of that?' O.K., nothing, really. I agree. But we have done some things that the best of liberals will not do."

Under Bernie, city workers became involved in running their government. Bosses received 7.5 percent raises, while union employees got 9 percent. Some of Bernie's fiscal maneuvers came directly from the workers themselves. "We're getting the workers involved in the day-to-day management," Sanders explained. "These guys have worked here for years. They said, 'You can cut here, you can cut there.' They know."[23]

Bernie would run unsuccessfully for governor in 1986 and for Congress in 1988. Then he won his seat in the House and has never looked back. In each of his three Senate runs, he has not received less than 65 percent of the vote.

In the Senate, Bernie operates in a unique fashion. Those of his colleagues who have been in DC for ages have staff alumni installed in powerful positions all over town. My first internship in Washington, DC, was in Massachusetts representative Ed Markey's office (this was before he won one of the state's Senate seats). Markey alums are spread throughout the city. They are lobbyists, or they are working in other legislative offices, or they are in the media. And they can be called upon to help at any time.

Harry Reid is perhaps the ultimate example of this. Team Reid is more like an extended family. After moving on from working for him, we might be on different sides occasionally, but our connection to Reid trumps momentary political disputes.

Bernie, by contrast, has no alum network in DC. He has worked in the city for thirty years, yet has almost no former senior staffers working for other politicians or in other institutions, whether in government or media. Even Elizabeth Warren, who has only been in the Senate since the Obama administration, has a brain trust beyond her Senate office, from her time at the Consumer Financial Protection Bureau and the Senate.

Bernie's former chiefs of staff include Huck Gutman, still one of his closest friends and now a poetry professor emeritus at the University of Vermont; Jeff Weaver, who worked as a lawyer but primarily owned a comic-book shop in his time away from Bernie; and Michaeleen Crowell, who left his Senate office just before the 2020 campaign began. She was the only senior Bernie staff member, as far as I know, who went to work at a corporate lobbying firm. Caryn Compton currently works as the chief of staff for Rural Utilities Services at the USDA.

Bernie's approach to campaigning also set him apart from other members of the Senate. He has rarely participated in high-dollar fundraisers with political donors, which made skipping the Liberty and Justice dinner even less of a decision for him.

It's not merely a matter of principle, though it is that. It is that the high-dollar fundraising is inefficient for Bernie. Early on in his career as the socialist mayor of Burlington, he built up a small following that would contribute in response to direct-mail solicitations. And Bernie's mail program today is unlike anything I've seen elsewhere.

Having worked for a firm that did direct marketing for Doctors Without Borders, Oxfam, the ACLU, and Planned Parenthood, I came to his office familiar with direct-mail strategy. In many ways, direct mail is still as sophisticated as online operations. The organizations that run mailing for political candidates and otherwise are not merely putting letters in the mail. The process involves polls, focus groups, test packages, and modeling.

Bernie's mail outreach is much simpler. A direct-mail letter from Bernie is just that—a letter from Bernie. Whenever we sent one from the campaign—which we did also, infrequently, due to the necessity of his personal involvement—he would struggle over the content, taking the process and his language very seriously. His letters would often end up four pages long and cover a vast range of topics and ideas that he believed were important. Most notable, though, was that his direct-mail letters would ask for contributions in the softest way possible, in the form of a simple reply card in the envelope.

But it worked. For decades people had been responding enthusiastically to Bernie's letters, and those checks were the fuel behind almost every one of his campaigns. He came to regard email as important as direct mail. While he couldn't write every single email himself, he was continually trying to make sure that we were treating the list with dignity and respect and not merely hounding people for money.

In April 2017, Tim Tagaris and I drafted an email for Bernie to send from his Senate campaign account. He responded, as he often did to drafts of speeches, that it was "85% of the way there"—meaning he would rewrite every word. Tim and I were at a baseball game at Nationals Park when his own draft came in. The email was now close to 1,000 words, and all the language that was designed to help raise money had been removed. I was depressed, thinking it was going to fail. Tim, on the other hand, was smiling. "You'll see," he said. A day later, that email, in Bernie's voice, raised close to half a million dollars.

One consequence of the 2016 presidential campaign was that Bernie Sanders had the best email lists in politics. What was often misunderstood about this list is that the people on it are loyal only to him, and dedicated to the singular project of advancing his political future. Remove Bernie, and its effectiveness evaporates. This is precisely what Our Revolution discovered. While the organization was spun off from the 2016 campaign with Bernie's explicit endorsement, they could never raise money or organize even at a quarter of the scale Bernie could off the same list. Here was more evidence that the storyline that Bernie "refused to share" his email list with the DNC was ridiculous. Bernie's list didn't even work for his own organization; it certainly wouldn't have worked for the DNC.

Bernie doesn't have an extensive DC alumni network. He doesn't have a fundraising network. He doesn't raise much money for the DSCC or for other members of the Senate with traditional fundraisers. And, partially as a result, he doesn't have a social life in DC. In 2017 and 2018, Jeff Weaver and I were his most common dinner companions. Most of the time, our conversations, often at mediocre restaurants, were focused more on political gossip and our day-to-day work than on the steps we would need to take to put together a presidential campaign (which, in this period, he still wasn't sure he wanted). Most senators build a life in DC. They have a large network of friends and a community with whom they socialize. Bernie simply didn't. It was not something he wished for, or felt he was missing.

The one thing Bernie wanted to do more than anything else when he was in DC was to go back to Vermont as quickly as possible. If a vote in the Senate caused him to miss the 2 PM American Airlines flight from National on Thursday, he would desperately try to make the 5 PM an hour away at Dulles rather than wait for the next direct flight from National Airport at 10 PM.

From the moment he arrived in DC on Monday afternoon (he never wanted to take the early flight) until the moment he left the city on Thursday afternoon, he was thinking about getting back to Vermont. Nothing would put him in a worse mood than if votes were delayed or it looked like he would have to stay in DC longer than usual for any other reason. Delays commonly resulted from a member of the Senate, frequently Rand Paul, holding up votes until he could get what he wanted, frequently a vote on some tangential issue that would lose by a wide margin. Bernie viewed this practice as showmanship with no point. "Ari, I live in an insane world where one member of the Senate can completely screw up everyone else's life."

Vermont, though, was his salvation. Bernie Sanders has one of the most consistent personalities I've ever encountered, but in Vermont he is a completely different person. It is as if an enormous weight is lifted off his shoulders when he arrives back in the state. Bernie in Washington, DC, is tense and mission-driven. He walks down the street at a fast clip. Even if he doesn't have anywhere to go, he is worried about being trapped in a conversation. To him, everybody has an angle, and everybody wants something. The one group of people he genuinely seems to enjoy are cabdrivers. Taxi drivers in Washington, DC, most often African immigrants, invariably cheer him on or stop for a conversation.

Another reason for his reticence about being in Washington, DC, is that he is always being watched, and anything he does will be reported on, often falsely. This disturbed him even when the resulting story in the media was positive. In October 2018, walking briskly toward the Capitol, he told a woman to be careful when crossing the street. The woman posted on social media that Bernie Sanders had just saved her life. News moved so fast that we heard about it before he arrived at the office. When we asked him about it, he was irritated that the story even existed. "Ari, I told her not to step into the street. Enough of this bullshit."

In Vermont, he would stroll down the street, chatting with people. He would have conversations on Church Street and in the supermarket. He isn't stiff, and he isn't rushed—except when asked to pose for a selfie. He often would say "very quick" when someone asked for a photograph with him. During the campaign Jeff and I would talk to him about his reaction—if you were going to take the selfie, why not be positive about it? The photo would likely be on the wall of someone's house for a long time, so why not make it the best experience possible instead of making it seem like an imposition? In truth, Bernie did not hate taking selfies. Rather, he was still genuinely confused and uncomfortable about his fame.

Becoming famous was a weird experience for Bernie Sanders. It surely is for anyone who is famous. But for Bernie, fame came very late in life. While he certainly had been a known entity in Burlington for the past forty years, he was a backbencher in the House and Senate for most of his career. Then in 2016 Bernie Sanders, at age seventy-four, suddenly became one of the most famous and recognizable people in the world. Both his voice and his appearance were unmistakable, and that fact in itself made him uneasy. He once asked me to stop calling him "Senator" in public because it would call too much attention to him. I responded by asking if he thought calling him Bernie would make it any better.

For Bernie, fame is double-edged. He hates the trappings of fame. In airports, he would often ask me whether people were taking selfies with him because they actually supported his ideas or just because they were excited about meeting a famous person. His newly achieved fame has only been important insofar as it can advance the issues he has cared about his entire life—the fight for equality, the fight for health care, the fight for justice. If he is just famous to be famous, it certainly isn't worth it.

At times during the campaign, he would point to the absurdity of his situation. One afternoon, we were driving in front of the US Capitol. I was sitting in the back of the car, Bernie in the passenger seat. We stopped at a red light, and a group of high school students standing on the corner, no doubt on a field trip, noticed Bernie Sanders sitting in the car next to them. They started screaming. High-pitched shrieks filled the car. Bernie rolled down the window, shook hands, and let them take selfies. The light changed and we pulled away, the kids still screaming. Bernie turned to me and said, "I'm like Mick Jagger," as he laughed.

Bernie is almost completely unaware of other famous people (not just Jeff Katzenberg). We would frequently run into someone famous, and he would have no idea who they were. In 2018, Bill de Blasio asked Bernie Sanders to swear him in as mayor. That morning in New York City, at a hotel next to City Hall, chef Tom Colicchio, the host of the TV show *Top Chef*, was having breakfast with his kids at the table next to us. (If you want to know what a world-famous chef orders for his kids for breakfast at his own restaurant, the answer is waffles.) After they finished, he came up to the table to introduce himself to Bernie. I told him, "Senator, this is chef Tom Colicchio." Bernie thanked him for cooking such a nice breakfast, not understanding that he wasn't coming from the kitchen. Colicchio was incredibly gracious and proceeded to talk to Bernie about some of the anti-hunger work he was doing. When he left the table, I turned to Bernie and said, "Senator, that is one of the most famous chefs in the world who has hosted a top-rated cooking show." Bernie replied, "Well, the breakfast was very good."

The evening before our encounter with Colicchio was a rare instance when Bernie took advantage of his fame. A few weeks prior, when Bill de Blasio called Bernie to ask if he would swear him in, I noted this was not a simple one-day trip from Vermont. To be at City Hall for the ceremony, Bernie would have to spend New Year's Eve in New York City. He considered this for a second, and said, "Do you think we could go see the ball drop?"

It was endearing. Despite his decades in Vermont, Bernie was still a Brooklyn kid at heart. No event is as big a nightmare to navigate. Hundreds of thousands of people, drunk and penned in together, waiting hours in the freezing cold. There was little chance we would get into Times Square on New Year's Eve without some sort of special access.

Of course, the mayor's office was more than happy to arrange an entire evening for us. I had a request of my own. If I was going to spend New Year's with Bernie and Jane, then my wife, Julie, would have to attend as well. Jane thought this was a fantastic idea. So, on New Year's Eve, Bernie, Jane, Julie, and I made our way to Gracie Mansion for dinner with the mayor and his family. Then we got into NYPD SUVs in order to travel by motorcade to Times Square. In traditional De Blasio fashion, after leaving dinner, the mayor kept us waiting in the cars for about thirty minutes.

With sirens blazing, we arrived in Times Square, and stepping out of the cars, were led, eventually, to a spot below the main stage.

We were standing ten feet from Mariah Carey as she sang—this year with cue cards, so she wouldn't forget her lyrics again, as she had during the 2017 New Year's celebration.

We were in and out of the chaos in under fifteen minutes, the crowd cheering for Bernie, and in bed in southern Manhattan by 12:30. The next day Bernie swore in the mayor in the bitter cold. I stayed inside City Hall during the ceremony. Even Bernie, accustomed to cold winters in Vermont, was eager to get it over with.

Bill de Blasio's relationship with Bernie was always intriguing to me. On a personal level, Bernie and Jane very much liked the mayor and his wife, Chirlane McCray. But De Blasio always seemed somewhat obsessed with Bernie. Beyond the normal ass-kissing progressive politicians engaged in, it was clear to me that the mayor wanted to be tapped by Bernie as his political and ideological heir. And this is just not something Bernie would have ever done.

De Blasio insisted on visiting Bernie and Jane in Vermont the following summer, spending a day in August at the Sanderses' "camp" on Lake Champlain. This resulted in pictures of De Blasio canoeing while Bernie sat on the lakeshore with no shirt on, taken by a New York tabloid photographer with a long lens.

On one trip to New York to campaign with De Blasio in October 2017, the mayor's office had the idea that Bernie and the mayor should ride the subway together. The senator was at the tail end of a long weekend of travel that had taken him to Canada and Puerto Rico. His original flight from Canada had been canceled, so he was already a little annoyed.

When I met Bernie in Penn Station, he was not amused with the situation. He would soldier through. I handed him his MetroCard. As a kid, he had used tokens, and he was worried he would be unable to swipe the card successfully—during the 2016 campaign Hillary was ridiculed in the New York media for needing five attempts to successfully swipe a MetroCard. It worked on the first try. The mayor's photographer caught him as he pumped his fist.

After waiting a few minutes on the platform, we got onto a sub-way car packed with commuters as well as reporters, staff, and photographers. One photograph of the scene was remarkable. Bernie and I appeared miserable, which we were, while De Blasio towered over us with a grin on his face.

De Blasio wasn't the only politician who was enamored with Bernie. Sometimes the feelings of desire and possession led to pathological behavior. Earlier that weekend, Bernie had visited Puerto Rico at the invitation of San Juan's mayor and Bernie's future campaign co-chair in 2020, Carmen Yulín Cruz. She had asked him to come in order to see firsthand the devastation caused by Hurricane Maria.

In the week before the visit, we reached out to the island's governor and offered to meet with him as well. The mayor and the governor were political rivals, and the governor, Ricardo Rosselló, knew she would be running against him in the next election. The two sides were not amenable to working together to make Bernie's one-day trip feasible. The governor wanted to greet Bernie at the airport and give him the initial tour. But the mayor had invited Bernie, so this was her role. We proposed numerous times later in the day to the governor, and when that didn't work, suggested that a phone call might suffice. The governor's staff was belligerent at this point, but we got the governor's phone number and said Bernie would call when he landed.

Katie Thomas, the senator's aide who was the primary author of his Puerto Rico relief bill, accompanied Bernie on the trip. When their flight arrived, I began to get a series of texts from her describing a demented situation. When Bernie deplaned, we had planned to meet the mayor at a specific exit, but some security guards were at the gate and tried to direct Bernie out a side door. He refused and continued to the predetermined meeting spot.

Bernie and Katie got in the mayor's car, with the mayor's son driving, and pulled away from the airport. In that moment, an armada of police cars swooped in with their sirens blasting. They were behind the mayor, demanding that they pull over. The mayor's son sped up, and a highway chase ensued. Finally, Bernie asked the mayor's son to pull over. The cars chasing them were the governor's motorcade. The governor wanted a meeting. I received texts with pictures of the two of them standing on the highway median engaged in conversation. So, the governor got his meeting in the end.

Sometimes Bernie's interactions with other politicians were not dangerous, but simply strange. In 2018 we flew to Minnesota to campaign for Keith Ellison, who successfully ran for state attorney general. While boarding a flight from Washington, we bumped into Minnesota senator Amy Klobuchar. She might be one of the more conservative Democratic senators, but she and Bernie have a good rapport. They entered the Senate in the same year and have worked on prescription drug legislation together. Klobuchar and her husband have visited Bernie and Jane in Vermont. Now, Klobuchar decided she and Bernie should sit next to each other on the flight, and switched to a center seat to make that happen. They talked for the entire flight.

When we arrived at Minneapolis–St. Paul International Airport, we learned that our driver's flight had been delayed, so we decided to take a cab to the hotel. No, Klobuchar noted, that would not be "Minnesota nice," so she insisted that she drop us at our hotel. While we waited for our bags, Klobuchar walked Bernie around the airport and introduced him to her constituents. It was one of the most incredible displays of political prowess I've ever seen. At a random time in the middle of an airport, Amy knew dozens of Minnesotans by name, by occupation, and by their families. Even Bernie was impressed. As he told me, "Ari, she works very hard. She is up until three in the morning and does more constituent work than anybody."

With our bags in hand, we headed outside. A Klobuchar staffer came to pick us up in a tiny sedan with five seats. Between the six of us—the driver, Klobuchar, Bernie, Josh Miller-Lewis, then Bernie's communications director, a videographer, and me—and our bags containing bulky video and photo gear for the trip, there was not enough room in the car. After insisting Bernie take the front seat, Klobuchar told Josh to sit on her lap for the twenty-minute ride to the hotel. On the way, she gave us a verbal tour of Minneapolis, while Josh had the most uncomfortable car ride of his life.

* * * *

BERNIE MIGHT NOT BE a typical politician, but the plan to limit our participation in the Liberty and Justice Celebration in Iowa in late 2019 made others on the campaign nervous. Ultimately other senior staffers heard about Misty Rebik and Pete D'Alessandro's idea to radically cut back on our presence at the event. "How many tickets did we have to the Liberty and Justice Celebration?" a number of senior staffers frantically asked those of us who had been in Iowa. The answer was, none. These staffers were in shock, and ran to Bernie to express their outrage. He would be onstage at the event and possibly face a hostile crowd, and they thought this was unacceptable. They called the state party to see if we could get any tickets, but the event had been sold out for weeks. We were stuck. It became a source of consternation within the campaign.

In my view, Iowa politics were Misty and Pete's specialty. They knew the state and the main players. Better than anyone else, they understood the ramifications of what they had proposed. I also liked the idea of no longer accepting the extortionate practices of the Iowa Democratic Party. Campaigns were spending themselves into the ground and had been for a long time. I was reminded of a meeting during the general election in 2004 when I was on the internet team for John Kerry's presidential campaign. Next to our area of the office in downtown Washington, DC, sat the political department. There were rows of desks, with each staffer focused on a different constituency. One time, a senior operative asked the lower-level staffers in the political department to introduce themselves. Each said which political group within the party they were responsible for speaking with. After about ten minutes of this, he screamed out, "Does anybody here talk to fucking voters?"

Every dollar that went to the Iowa Democratic Party was a dollar we weren't spending to talk to voters, not only in Iowa but across the country. The state was critical because it went first. Bernie needed to win it, and a bad performance could end his campaign. But the people who attended the official Democratic Party would not caucus for us.

The night of the dinner, we held our "March Against Corporate Greed," as planned. Thousands of Iowans joined us as we walked to the venue where the official dinner was taking place. It was precisely the type of celebration Bernie loved, working-class people, of all ages and races, joining together to make themselves heard. Our supporters split off and went to a dinner event and organizing training hosted by the campaign across the street. Bernie went into a backstage room to prepare for his speech to the state's Democratic Party.

The night's news was already dominated by the fact that Beto O'Rourke was dropping out of the race and would not appear at the dinner at all. After launching his campaign with the largest first-day fundraising haul of any candidate, Beto developed a reputation for campaigning harder than anyone else, particularly in Iowa, where he would sometime hold up to a dozen events in a single day. But it didn't matter. The energy around him was a media bubble. That bubble popped, and that was it.

He was not the only candidate who experienced this. National media narratives always play an immense role in voter decisions, but in this cycle, the effect felt bigger than ever. Both Beto and Kamala Harris had their positions inflated by media attention, only to be revealed as weak.

Bernie was worried before his speech. "Ari, I am walking into enemy territory." He knew the room would be filled with other candidates' supporters, and none of his. He also knew that many in Iowa, especially those predisposed not to like him, would be angered by our campaign's effective boycott of the event.

The nervousness on display in our hold room never appeared on the floor of the convention hall. Bernie strode out and spoke to a cheering audience—a surprisingly positive reaction. All the other candidates' sections were decked out with banners. People had signs and noisemakers. Campaigns had paid tens of thousands of dollars just to put banners in the hall. If you walked into the room with no prior knowledge of American politics, you would not even know that Bernie Sanders was a candidate, let alone a formidable one.

The content of Bernie's speech ended up not mattering much. What reporters were interested in was the fact that Bernie used a podium. While every other candidate chose to speak with a hand-held mic, we had requested a podium. Why? Because Bernie always likes a podium. It made him feel more comfortable when giving even a short, ten-minute speech. I got more than four dozen texts during his speech asking if the podium was a means of supporting himself, post–heart attack. In the end, I don't think the press or the other campaigns even noticed that none of our supporters were in the hall.

CHAPTER 7

"Rallying the people"

DURING MY FIRST MEETING WITH BERNIE IN LATE 2016, when I was interviewing for a job with him, our conversation centered on planning rallies to fight for the Affordable Care Act, which we knew would be threatened by the GOP. After identifying as an independent throughout his entire career, Bernie was asked by Chuck Schumer, following the 2016 election, to become a member of the Democratic leadership team. His specific responsibility was for outreach, taking a lead role selling the Democratic agenda and the failures of Trump's presidency. He took that responsibility seriously. Bernie knew other members of the caucus were more skilled at the inside game—and would have a better shot of wooing John McCain, Susan Collins, Lisa Murkowski, and other Republicans in the hopes they would buck their party and vote against the repeal of the Affordable Care Act. Not only is Bernie not good at this type of politics—he also doesn't place much value on it. He is a successful grassroots politician because he genuinely believes change comes from outside Washington. He sees the inside game as slow, plodding, and biased toward incremental adjustments to a completely broken system. His heroes and role models are those individuals who created mass movements, including Martin Luther King Jr. and Eugene Debs. Grassroots action may also take time to produce change, but when changes comes, it does so as a tidal wave.

Bernie is well aware that other senators were more knowledgeable about the policy details of the Affordable Care Act. It's not that he is ignorant about policy. He simply recognizes others are better at the nitty-gritty work. Bernie's talent is expanding the realm of the possible and rallying people to his side.

For the same reasons, Bernie is not a creature of the Senate floor. Harry Reid, even before he was a member of the Democratic leadership, struck up a friendship with Senator Robert Byrd of West Virginia, who had spent a lifetime in the Senate and probably knew more about floor procedure in the chamber than any human who ever lived. Through Byrd's tutelage, Reid learned how the Senate functioned in all its (often strange) particulars, and that was his strength as the Democratic leader. Bernie has never bothered with arcane rules, even though as a ranking member of the Senate Budget Committee he would play a significant role in managing the floor process to defend the Affordable Care Act against Trump and a GOP-controlled Congress.

In his mind, defending the ACA would require leaving DC, traveling the country, and especially red states such as West Virginia, speaking directly to voters. Bernie believes in the persuasive potential of conversation. For a politician with a reputation for avoiding glad-handing, Bernie has an abiding faith in the goodness, decency, and intelligence of ordinary people, regardless of party. Go out. Speak to people. Make your case directly. And you can change minds.

This is why Bernie loves rallies. He doesn't love them because they allow him to bask in adulation. He loves them because they provide a way to connect with a lot of people at once. In his view (and mine), politics has become too impersonal and too driven by a never-ending cycle of fundraising, consultants, and television ads. As Bernie sees it, most political events are fundamentally fake. They are staged dramas for the cameras, put on by advance staff more concerned with their next gig and political connections than with improving people's lives. When Bernie goes onstage, the clips and the press matter less than the people he is talking to.

"Rallying the people" is what he calls it. The practice is as fundamental to his political identity as is Medicare for All. One of Bernie's defining characteristics as a politician is that he doesn't just want to convince people of his beliefs, he wants to persuade people to engage in politics in the same manner he does.

His most significant and frequent complaint about working with the Clinton campaign in the fall of 2016 was precisely that they were more concerned with the images than with the people attending their events. He would describe leaving the stage at a rally put on by the Clinton campaign and asking the staff how many people had attended. Instead of responding with a number, they would talk about how good the event looked on television, not the number of people who attended or the grassroots actions taken. This was the cardinal sin, to Bernie.

As a member of the Senate Democratic leadership, Bernie would use rallies to fight for the Affordable Care Act. This was an admittedly uncomfortable position for him. Since the deaths of Paul Wellstone in 2002 and Ted Kennedy in 2009, Bernie Sanders had been waging an incredibly lonely fight in the Senate for Medicare for All. He believes, in the core of his being, that private insurance companies are evil—that they exist solely to profit from the misery of those who are sick and that they stand in the way of people getting the care they need.

While expanding Medicaid and providing wider access to the private insurance market, the Affordable Care Act actually increased the power of the insurance industry in the United States. A portion of the left would have been happy to let the Affordable Care Act die. Ultimately, they argued, the pain created by tens of millions losing their health care would force the creation of a better and more robust single-payer system. Bernie rejected that idea. For him, despite its faults, the Affordable Care Act had saved hundreds of thousands, if not millions, of lives.

Furthermore, because of Bernie's advocacy, the ACA included

one of the largest expansions of Community Health Centers since that program began in 1964, as Neighborhood Health Centers, after the passage of Lyndon Johnson's Economic Opportunity Act. These federally subsidized facilities allow people to receive primary care and sometimes dental care at low or no cost. Allowing Trump and the Republican Party to repeal the ACA would condemn tens of thousands of Americans, especially those with preexisting conditions and without access to the employer health care market, to death. It was not an option; Bernie never considered it.

Harry Reid loves to tell the story about how he inserted $11 billion into the Affordable Care Act to fund Community Health Centers, at Bernie's request. "You tell reporters, Ari, if they don't believe this is true, they can just call me," Reid said to me on multiple occasions.

In the spring of 2017, Bernie became almost single-minded: our staff would work on saving the Affordable Care Act from Donald Trump.

The common view of Bernie as someone who doesn't play well with others and is happier going off in his own direction was also demonstrated in this period. For example, in early 2017, after the Senate rejected an amendment to the budget bill that called for the importation of prescription drugs, which would have reduced prices in the United States—Bernie was upset. The staffer driving his effort, Warren Gunnels, staff director of the Senate Budget Committee, is not known for communicating in subtleties. He is the longest continually serving Bernie staffer, and is the embodiment of Bernie's politics and policies. He will fight vigorously with other staffers and even members of the Senate who he feels are standing in his or the senator's way.

When the Senate rejected the amendment, Warren and Bernie walked off the floor and, in front of a crowd of reporters, they implied that Democrats who voted against the amendment, without naming names, were sellouts to the pharmaceutical industry. This group included New Jersey senator Cory Booker and Pennsylvania senator Bob Casey. The comments set off waves of recriminations both online and within the Democratic caucus. Unlike earlier in his career, Bernie would have to engage in something unfamiliar to him: a balancing act. He was no longer a lone wolf. Now he was a member of Senate leadership. Ultimately the two Senators would strike a compromise with Bernie and join him in introducing a drug importation bill later that Congress.

*　*　*　*

THE SECOND WEEK OF JANUARY 2017, Bernie Sanders held what he called "our first stand." This was his first majority initiative doing outreach as a member of Senate leadership.

The plan that was hatched in the December meeting in which I interviewed for my job—for Democratic senators to hold a series of rallies in their states in January, demonstrating unity against Donald Trump and Republican efforts to repeal the Affordable Care Act—had found support within the Democratic caucus. Bernie, along with Senate Democratic Leader Chuck Schumer and Michigan senator Debbie Stabenow, would hold a large rally in Macomb County, Michigan.

Macomb, a suburban county north of Detroit, was one of the areas of the state that flipped from Obama to Trump in the 2016 election. Its economy had been harmed by neoliberal trade treaties that resulted in factories being shut down as manufacturing jobs moved overseas. The county is populated with white working-class voters who had not only voted for Donald Trump, but had left the Democratic Party. To Bernie, these were the very voters whose lives would be turned upside down if the Affordable Care Act was repealed.

While the Democratic Senate leadership would rally in Michigan, other members of the caucus as well as Democrats in the House were asked to hold their own events around the country. This was risky. It was one week before the Women's March, which was already shaping up to be one of the largest-ever gatherings of progressives in American history. We had real questions about whether people would be willing to show up for direct actions two weeks in a row. There were also questions about whether senators and House members would be willing to participate in rallies so close to the inauguration. And would progressive groups promote the ACA events on their email lists?

It turned out our worries were unfounded. That day in Michigan, more than 8,000 people came out in a freezing cold parking lot to rally for the Affordable Care Act. Eight thousand is a large crowd in Michigan at the height of a presidential election. Eight thousand for a losing presidential candidate and a few senators is unheard of. But large crowds gathered not only in Michigan but at least eighty-six events around the country.

"Our First Stand" rallies were Bernie's first successful act as a member of the Democratic leadership. He was so pleased with the results that he decided he wanted to re-create them, so we put together a second set of rallies in February. The lesson of this second set of rallies was that other than Bernie Sanders, members of the caucus were generally uninterested in regularly holding large rallies.

Bernie expressed amazement at this fact. His fellow Democratic senators would travel across the country, fundraising at every stop, but never meet with real people. Fundraising, of course, meant spending time in a few donor-rich, affluent areas. A very large portion of national fundraising takes place in New York, Los Angeles, the Bay Area, Chicago, Boston, and Florida. In the summers, people go to Martha's Vineyard, Nantucket, and the Hamptons. Bernie had stopped making those fundraising trips years earlier, which was part of the reason he had the time and the ability to visit places other members ignored. For the second series of rallies, Bernie went to Kansas and held a large rally with the state's Democratic Party.

Now the question became, what next? While we had received

a reprieve before the April recess, because Republicans failed to pass their bill that would repeal the Affordable Care Act through the House of Representatives, they would not give up. With control of both houses of Congress, they saw repeal as a task they had to carry out to satisfy their base. As long as the debate continued, Bernie wanted to keep the grassroots involved.

At the same time, Bernie had a second priority: the reintroduction of Medicare for All. There is no single piece of legislation Bernie Sanders is more identified with than his bill to bring single-payer health care to every American. The idea was not his. President Harry Truman had advocated for a Medicare-for-all system, and when President Lyndon Johnson signed Medicare into law in the 1960s, it was designed as a stopgap measure on the way to a single-payer system. First, Johnson would prove the success of the program for seniors. Then his administration would take the obvious step and expand coverage to everyone else. But the second step never occurred. Medicare for All has been viciously attacked from the moment Truman proposed it. At the height of the Cold War, the American Medical Association hired a Hollywood actor and pitchman named Ronald Reagan to persuade Americans that Truman's proposal was socialism. The quest for universal coverage continued post-Johnson with various members in the Senate, most notably Ted Kennedy and Paul Wellstone, who led what became an increasingly lonely campaign.

During his campaign for president in 2015 and 2016, Bernie did not actually introduce his own Medicare for All bill. Early 2017 was finally the time to do so. Lori Kearns, Bernie's chief counsel, was primarily responsible for the gargantuan task of writing the Medicare for All bill. As Donald Trump had so artfully noted, "health care is complicated." Changes to health care impact not only nearly 20 percent of the economy, but the lives of most if not all Americans.

Fear drives much of the discussion around our health care system. All of us are afraid of getting sick, of what a doctor's visit will cost us, of the results of tests, and of losing our coverage. Opponents of change know this and rely on fear to prevent progress. Barack Obama experienced this firsthand when he passed the Affordable Care Act—a bill that did not fundamentally change the profit model that drives our health care system. At the most basic level, Bernie Sanders wants to destroy the current system—or, at least, the incentives driving insurance companies' actions.

Initially, we had planned to introduce Medicare for All in the spring. Lori worked up a draft, but it became clear to us that it wouldn't make sense, politically, to introduce the bill while fighting to preserve the Affordable Care Act. This allowed Lori to spend an additional few months building support within the Democratic caucus necessary to bring as many cosponsors to the table as possible. That number would be our key metric. Previously, not a single member of the Senate had cosponsored Bernie's bill. If we could get five other senators to sign on to Medicare for All legislation, we would view it as a success, even though we obviously had no illusion the bill would become law in 2018.

In the meantime, we went on a tour over April recess that was initially supposed to focus on health care. After the House failed to pass Donald Trump's health care bill in April, we shifted to a "Unity Tour" with Democratic Party chairman Tom Perez. But as it became clear Republicans were ramping up their efforts again, we returned to the plan for ACA rallies. We would not do large-scale rallies in the big blue states. Bernie's goal during June and July was to travel to red states and more rural areas to argue that ending the Affordable Care Act would be a political mistake for local politicians.

Bernie often expected these events to materialize out of nowhere. On one particular Wednesday, he called me into his office, asking what we could do that weekend to combat Trump and the Republicans. I paused for a second, fatally, which allowed Bernie to answer the question for himself: we should do rallies in Pennsylvania, Ohio, and West Virginia.

It was not only a Wednesday; it was also around 5 PM. He wanted the first rally to take place on Friday. We now had a monumental assignment in front of us. Over the next few hours, I worked with MoveOn.org and other organizations, put an advance team on the ground in each of the states, and found venues and speakers. Within twenty-four hours we publicly announced the tour. When Bernie landed in Pittsburgh that Friday, 2,000 people were waiting for us at the city's convention center. We had a full lineup of speakers ready to go, people whose lives would be upended if they lost their health care.

Afterward, as we pulled out of the venue to drive to Columbus, Bernie asked me if I would like steak for dinner. Sure, I said. He then said, "Have you ever eaten at the Outback Steakhouse?"

"No, Senator," I replied.

"Their rib eye is delicious."

Phil Fiermonte, who had worked for Bernie since his first mayoral race, was driving eighty-five miles per hour out of the city while also googling Outback locations. He found one in St. Clairsville, Ohio. At about 9 PM that evening, Bernie Sanders, four staff members, MoveOn staffer Ben Wikler (later chair of the Wisconsin Democratic Party), and a coterie of reporters walked into the rural Outback Steakhouse, to the delight and confusion of the locals enjoying drinks on Friday night.

We ordered our dinner, and at the end of the night Bernie took selfies with other customers. One woman said she was praying that he would stop killing babies—a reference to abortion—but other than that, the interactions were positive.

Leaving the restaurant, Bernie said to me, "Ari, how was your steak? I bet it wasn't any worse than the ones you get at that Rahm Emmanuel place you and Jeff like to eat at." The "Rahm Emmanuel place" was BLT Steak, a high-end steak house a few blocks from the White House. The reason Bernie calls BLT the "Rahm Emmanuel place" is that once, after a meeting a block away at AFL-CIO headquarters, he walked in expecting a moderately priced steak house. He saw the former White House chief of staff as well as the prices on the menu, and promptly exited. It is an objective fact that a steak at BLT Steak is better than the steak at Outback. Bernie will never agree.

Bernie's opinion on steak is suspect. In August 2018, I was in Burlington, where Warren Gunnels and I were helping the senator with his book, *Where We Go from Here*. Bernie asked us if we wanted dinner and suggested "steak."

"Steak" can mean a number of things, when Bernie says it. In DC, "the steak place" might refer to Pizzeria Uno in Union Station, where they will serve you a burnt piece of shoe leather. "Going for steak" with Bernie in Burlington meant a Japanese hibachi restaurant that was at least OK, though I would never classify flying shrimp and onion volcanoes as "steak." On this day, Bernie meant that we would grill in his backyard.

First, Bernie and I went to the supermarket in his Chevy Aveo. Contrary to internet rumors spread by conservatives, Bernie Sanders drives perhaps one of the worst American cars ever made. As he has told me about its origins: "I went to the lot and asked them for their cheapest car." It is a terrible vehicle—tiny and ill-equipped for Vermont winters. I once watched him drive up an icy hill in a Vermont winter, questioning both how he survived and his sanity.

At the supermarket, Bernie was quick and efficient. He purchased a large London broil, frozen peas, and a quart of ice cream, and we were on our way. Back at his house, he took the steak right out of the packaging and tossed it on his cold propane grill. Only then did he turn it on. This guaranteed the steak would have no sear, and the juices would run right out of it. He put the package of peas in the microwave, flipped the steak once, and ten minutes later, we had a bone-dry steak and slightly cold peas.

I questioned the culinary quality of this meal, though Warren loved every bite. "God, Bernie, this is one of the best steaks I've had," he said. "Ari, I don't understand what you are complaining about."

Until Bernie had his heart attack, the Outback Steakhouse was one of his favorite restaurants. When on the road, he found a certain level of comfort in fast-casual dining places, even though they were parts of large corporations whose power and influence he so often decried. Bernie understood this, of course, but I think he found comfort in knowing exactly what he'd get when he walked into one of these restaurants. As he told me: "Ari, what I like about Outback is, the food is good, the people are nice, and the staff doesn't come to the table and bug you a million times." I had never eaten at Outback before this trip, but I would become a regular patron, dining there dozens of times with Bernie over the next three years.

The trip continued to be eye-opening for me. I had only been working for Bernie for a few months, and this was only my second time on the road with him.

I learned that Bernie had a particular formula he wanted at events. First, music was essential—there always had to be live music; the genre was unimportant. Throughout my time with Bernie, everyone from reggae to bluegrass bands, from local garage bands to some of the biggest musical acts in the world, performed at our events. For Bernie, it was about creating an environment that went beyond politics. Political gatherings should be community events, and, above all else, should be fun.

Bernie was also focused on the other speakers at his events. In his view, they were there to tell their own stories. Bernie had a platform, and he was happy to share it. But he didn't want local politicians spouting pabulum. Often, though, it was not easy to keep the politicians at bay, because so many requested speaking roles and got very upset when they were told they would not be part of the program. On this tour, Bernie was not happy with the lineup of speakers. They were too political and, he believed, too focused on Trump; there was not enough about how ending the Affordable Care Act would impact the lives of everyday people. At least, this was true until we reached West Virginia.

One of the speakers at our rally in Charleston was Rusty Williamson, a local tattoo artist from Nitro, a town named for its production of nitrocellulose for ammunition during World War I. Rusty had recovered from testicular cancer to become one of his state's leading advocates for medical marijuana and Medicare for All. He was incredibly moving onstage, as he told the story of his health struggles. He was precisely the type of natural speaker, and leader, Bernie gravitated toward. He pulled me aside backstage and said, "See Rusty? That is who I want at every rally." Rusty, inspired by Bernie, would run for the state legislature in West Virginia in 2020, winning the Democratic primary in his district.

After the rally speech, we headed to Chuck Yeager Airport in Morgantown for the short flight back to DC. The airport's only food option is a pizza place just before security. Our group decided to stop to eat before boarding. As we entered the restaurant and were seated, we heard screaming in the kitchen. We couldn't make out what the man was saying, but it sounded like someone was extremely angry.

Bernie asked what was going on, and I replied that it must be a Trump supporter. Driving through the state, we encountered very little antipathy, even in deep-red areas. At a truck stop where Bernie used the restroom, an overweight white man with a mullet turned his pickup truck around and sped toward us. It turned out he was a supporter who was just excited to see Bernie. Now, as the screams in the pizza shop's kitchen grew progressively louder, it became evident that someone was very unhappy Bernie was in their place of business.

Suddenly a chef burst into the dining room, charging toward our table. Two of his coworkers were trying to restrain him. Phil Fiermonte and I got up, as though ready for a physical confrontation. Then we heard what he was saying. Though most of it was still hard to make out, one line was clear: "She was a beautiful woman, and she went to China to help people, and you destroyed her. YOU DESTROYED HILLARY."

At this point, his coworkers dragged him back to the kitchen. Bernie remained sitting calmly at the table, and said, "Well, I guess Hillary had one supporter in West Virginia."

Our ACA tours continued throughout 2017, as Republicans continually threatened to reintroduce their failed bill. We would do two more rallies in West Virginia. Bernie's strategy was straightforward: States like Kentucky and West Virginia were among the poorest in the country and led by Republican politicians who didn't care at all about their most vulnerable citizens. If Bernie could show at least some locals that there was a better way, these trips would be worth it, even if they didn't result in flipping a state blue.

Being out on the road was fuel for Bernie. It was where he found the most joy—sometimes at the expense of his staff. Armand, our videographer and frequent travel companion, was vegan. The problem with Bernie and veganism starts with the fact that he cannot pronounce "vegan." He says "vay-gan." More importantly, our stops at the Outback and other chain restaurants were not exactly vegan-friendly, and Armand had difficulty finding food.

At one point, we were driving through Wisconsin between Racine and Green Bay, and Armand asked if we could stop at a vegan sandwich shop ten minutes off the road. Bernie said yes, and we set the GPS. It turned out the restaurant was a stand inside a public market in downtown Milwaukee. As Armand ordered his lunch, a selfie line formed around Bernie. Dozens of people lined up. Armand, as our photographer, was going hungry—every time he tried to take a bite of his food, another person would hand him their phone. For some reason, Bernie thought this was the funniest thing he had ever seen and could not stop laughing. Armand, though still hungry, also managed to see the humor in the scenario.

Bernie always seemed to dread our trips, nervous about what he would say onstage and already feeling a bit tired. But the moment he stepped onstage at the first rally of a trip, he was transformed. It wasn't the crowd size that gave him energy—though Bernie does love a big rally—it was the fact that he was out of DC and connecting with people who were there because they cared about their communities. We would continue to travel the country through June and July, rallying the people in defense of their own health care, until John McCain's decisive thumbs-down vote in the Senate in late July ended Republican attempts to repeal the Affordable Care Act.

* * * *

AS AUGUST RECESS APPROACHED, it was finally time to start moving toward introducing Bernie's Medicare for All bill. Lori Kearns and another staffer, Marissa Barrera, spent much of the summer working with seventeen other Senate offices to assemble the bill. There were numerous forces, often with competing interests, trying to influence the legislation—even beyond those opposed to Medicare for All. For years, supporters of Medicare for All had been in the wilderness. This was the most serious bill-writing process in a long while, and they wanted their policy preferences included.

Additionally, because health care plays such a prominent role in our lives, numerous side issues became serious obstacles. The lessons we learned during the drafting process served our campaign well as we entered the debate on health care in 2019, by which time we had spent a great deal of time answering questions other candidates and their staffs were trying to respond to on the spot.

For example, there was the question of how to deal with immigrants. While the issue might seem outside the scope of a health care bill, how immigrants would be covered was a particularly contentious point. Even stickier was how to deal with undocumented immigrants within a health care bill. It is no small matter, on a practical level: the more people you leave out of the system, the greater the cost to other patients and the government when uninsured people fail to pay hospital bills. During pandemics, you risk people spreading disease because they can't get the care they desperately need. Bernie saw it as a basic moral question, similar in some respects to his view of the rights of imprisoned people to vote. As he said when we discussed the issue with him, "If we say health care for all, we mean health care for all, and that includes legal immigrants and the undocumented."

A second major issue for any universal health care bill is abortion. To Bernie and other progressives, abortion is reproductive health care, and reproductive health care must be covered. This would mean unraveling the Hyde Amendment, which blocks federal money from being spent on abortions. To Bernie, this was also a basic moral question. The Hyde Amendment prevents women from receiving necessary medical care. Therefore it must go.

The main interest group that had backed the bill from the start was National Nurses United. NNU, a union of more than 100,000 nurses, was then run by RoseAnn DeMoro, who was so close with Bernie that she attended the meeting in my apartment in 2018. RoseAnn and her organization were tough political streetfighters. The union was concerned that Bernie might moderate his position to win more cosponsorships in the Senate. Two overriding issues were at the top of their minds. The first was copays. How much would Americans have to pay each time they went to the doctor's office? It is widely understood that any charge, even a de minimis one, reduces people's access to care. Yet many experts believe these charges are necessary to prevent people from overusing health care services.

The nurses demanded that the Medicare for All system our bill would create involve no copays. Our office was divided on the matter. One side felt it was necessary to win over cosponsors and reduce the cost of the legislation. A second argued that health care was a human right, and any obstacle to access cut into that basic right. Bernie's guidance was unambiguous: all copays were out, with the exception of a small one for prescription drugs. This also allowed for a clear political message: no copays, no premiums, no deductibles, though he did allow for a small copay, no more than $200 per year, for prescription drugs.

The second overriding issue raised by NNU—one that would ultimately create doubts among Medicare for All activists about Elizabeth Warren's health care policy during the campaign—was the timeline for implementation. For decades Medicare for All advocates pointed to Medicare's one-year implementation in 1965 as their North Star. Most policy experts were not comfortable with this timeline, however, and other supportive members of the Democratic caucus were divided. Nobody believed it was possible to implement Medicare for All in a single year. Al Franken's staff occupied the outer boundary, believing the bill should provide for a multidecade implementation process, slowly making more people eligible for the federal program every year.

Ultimately, a four-year compromise plan, written by Kirsten Gillibrand, emerged. In the first year, the eligibility age for Medicare would drop to fifty-five while also covering all people up to age twenty-five. The window would tighten annually until everyone in the United States was covered.

Private insurance could still exist, but only for services not already covered in the bill. We were trying to avoid creating a two-tiered health care system—one for the wealthy, one for everyone else. Our bill allowed for people to pay out of pocket and choose not to have insurance, but once they made that choice, there would be severe restrictions on enrolling in the public program. Only the very rich would ever dream of opting out, and even then, the decision would be financially questionable.

Throughout August, Lori continued to improve the bill, sending new language back and forth to Legislative Counsel, the office that all senators use to formally draft their legislation. Finally, our office set a deadline. We would introduce the bill in September, for the first week Congress returned from its August recess. But how much support would we receive?

Bernie's Medicare for All bill, previously known as the American Health Security Act when he introduced it in 2009, 2011, and 2013, had never received a single cosponsor in the Senate, so any support would be an improvement. In retrospect, our lack of confidence seemed irrational. But at the time, we were worried that fewer than five other senators would support the legislation. This would be viewed as a failure. We were so concerned about the bill not finding any support that I made a bet to spur on our efforts. If we got five cosponsors, I would run around the Capitol wearing a cape and with Lori's dog Smokey—a tiny Havanese—on my head.

Just as we announced our deadline, we received word that we had our first cosponsor on the bill: California senator Kamala Harris would sign on to the legislation. Her staff informed us she was likely to announce her support at a town hall she was holding that evening. We watched, unsure whether she would actually do it. Her announcement was a huge breakthrough. It would add the necessary pressure on others: with Harris on the bill, other 2020 aspirants would join. The one big question was whether Elizabeth Warren would cosponsor the bill. Other offices, even some that would never consider cosponsoring, had participated in our working group that drafted the legislation. However, Warren's office had remained unresponsive. We heard rumors that her staff pushed hard to convince her not to join the bill. This created a very real problem for us.

Part of my job was to collect endorsements for the legislation from progressive groups. There were several organizations, most notably MoveOn, that would not sign onto the bill unless both Sanders and Warren were behind it. It would be politically risky for them to do otherwise. This was expressed to me by their staff in no uncertain terms. Our fear was that other progressive groups could hold off from supporting the bill as a result of MoveOn's decision.

The push for cosponsors had two main goals. First, we wanted to advance toward making the legislation a reality. That meant we needed more public support. The more groups that supported us, the more members of Congress would feel comfortable getting on board—and the more members, the more additional groups would join.

The second, though more immediate, goal was to tie other 2020 candidates to the bill. The more members who signed on and who were also potentially running for president in 2020, the more difficult it would become to attack Medicare for All during the primary. Bernie was still unsure whether he would run or not. If he did run, having as many other candidates on the bill as possible would be a way to deflect criticism of the bill. If he did not run, support for the bill would still position Bernie as a leader on the issue within the Democratic Party. Those who were running for the Democratic nomination would have little choice but to rally around the bill in an attempt to win his endorsement.

Health care was one of the most critical issues for Democratic voters, including specific, and vital, voting blocs, such as Latinos. The more potential candidates on our bill, the more territory would be ceded to Bernie. In debates, candidates would be forced to defend the idea as their own, at least in part.

Once someone signed on, moreover, they would have a hell of a time backing away from Medicare for All—as Kamala Harris would find during the primary.

This strategy was in part based on a conversation that took place years earlier, when I was seated next to the infamous anti-tax activist Grover Norquist at a dinner in Washington, DC. At some functions, hotels have a habit of putting the dessert on the table right in front of you when you sit down. It stares at you through the salad and dinner courses. Everyone at the table engages in a silent game of chicken to see who will be the first to eat it. Grover immediately ate his cupcake after sitting down. He might be one of the most toxic activists in the history of Washington, DC, but this was an idea I could get behind. I asked why he didn't wait. Grover replied that the fire alarm could go off or something else might force him to leave. Why go without dessert when it was already in front of him? He was right.

I also asked him about the no-tax pledge he had successfully convinced most GOP politicians to sign over the years. What made it so effective? Grover responded truthfully. It was self-enforcing. Once a politician signed the pledge, they were locked in. His organization wouldn't need to spend money to attack apostates; the conservative base would bring fire and brimstone if a politician violated it.

Our strategy relied on the same insight. The signatures of any likely candidates, at least during this presidential cycle, were written in blood. Medicare for All was extremely popular among the Democratic electorate. There would be an enormous political price if a candidate was perceived to have flip-flopped on the issue.

About a week before we introduced the bill, Warren asked for a meeting with Bernie. She came over to the office and went in alone, without staff. The two of them met for about thirty minutes. We held our breath outside. When she left, we piled into Bernie's office, and he told us, "She is on the bill."

By the time the bill was introduced, we had sixteen cosponsors, including every Democrat in the chamber considering a presidential run. The group included Warren, Gillibrand, Harris, Cory Booker, Jeff Merkley, and, to our surprise, Al Franken.

The oddest cosponsor, though, and the one we still do not understand, was New Hampshire senator Jeanne Shaheen. Her staff had not participated in the drafting of the bill. She didn't show up at the launch event, and in the next Congress, she didn't sign on. But for some reason that remains unexplained, she was with us that day.

The press conference on September 13, 2017, to introduce the bill took the shape of a celebratory rally. We printed giant banners that said "Healthcare is a human right" and placards with "Medicare for All" on them. We had invited people with medical horror stories as well as doctors and nurses to speak in support of the bill. And member after member—presidential candidate after presidential candidate—stood up in support of the legislation.

* * * *

MEDICARE FOR ALL was front and center throughout the 2020 primary, as we expected it would be. When Harris tried to step back from her support for the bill, she paid the expected price. Other candidates hugged Bernie tightly during the debates, as we predicted they would. Kirsten Gillibrand bragged onstage about writing the portion of the bill dealing with the implementation timeline, while Elizabeth Warren declared, simply, "I'm with Bernie."

Yet in mid-November 2019, Warren made what we viewed as a mistake when she, too, tried to move away from Bernie. Medicare for All was the centerpiece policy of Bernie Sanders's presidential campaign. Part of the issue came down to the question, "How are we going to pay for it?"

Study after study shows that Medicare for All would save our country money. We are expected to spend approximately $50 trillion over the next ten years on health care, under the current system. That figure includes health insurance premiums, copays, out-of-pocket expenditures, and government spending on Medicare, Medicaid, and CHIP, along with various tax deductions and credits that fund health care. If everything was filtered through a single program, the resulting efficiencies would reduce costs.

If all those expenses were put on the federal government, government expenditure on health care would obviously increase. Bernie was clear and straightforward about this: instead of paying premiums to a private insurance company, you would pay a tax. The vast majority of Americans would spend less money on health care.

When reporters asked, "How are you going to pay for it?" what they were really asking was, "Are you willing to raise taxes on the middle class?" Bernie answered honestly: yes.

Warren put herself in a bind by answering no. She would now have to release a plan to cover the costs of a single-payer system. This strategy did not make sense. If she were planning on breaking from Bernie on the issue, the time to do it would have been in April or May, so that the issue would be resolved in the media by the time people were paying close attention in the fall. Instead she would release her plan in November. According to reporters, it would come in two parts. First would come the financing part. Second would be the implementation part.

The night before she released the first part, we started getting phone calls from reporters asking us to respond. This was odd, because we didn't know what Warren's plan was. I and other Bernie staffers tried to extrapolate what she would propose based on what we were hearing from the press. This created an impossible puzzle. Warren made the commitment that she would not raise taxes on the middle class to fund Medicare for All. This left limited options for raising the revenue needed to pay for universal health care.

Our nightmare scenario was that she had found some brilliant solution that our team had not thought of. This would have been less of a political nightmare than a personal embarrassment. If Bernie had to say that Warren had come up with a great plan to finance Medicare for All, so be it. But we had spent years on the question. Lori Kearns knew more about the issue than any other policy expert, and many of us weren't far behind. Could Warren and her people have come up with some solution we weren't thinking of?

In the end, it was Josh Orton who puzzled out what her plan was. They would either use an employer-side payroll tax or a head tax. It was the only way they could hit the revenue number necessary to offset the costs of single-payer insurance. The problem was that either tax would, at a technical level, violate the notion that Warren was not going to raise taxes on the middle class. Because the employer pays them, these taxes would still be factored into the cost of payroll. A straight payroll tax increase would be difficult for our campaign to object to because Bernie's own plan included one as a pay for. But the head tax was not acceptable from a policy perspective. It would essentially charge companies a flat fee per employee for their health care, a practice that placed the greatest burden on lower-wage workers. If companies had to pay $7,000 per worker, this would mean a 20 percent increase in the total cost of compensation for a $35,000 worker versus a 3.5 percent increase for a worker making $200,000 per year. A payroll tax like Bernie envisioned would keep the percentage the same regardless of salary, meaning companies would have to pay more for a $200,000 worker than they would for a $35,000 one.

Warren had chosen a head tax, a fundamental contrast with Bernie's philosophy that all government taxes and fees had to be progressive. There was no chance he would go along with her plan. I think Warren was genuinely surprised by this result. She and Bernie played phone tag the next day, but they finally reached each other while our plane was preparing for takeoff in Manchester, New Hampshire, for

Iowa. He expressed his concerns with her plan. I couldn't hear what she said in response, but it was a curt conversation.

When Bernie was asked about Warren's plan by the media a few days later, he was unequivocal. "I think we have a better way, which is a 7.5% payroll tax, which is far more I think progressive because it'll not impact employers of low wage workers but hit significantly employers of upper income people."[24]

A few weeks later, Warren unveiled her strategy for implementing Medicare for All. Bernie's plan had the four-year implementation period designed by Kirsten Gillibrand. Warren said she would wait until the third year of her term in office to begin pushing for Medicare for All, extending out the calendar to seven years.

For activists who had spent decades fighting for Medicare for All, even four years was too long to wait. As Grover Norquist had explained to me, the most powerful pledges are self-reinforcing. We didn't have to do anything to fight against Warren's plan.

When the Warren campaign was asked what she was referring to when she complained about negative attacks from our campaign, they cited our response to her health care plan, among other issues. On two levels, this seemed mistaken. First of all, activists controlled the message. There had been times in 2017 and 2018 when they protested against Bernie over both the timeline of our Medicare for All bill and the lack of coverage for long-term care—though this problem was fixed in the 2019 version. We couldn't have stopped them from speaking out even if we wanted to.

Second, her plan seemed like an act of arrogance from their camp. The whole theory behind their plan was that despite our team's years of work on this subject, they could somehow devise a way around the political attacks that would come with the admission that taxes would go up.

Instead of blunting attacks from Pete Buttigieg and other moderates, the Warren team's rollout of her health care plan only led

to increased aggression from the left side of the party. Simultaneously, because of our endorsements from AOC, Omar, and
Tlaib and the ads on the air in Iowa, we were steadily rising in the
polls. By the third week in November, Bernie was back solidly in
second place, with Joe Biden in our sights.

CHAPTER 8

"Do you think Hannah Montana will campaign in Montana for us?"

BERNIE HAS LONG HELD THE IDEA THAT IF YOU RECOGNIZE people's intelligence and treat them with respect, you can bridge even broad political divides. He loves large crowds but didn't want his campaign to merely be a series of rallies at which people could come and cheer, with politics becoming a sporting event. On our trip to Iowa in early November, joined by AOC, Bernie would do something different. We would host a conference in Des Moines with several hours' worth of panels and speakers focused on climate change. While Medicare for All was and is Bernie's signature issue, he is most immediately concerned about the threat of climate change.

This was another example of Bernie's being well ahead of the curve. During a debate with Hillary Clinton in 2016, pundits laughed at Bernie when he said that climate was our greatest national security challenge. The commentators said it showed his liberal naivete and made him appear to be a less serious candidate. Four years later, on the Democratic debate stage, his was now the consensus view.

Bernie also understood that climate change was a critical motivating factor for so many young people involved in our campaign. He will likely not be around for the worst consequences of warming if we continue to pump carbon into our atmosphere at the current rate, but for our campaign's young staffers and supporters, it is a matter of life and death. Bernie absorbed their sense of urgency, coming to view climate change similarly to Medicare for All in at least one specific way: As a member of Congress, he had access to the best health care in the world for decades, yet that didn't stop him from fighting for others to have the same level of care. Likewise, he might not experience the worst impacts of climate change, but he was fighting for those who would.

The conventional wisdom stated that AOC was not, and simply could not be, popular in Iowa. But this was untrue. Our rallies there were the largest in the state at any point in 2019. But Bernie was still more excited about the climate conference. Nearly 2,000 people attended the event. What was amazing to me was that, hours into the event, the audience was still enraptured by the conversation.

The stage was adorned with blown-up illustrations by New York artist Molly Crabapple, giving it the feel of something different from, and bigger than, a standard political event. Bernie and AOC were onstage together, uniting two generations of progressives, discussing what they both viewed as the most important political project of our time. Bernie has a habit of calling our work "revolutionary," even when it really isn't. On that day, though, he was right.

From Iowa, we took off for California. On our first stop we received the endorsement of National Nurses United. This support mattered a great deal to Bernie. NNU has been on the front lines of the Medicare for All fight for decades. As nurses, its members were the best surrogates for Bernie on the issue, speaking for universal health care out of personal experience with the problems within our current system. In 2016 NNU was one of the few national groups to endorse Bernie, and that fact remained planted in his mind. But while we were in Oakland to hold an event with the union, disaster struck.

We had been scheduled to host a series of rallies in the central and southern parts of the state, culminating in an appearance at the California Democratic Party Convention. With less than forty-eight hours' notice, our permits for the Los Angeles rally had been pulled by law enforcement. We were stunned. We immediately tried to appeal the decision but got nowhere with local officials.

Bernie was strident. "What if I do the rally anyway? Fuck 'em. Let them arrest me."

I explained that that just wasn't possible. Without the permits, we'd have no stage, no sound, no way for the press to see him. It would be a chaotic, unsafe situation.

Our advance team fanned out across the area, looking for a new rally venue. We found one at a high school a few blocks from the original site. Staffers Facetimed me as they jumped the fence in the dark of night to tour the site and determine if it would work. It was actually a perfect spot to hold a rally, and we wouldn't need the same permits that had been denied at the original site.

The next day our trucks carrying staging, sound, and lighting equipment as well as a bike rack circled the new site as we waited for the school administration to finish a meeting and print the necessary permits. We didn't know if we would get them in time. For all our nervousness, the call came in: we had our permits and the rally was a go. It turned out to be one of the best event locations of the entire campaign. The school's outdoor basketball courts and the balconies overlooking the rally site filled to the brim, with the crowd wildly cheering Bernie's speech. The event also saved me the horror of trying to prevent Bernie from holding a wildcat rally in Los Angeles. His threat was not an idle one. I believe he would have marched straight into that park with a bullhorn, permits be damned.

Before the CA Democratic Party event, Bernie was scheduled for an interview that was worrying him. It was with Bernie Sanders—at least the closest approximation of Bernie Sanders. James Adomian is a comedian who does one of the best imitations of Bernie, even better than Larry David's. Dressed in full Bernie costume, he would interview Bernie.

An hour before the interview, Adomian was setting up. Bernie called. "I don't think we should do this." Faiz and I spoke with him, and found that his fear was rooted in humility more than anything else. Bernie spoke frequently in front of thousands, and is legitimately funny, especially in private, with great comedic timing. Yet here he was, concerned about a comedian. We assured him it would be great, and it ultimately was. For me, it sank in during the interview that the reason Bernie is so good at what he does is that he doesn't have the traditional politician's bravado. On some level, he still couldn't believe how far he had come since that first mayor's race in Burlington in 1980. He had spent the first part of his political "career" as the perennial candidate who had no chance at winning. As a backbencher in the House of Representatives and in the Senate, he was a gadfly who could easily be ignored. And he was still that person, in many ways, despite his soaring popularity since the 2016 campaign.

Following Bernie's heart attack and with our subsequent rise in the polls, he was starting to feel increased pressure. Any mistake could end his presidential ambitions. While we found the interview with Adomian fun, Bernie was uncomfortable not only due to the intimate adulation, but because it was a stress point. What if he slipped and said something off, leading to days of controversy? Faiz and I understood that Bernie is a topflight performer, even if he hates the idea of consciously putting on a show. With Adomian in fine form himself, the interview was a low-risk, high-reward event, showing a humorous and personal side of Bernie that I knew well, but that is rarely seen. What was remarkable is that even ten minutes before the interview he was still thinking about canceling, but he walked into the room and exceeded everyone's expectations, his own most of all.

At this point, we were campaigning without a break, immediately leaving California to attend a Nevada Democratic Party dinner honoring Harry Reid. We would go right from there into debate prep at a hotel on the outskirts of Las Vegas, for the upcoming debate on November 20 at Tyler Perry Studios in Atlanta. The most touching moment of that evening occurred after the dinner.

Reid gathered all his alums who were now on competing presidential campaigns for a photograph. The message was clear: we were competing against each other, but we were still family. Confined to a wheelchair following treatment for pancreatic cancer, and wearing a hat to cover his bald head, Reid wheeled into the middle of the staff. Bryan, our campaign photographer, volunteered to take the photo. The other presidential candidates were waiting to greet Reid and stood to the side, understanding what the moment meant to many of us.

Harry Reid and Bernie Sanders are very different politicians, but each man's political values arise out of personal experience. Reid was the dirt-poor son of an alcoholic hard rock gold miner who grew up in Searchlight, Nevada, a failed mining community in the middle of the desert. His mom made ends meet by doing laundry for some of the thirteen local brothels. Reid, in his own words, "learned to swim at a whorehouse."[25] He credits the owner of that brothel, Willie Martello, with teaching him "honesty" and giving him his largest Christmas present every year: a five-dollar bill. (This happened to be the price of services at Martello's establishment, the El Ray.) Reid hitchhiked forty-five miles to high school, boxed his way to college at Southern Utah University, worked as a Capitol Police officer through law school at George Washington University, and rose through Nevada's political ranks when his high school boxing coach and mentor, Mike O'Callaghan, became governor. He was the gaming commissioner caricatured in the Martin Scorsese movie *Casino*, who in reality shut down the mob and paved the way for the corporate casinos that now line the Strip. His car was bombed, and once, while the FBI was watching, he beat up singer LaToya Jackson's future husband after he attempted to bribe him.

Reid rose through the Senate to become majority leader by being one of the most hard-nosed and smartest inside players ever to walk in the chamber. A friend of his once told me that the desert outside Las Vegas was littered with the bodies of those who stood in his way. He was speaking hyperbolically (I think), but also paying Reid a compliment.

Reid was always more progressive than he let on, and he also hated Republicans, almost as a matter of temperament. The proudest moment of his life was not any political accomplishment, but when, as a teenager, he saved enough money doing work after school that he could afford to buy his mother a new set of teeth. I knew him to be gruff, the kind of person who would hang up the phone without saying goodbye.

But his former staff loved him. With his health deteriorating, I and other former Reid staffers at that dinner knew it was possible we would be saying goodbye to our friend. Even powerful colleagues stood to the side to let him have a moment with his staff. One presidential candidate, though, seemed oblivious. As we set up to take the photograph, Andrew Yang jumped in front of Reid, flashing peace signs as his own photographer took a picture.

By this point in the race, debate prep had become relatively routine, as had the debates themselves. We encountered the same narratives and storylines, the same questions from reporters, and very little that was new or interesting. The debates were good for fundraising but mattered less and less in the polls. The debate in Atlanta just before Thanksgiving seemed less important than any prior one. We rested and prepped at the hotel outside Las Vegas. When we were about to fly to Atlanta, we got a call.

Ariana Grande was giving a concert in Atlanta the night before the debate, when we would be in the air, flying east. Her mother, Joan, was a Bernie supporter. Would Bernie like to join her and possibly collect the endorsement? The more immediate question, at least for the staff, was whether Bernie knew who Grande was. While Harry Reid takes an avid interest in celebrity culture (in the lead-up to the 2006 midterms, Reid engaged a reporter who was profiling Reid for the *New York Times* in a conversation about the travails of Britney Spears as easily as he talked about Senate floor procedure), Bernie couldn't care less.

However, sometimes Bernie could surprise me. Back in September a phone call came from someone in Los Angeles claiming that Miley Cyrus was considering endorsing Bernie. (This endorsement never happened.) We never knew whether to trust calls from Hollywood types or their handlers. When Bernie heard the news, he turned around in the car and said with a straight face, "Ari, do you think Hannah Montana will campaign in Montana for us?"

How did Bernie Sanders even know who Hannah Montana was? We soon learned that years before, when he was shopping for gifts for his grandchildren, everything in the store was Hannah Montana–related. That was how he was introduced to Miley Cyrus.

Once it was explained to Bernie who Ariana Grande was, he became excited. We changed our flight schedule and took off hours earlier for Atlanta. On arrival, we went right to the State Farm Arena downtown. Bernie went to her dressing room, and they met and spoke. Bernie came away impressed by another young person. "These young people, that generation is so smart," he said upon leaving the meeting. We watched the concert from a box in the arena. Bernie was taking mental notes on an Ariana Grande concert. "This is amazing. How many people follow her every move. I want to make politics as popular as this."

We predicted that the Atlanta debate would be unimportant in the story of the 2020 primary, and we were proven correct.

But post-debate, our campaign held a rally at Morehouse College, one of the most important HBCUs in the country. The appearance was pitched by Terrel Champion, who was now part of the policy team.

As a Morehouse alum, Terrel introduced Bernie onstage. It was one of the most heartfelt speeches of the campaign. Terrel was one of the few people on staff who had a deeply personal relationship with Bernie. His speech spoke to that connection, and to why, as a young Black man and a recent graduate of an HBCU, he was supporting our campaign. Bernie did not listen to many introductory speakers, using those last moments to prepare for his own remarks. But in this case, Bernie sat behind a curtain just offstage, with a beaming smile, as Terrel spoke. My sense was that, for Bernie, hearing how much he meant to Terrel, not only as a political inspiration but as a person, meant a great deal.

After Atlanta, we had another short swing through New Hampshire and then on to New York to appear on Jimmy Fallon's show. We knew that the break for Thanksgiving would be our last. The final two months before the Iowa caucuses would be a sprint, and now we would also have to contend with Donald Trump's impeachment trial in the Senate, which would take Bernie off the campaign trail for weeks, just as we were arriving at the most critical moment of the primary.

*   *   *   *

AFTER THANKSGIVING we structured our schedule around the final debate of the year, on December 19 in Los Angeles.

From our first campaign strategy meeting in my apartment in early 2018, we had always treated California like the fifth early state. We began to staff up there in the spring and had made numerous trips, often built around giant rallies. Other campaigns didn't seem to be focusing nearly as much on the state. Reporters had been insisting, during my conversations with them throughout the campaign, that Kamala Harris's home state advantage might be too much to overcome. This mystified us. When we looked at her home state approval rating, it consistently rested well below 50 percent. Many Democrats, especially those in Southern California, simply had no familiarity with her, even after she had won several statewide races for attorney general and then the US Senate. Bernie, in contrast, was immensely popular in the state, particularly among Latinos. We also knew that we would have the financial resources to go on air early in the state, while also boasting a larger, more sophisticated organizing program on the ground.

In November, it increasingly looked to us as though Harris would not only lose her home state, but she would lose badly. Ultimately her campaign recognized the problem, too—and this was one reason that, early in the month, she dropped out. For us, it wasn't the ideal outcome, because her vote in the state would likely go to another candidate, not Bernie. The trip to California in December became even more important because it would likely be Bernie's last time in the state until after the New Hampshire primary in February.

Bernie had barely been in the Senate since July. In truth, his absence made no difference to governance. The overwhelming majority of the votes Mitch McConnell brought to the floor were for judges who would easily be confirmed, based on the GOP's simple majority in the chamber. No real business of the country was getting done, because the Republican Party had no other business beyond confirming conservative judges and passing tax cuts for the wealthy and large corporations. For the impeachment trial, every senator would need to be in their seat for extended periods of time as evidence was presented against the president. They wouldn't be giving speeches or grandstanding. They would essentially be locked in a room for six days a week.

We would spend December planning for numerous contingencies, including quick flights in and out of Iowa, surrogates to host rallies and other events, and called-in appearances by Bernie from his office in DC. We even priced out a holographic Bernie and considered deploying it, but the cost of doing it well was simply prohibitive, and it was all too much of a gimmick, anyway.

All of that was to come, and it heightened the importance of our final West Coast swing of 2019. Because of the three-hour time difference and the five-hour flight, it would be nearly impossible for Bernie to return to California during the impeachment trial. It basically took an entire day to cross the country; even on a private jet, red-eye flights took a toll, and any upside was almost never worth it.

Following the debate in LA, we would hold rallies in California, concluding with an evening rally at a high school overlooking the border with Mexico. The campaign was peaking. Far removed from the slog of the summer, now Bernie seemed to breeze through three rallies a day. After that event we had one final event of the trip—a major rally with AOC at Venice Beach.

Members of our advance team who happened to live in Venice Beach pitched the rally. No one had ever held a rally of the size we were planning in that spot before; our goal was to create a West Coast version of the Queensbridge rally—a huge, animated crowd coming out to hear Bernie and AOC. One big difference would be the celebrity presence. Though Bernie found celebrity culture mostly confusing, he understood that in LA, it mattered more than elsewhere.

Before the rally in Venice, AOC and Bernie hosted a meet-and-greet with around a hundred celebrities and other LA people. Photographs of the event are surreal. Tim Robbins and Danny DeVito taking selfies. I joked around with Werner Herzog, who was then starring in *The Mandalorian*, and chatted with Kim Gordon of Sonic Youth, one of my favorite bands from high school. Jeff Ross, famous for his appearances on Comedy Central's roasts, was there, intently listening to Bernie and AOC's speeches.

That celebrities were embracing Bernie was just more evidence that our campaign was gaining momentum. We had not begun daily tracking polls yet but were growing in confidence. We felt as though the nomination was within our grasp, even if we were still in second place, and even though the primaries hadn't begun.

The event in Venice Beach was spectacular, a fitting West Coast counterpart to the Queensbridge rally. Afterward, as Bernie, his family, and AOC flew to Las Vegas for an evening rally, we were more upbeat than at any point in the campaign. The Las Vegas rally in an absolutely packed high school gym only further encouraged us. Bernie was so energized by the crowd, he briefly forgot something that in other times would have been playing on his mind and worries: later he would be on a red-eye to New Hampshire, to attend a Christmas pageant with his grandchildren.

After Bernie left, AOC, her boyfriend, Riley, and a handful of Bernie staff, myself included, went to the movies to see *The Rise of Skywalker.* It was a last moment of rest before the final sprint began.

* * * *

FOLLOWING THE BRIEF PAUSE for Christmas, we returned to New Hampshire, with Bernie hosting a Christmas social event for union workers. Attendees learned something about Bernie that not many people outside Vermont know: he loves to dance. As the music played upbeat pop music, Bernie danced his way through the evening with any partner who would have him. It's generally a tradition that on his birthday, Bernie hosts a dinner and dancing cruise around Lake Champlain, and he is usually at the center of the action throughout the night. On the dance floor, the stiff and gruff demeanor fades away, and Bernie is smiling and happy, swept away by the music.

After barnstorming across New Hampshire during the final days of 2019, we flew to Iowa for a few days of campaigning and a New Year's party. At the party, Prince's former band, the New Power Generation, played into the night. Finishing his speech, Bernie asked me whether he should join in and dance, but he decided it was better to rest up for the campaign ahead. As the event ended, the advance staff retreated to the hotel suite and kept the party going. I gave a very drunken toast, thanking the team and letting them know we were on the way to victory. It felt like an obvious thing to say.

We awoke the next morning to the arrival of our latest campaign tool: a bus wrapped in Bernie graphics. I had insisted on a touch of humor—a front panel reading #NotMeBus. The bus offered a more comfortable way of getting around the state than our typical SUVs. Bernie had a cabin with a door and therefore could have some private time while crisscrossing the state. At least we expected he would. Bernie found he didn't like the bus very much, preferring to spend his hours on the road riding in his SUV. At this point, the impeachment trial was about to begin. We were still trying to figure out how we would campaign for president in a hands-on, grassroots state without our candidate.

It was in this stretch that everything seemed to blur together. We were always on the move. Momentum was clearly behind us that week in Iowa. Our press corps was growing by the day. Then came the hard evidence we had been waiting for. The *Des Moines Register* poll is considered the gold standard in the state. Conducted by Ann Selzer, its results are seen as almost infallible. This poll's release would give us a clear sense of whether reality matched our perceptions.

The last time the poll had run, before Bernie's heart attack, we had come in fourth. If we were still in that position, we would be effectively done, at least to the media, though the media would then shape the public's views, of course. I sat in my room at the Des Moines Airport DoubleTree obsessively calling every reporter

I knew who might have access to the results of the poll. Finally, we struck gold.

"You are going to be very happy," the text from a friend read.

"How happy?"

"As happy as you could be."

Thirty minutes later, Josh Orton had the numbers. Bernie, against all odds, was now leading Warren by three points, followed by Buttigieg and Biden. We were elated. A campaign that had been dead three months ago, with terrible polling and the candidate in the hospital after a heart attack, would now be the favorite to win the Iowa caucuses. We were surging, somehow, at exactly the right moment.

Bernie, as always, brought us down to earth. "Guys, I don't know how much I believe these polls," he said. We had work to do: not only was impeachment coming, but another debate was, too—and this one would not be as forgettable as the last.

CHAPTER 9

The Bernie Doctrine

ON JANUARY 3, 2020, WE WERE ON THE ROAD IN IOWA when news broke that Iranian general Qasem Soleimani was killed by a US drone strike near the Baghdad airport, an assassination ordered by Donald Trump. We arrived in Cedar Rapids and Bernie, Faiz, and I went to the restaurant on the top floor of our hotel to work on a statement in response.

Soleimani was not a sympathetic figure. He was a terrorist who had launched attacks that killed Americans, and was a clear enemy of our country. At the same time, it seemed as though his killing could set off a war with Iran—the longtime goal of many neoconservatives. They had a history of using any excuse to increase tension and attempt to force the United States into their dream conflict. Bernie viewed this as incredibly dangerous. The Iraq War was one of the worst foreign policy disasters in American history, and he believed a war with Iran would be even worse.

The first draft of a statement came from Bernie's office in Washington, and it sounded similar to other Democrats' statements—it condemned Soleimani, but also suggested the problem with the assassination was an issue of process. Bernie felt this was evasive. Our final statement, released on Twitter, said: "When I voted against the war in Iraq in 2002, I feared it would lead to greater destabilization of the region. That fear, unfortunately, turned out to be true. The United States has lost approximately 4,500 brave troops, tens of thousands have been wounded, and we've spent trillions. Trump's dangerous escalation brings us closer to another disastrous war in the Middle East that could cost countless lives and trillions more dollars. Trump promised to end endless wars, but this action puts us on the path to another one."

The action taken by Trump was wrong, and Bernie condemned it in clear terms. There was no hedging with contradictory statements about evil mullahs. The next day, we held a town hall at the National Motorcycle Museum in Anamosa, Iowa. On the way, Bernie, Faiz, and I worked on a speech focusing on the assassination. He wanted to use the event to highlight a central flaw in American foreign policy, which time and time again had taken us to the edge of war—and beyond. That morning he was forthright as ever: "This is a dangerous escalation that brings us closer to another disastrous war in the Middle East, which could cost countless lives and trillions more dollars, and lead to even more deaths, more conflict, more displacement in that already highly volatile region of the world."

Noting his lonely opposition to the Iraq War seventeen years prior, Bernie stated, "Let me repeat a warning I gave in 2002 during the debate over the war in Iraq: 'War must be the last recourse in our international relations. And as a caring nation, we must do everything we can to prevent the horrible suffering that a war will cause.'" Bernie continued, "As the former chair of the US Senate Committee on Veterans Affairs, I have seen up close the pain, death, and despair caused by war. I've gone to too many funerals in my own state. I've talked to too many mothers who have lost their kids in war. I've talked to too many soldiers, men and women, who have come home with PTSD, who have come home without arms and without legs." He concluded by tying a foreign policy message to his message about the political economy: "And I know that it is rarely the children of the billionaire class who face the agony of reckless foreign policy. It is the children of working families."

Bernie had grown more confident talking about foreign policy since his first campaign for president. He understood that his ideas and philosophy had been proven right repeatedly. For me, nothing better demonstrated his command of foreign policy—or how he would engage with other nations as president—than an intimate lunch with the then Iranian foreign minister Javad Zarif in 2018.

The meal took place at the New York residence of Iran's UN ambassador, across from Central Park and about a block from the Metropolitan Museum of Art. Over multiple courses in a dining room where Western art adorned the walls, the two men went back and forth like fencers. While Bernie was staunchly opposed to even the thought of war with Iran, he was no fan of their regime. He had been leading the effort in the Senate to stop American support for Saudi Arabia's war in Yemen, a proxy war against Iran. But if Zarif thought he was talking to an ally, he was soon corrected.

As Zarif complained about Saudi influence in Washington, and the kingdom's generous spending, as much as $250 million used to influence *both* parties, Bernie pressed him to end Iran's role in a war that had caused a humanitarian catastrophe. Zarif was evasive, suggesting the key to ending the conflict was talking to the Russians. The former foreign minister is fluent not only in English but in American politics. During the meeting, he made several jokes about Jared Kushner and his family's financial troubles with their building at 666 Fifth Avenue. He knew that it was both strategically silly and a political nonstarter for Bernie to engage in a dialogue with the Russian government on the issue. Zarif's pleas of innocence on behalf of his government fell on unsympathetic ears.

Also at the table was a moderate Democratic congressman. He eventually got a word in edgewise on behalf of a constituent in prison in Iran. Zarif was spouting some pabulum about Iran's independent judiciary when Bernie interrupted. "Mr. Foreign

Minister," Bernie said. "You talk about $250 million in public relations that Saudi Arabia spends. You know what would get *you* some good PR? Freeing this man." Zarif, for the first time in the meeting, was left speechless.

Leaving the building, Bernie turned to me and Matt Duss, his foreign policy advisor, patted his stomach, and said, "Those guys are assholes, but that lunch was delicious."

A Bernie Sanders administration would have meant fundamental change in many respects, but given the power of the president in foreign policy, the quickest and most dramatic transformation would have been in the United States' self-professed role in the world. In 2016, Bernie's limited foreign policy experience was considered a weakness because he was campaigning against Hillary Clinton. The former secretary of state had led US foreign policy during Barack Obama's first term, traveling to hundreds of countries. In truth, Bernie undersold his own expertise. He was right not only about the Iraq War, but about the destructive impact of neoliberal trade policies on the American manufacturing base. One of his first votes in the House of Representatives was in opposition to George H. W. Bush's Gulf War. Reading the transcript of the speech he gave in that moment, it is remarkable how prescient Bernie was:

> *Despite the fact that we are now aligned with such Middle Eastern dictatorships such as Syria, a terrorist dictatorship, Saudi Arabia and Kuwait, feudalistic dictatorships, and Egypt, a one-party state that receives seven billion dollars in debt forgiveness to wage this war with us, I believe that in the long run, the action unleashed last night will go strongly against our interests in the Middle East. Clearly the United States and allies will win this war, but the death and destruction caused will not, in my opinion, soon be forgotten by the Third World in general, and the poor people of the Middle*

East in particular. I fear very much that what we said yes-
terday is that war—and the enormous destructive power of
our armed forces—is our preferred manner for dealing with
the very complicated and terrible crises in the Middle East.
I fear that someday we will regret that decision, and that we
are in fact laying the groundwork for more and more wars
for years to come.

Bernie was correct about that war, in the sense that while we easily won a military victory, it ultimately put us on the path to another war—and quagmire—in Iraq. Nearly thirty years later, Bernie's words rang true for other, even more obvious, reasons. In hindsight, it is also hard to imagine how difficult a vote against the first Gulf War must have been for a freshman member of Congress. While Vermont is now considered a solidly Democratic state, Bernie had just replaced a Republican in Congress in a tight three-way race. Also, Bernie wasn't simply running for reelection against the Republican Party. He knew he would likely face opposition from Democrats as well. After the vote he walked off the House floor and remarked to Jane that he likely just lost his seat in Congress.

Of course, he ended up winning his seat over and over again. But, like many of those in DC with a track record of being correct and not following conventional foreign policy wisdom, he had often been marginalized and forced to the fringes because of his opposition to military adventurism. Voting against militarism and defense budgets does not make any politician popular with the Council on Foreign Relations crowd.

For a long time there has been a bipartisan consensus on the use of military force. While often remembered as a partisan act carried out by a reckless Republican administration, the Iraq War was supported by the leadership of both parties. Joe Biden, as chair of the Foreign Relations Committee in the Senate, helped usher the bill through the Senate. The body's leaders, Tom Daschle and Harry Reid, supported the war.

Bernie, by contrast, helped lead the opposition to the second war in Iraq on the House floor. It may be hard for younger Americans to understand how this was possible, but in the early years of the war, being against it was considered a politically toxic stance. There are now some people on the left of the foreign policy spectrum who at the time accused progressive opponents of the Iraq War of being fifth columnists. It was only with the rise of Howard Dean in the 2004 Democratic primary that opponents of the war were galvanized into an effective political force. Even then, Dean was the subject of an attack ad morphing Dean's face into Osama Bin Laden's. It was produced with the help of Robert Gibbs, who would go on to be Barack Obama's press secretary.

On the day in 2003 that the House of Representatives voted to go to war in Iraq, I was having lunch in the House's Longworth Cafeteria with a friend who had also begun his career as an intern in the office of then-representative, now-senator Ed Markey. Ed walked up to our table to ask how his "two favorite interns" were doing.

He then asked us how he should vote on the resolution. We both responded that he should oppose it. The Iraq War was a mistake, and the evidence showed that Saddam Hussein did not possess weapons of mass destruction. Bob Graham, head of the Senate Intelligence Committee, had said as much. Markey, however, was trying to teach us a lesson. He told us he would be voting for the resolution. His rationale was that it was critical, with the midterm election coming up, that Democrats not look weak on national security. Democrats who voted for the war stamped their names on George W. Bush's foreign policy. When the war in Iraq inevitably went bad, as predicted by many, Bernie included, they were then in part responsible for its failure. The Democratic Party saw candidate after candidate weakened by their support of the Iraq War.

During the 2004 campaign, John Kerry's "I voted for it before I voted against it" comment about funding the Iraq War was, to many, the moment he lost the election. It signaled a weakness that allowed the right to paint him as a coward instead of the decorated war hero he is. An old friend of Kerry's confessed to me after that election that Kerry would not have been so inarticulate if he had done what was truly in his heart at the time—vote *against* the war in Iraq, which he knew was wrong, and *for* funding the troops (the "I voted for it before I voted against it" vote). Instead, his campaign was curtailed in its ability to attack George W. Bush for the war. It was Kerry's war, too.

Four years later, one factor which ultimately separated Barack Obama and Hillary Clinton in the minds of many progressives was that Obama had stated his opposition to the war in Iraq—though he never had to cast a vote on it in Congress. Clinton, on the other hand, was stymied not only by her vote for the Iraq War but also by the approach of her chief strategist, Mark Penn, who encouraged her to not back away from her support for the war, even while the majority of Democratic primary voters were angered about the continued commitment of American troops to the region.

During the 2006 election, when Bernie Sanders would win his seat in the Senate, one of the principal strategies Rahm Emmanuel, as head of the DCCC, deployed in House races was to recruit conservative candidates with military backgrounds. Even as the country turned against the war in Iraq, the official arm of the Democratic Party was still intent on keeping the anti-war left at bay, if not on crushing it. This occurred even though MoveOn.org, perhaps the largest organization opposed to the Iraq War, was one of the most significant political contributors that cycle.

The conflict within the party was apparent to me while working for Harry Reid in 2005–6. Reid was sick over his vote for the Iraq War. He despised George W. Bush and often could not contain his disdain, publicly calling him a loser and a liar. Reid moved from supporter of the war to cosponsor of the Feingold-Reid bill, which was the main legislative response of the left wing of the Democratic caucus to the war in this period. The bill would have created a binding deadline for withdrawal from Iraq.

At a staff level, there was a great deal of trepidation about his position. One senior staff member pulled me aside and claimed that my internal advocacy for withdrawal from Iraq, and the fact that I had Reid's ear on the issue, was putting the entire Democratic Party at risk. This person explained to me that at the end of the Vietnam War, liberals "spitting on soldiers" cast Democrats as weak on defense for a generation. In my superior's mind, opposition to the Iraq War was the modern equivalent, not only a losing electoral strategy for 2006 but one that could haunt the party for decades to come.

Bernie Sanders spent decades as one of only a few voices supporting an anti-interventionist position, along with a few other lonely voices such as California congresswoman Barbara Lee and Wisconsin senator Russ Feingold. During the 2016 campaign, while his values were more aligned with those of Democratic voters than ever before, he was not entirely comfortable addressing foreign affairs on a stage with Hillary Clinton. Yet, perhaps Bernie's best debate moment of the campaign came when he called out the foreign policy "blob" in Washington, DC, and Hillary Clinton's participation in it, specifically the mentorship she received from Henry Kissinger. "Hillary talked about getting the approval or the support or the mentoring of Henry Kissinger. Now I find it kind of amazing because I happen to believe that Henry Kissinger was one of the most destructive secretaries of state in the modern history of this country. I'm proud to say that Henry Kissinger is not my friend," Bernie said.

Punctuating the attack, he went on: "I will not take advice from Henry Kissinger. And in fact, Kissinger's actions in Cambo-

dia, when the United States bombed that country, over—through
Prince Sihanouk, created the instability for Pol Pot and the Khmer
Rouge to come in who then butchered some 3 million innocent
people—one of the worst genocides in the history of the world.
So count me in as somebody who will not be listening to Henry
Kissinger." What is consistently remarkable about Bernie Sanders
is that he tells the truth, something no other politician does, at
least not as bluntly or as frequently.

* * * *

THOUGH HE HAD long demonstrated good judgment and a strong
moral compass in the area of foreign policy, Bernie still felt, after
2016, that he needed to become more knowledgeable and comfortable on the subject.

As I was joining Bernie's office in early 2017, Faiz Shakir was
recruiting Matt Duss to come on board as well. Matt, who would
be part of the lunch with Zarif in 2018, was a longtime think-tank
foreign policy analyst who represented the left flank in many Democratic foreign policy debates. Faiz and Matt had worked at the
Center for American Progress together, but both had been chased
out when the institution moved right and became Hillary Clinton's personal policy shop.

When he was hired by Bernie, Matt had been running a small
organization, the Center for Mideast Peace. Bernie offered him a
chance to bring his work inside the government. The most important thing Matt did for Bernie was to help him see how correct his
instincts were. He brought in numerous foreign policy experts to
meet with Bernie. The more of these conversations Bernie had, the
surer of himself he became.

In the fall of 2017, Bernie was invited to give a speech at Westminster College in Fulton, Missouri. The tiny college in a small
town had been the site of Winston Churchill's Iron Curtain speech
in 1946, which helped shape the Cold War. The college regularly

hosts luminaries from around the world to deliver what is known as the Green Foundation Lectures. This would be an opportunity for Bernie to lay out his foreign policy vision.

Foreign policy speeches, I found, are especially hard for Bernie. On economic matters, where he is most at home, he has an approach he has honed over decades. While the media finds it boring—"at a time of massive income and wealth inequality, where the top 1 percent . . . "—the message is effective, and Bernie delivers it perfectly every time. But for him, foreign policy speeches typically cover new territory, in part because there is so much more territory to cover.

Matt Duss began drafting the speech weeks in advance. As with any speech, regardless of subject, Bernie procrastinated until the day we were supposed to leave for the event and then declared the entire speech would need to be rewritten. He looked at me that morning and said, "You ready to work hard this evening?"

An hour later—two hours before we were supposed to leave for Missouri—I was tucked in a fetal position on the floor of my office, my stomach feeling as though it was going to explode. A Gatorade did not revive me.

I made my way down to the nurses' office on the first floor of the Hart Office Building. Most people do not realize that the Capitol complex has a number of doctors' and nurses' offices readily available to members and staff. When I walked in, the nurse looked at me as though I was another staffer nursing a hangover, needing a quiet place to lie down. As she talked to me, I proceeded to vomit across the reception desk.

She immediately took me to the back of the office and offered me a cocktail of medications. Matt got in touch and let me know he could handle the trip himself, except that we were going to San Francisco from Missouri to speak at the conference of National Nurses United, one of the unions that was most supportive of Bernie. It was a hugely important event, and no one else was prepared to staff it.

After throwing up a few more times, I finally began to feel better. The nurse gave me a toothbrush and some mints. I cleaned myself up and was soon riding to the airport with Bernie.

During a layover in Chicago, Bernie and Matt went to Stanley's Blackhawks Kitchen in O'Hare. My stomach could not absorb food yet, so I opted out. Bernie walked across the hall to an airport bookshop displaying copies of his bestselling book, *Our Revolution*, and held an impromptu book signing. In the bookstore a customer was thumbing through another book about the 2016 election. Bernie walked up behind the person and said, "Don't believe everything you read." The customer looked up and saw Bernie. The look on that person's face was priceless.

When we arrived at Westminster College, we still hadn't started working on the speech, but our hosts wanted to give us a tour of the campus. Churchill's speech decades earlier still dominated the campus. Giant slabs of the Berlin Wall with cutouts made by Churchill's granddaughter were displayed with pride. We were shown the gym where the original address was given. A lone student playing basketball seemed genuinely shocked that Bernie Sanders was standing on the court.

At the bed and breakfast just off campus where we would be staying, the college had reserved the room for Bernie where Margaret Thatcher had slept when she visited the campus in 1996. Hearing this, Bernie said, "Nope. I'll take another room." I would end up sleeping in the Thatcher bed while Bernie bunked across the hall.

We still had a speech to write.

In the dining room, we finally started drafting. Bernie wanted not only to discuss specific foreign policy matters, but to lay out his foreign policy doctrine. Because he had fundamentally disagreed with the interventionist foreign policy of previous administrations and rejected neoliberal trade deals, many people wrongly thought of Bernie as an isolationist. But Bernie has a global vision of his own, though informed by decades of left thinking.

He saw imbalances that allowed powerful forces to profit through trade and war. He saw corrupt regimes like Saudi Arabia's that got away with literal murder while remaining in good standing with the United States. He saw aligned right-wing authoritarian regimes wreaking havoc across the globe, realizing their frightening nationalist plans while in many cases only encountering a tepid response from the American left.

Bernie, in contrast, believed in bringing people together within the United States but also across borders. There is the oft-used attack on Bernie over the fact that he and Jane took their honeymoon in Russia in 1988. At the beginning of the 2020 cycle, a video even circulated online that had been taken during their trip. Clearly shot with a 1980s camcorder, it shows Bernie and a group of their Burlington friends sitting clad in towels in a Russian sauna, drinking vodka and singing Woody Guthrie's "This Land Is Your Land."

While there was nothing nefarious in these clips, the true story was more complex. As the Cold War was coming to a close and President Ronald Reagan was encouraging more outreach with the Soviet Union, Bernie had established a sister city program between Burlington and Yaroslavl, Russia, a city north of Moscow. When he talks about the program, which continues to this day, he fondly remembers students from the city visiting Burlington and making friends with their American counterparts. He believed this type of cultural exchange and person-to-person diplomacy was critical to creating a more peaceful world.

Fueled by chocolate chip cookies, Bernie, Matt, and I huddled around my laptop and wrote the speech he would give. I was prouder of the final product than I was of perhaps any other document I worked on while in Bernie Sanders's office.

The speech, given that afternoon, expressed a type of hope often absent from our foreign policy debates: "I am not naïve or unmindful of history. Many of the conflicts that plague our world are long-standing and complex. But we must never lose our vision of a world in which, to quote the Prophet Isaiah, 'They shall beat their swords into plowshares, and their spears into pruning hooks: nation shall not lift up sword against nation, neither shall they learn war anymore.'"

Bernie expressed the belief that "the goal is not for the United States to dominate the world. Nor, on the other hand, is our goal to withdraw from the international community and shirk our responsibilities under the banner of 'America First.' Our goal should be global engagement based on partnership, rather than dominance. This is better for our security, better for global stability, and better for facilitating the international cooperation necessary to meet shared challenges."

He soon arrived at the core of the speech and of the Bernie Doctrine: "In my view, the United States must seek partnerships not just between governments, but between peoples. A sensible and effective foreign policy recognizes that our safety and welfare is bound up with the safety and welfare of others around the world, with 'all the homes and families of all the men and women in all the lands,' as Churchill said right here, seventy years ago."

In conclusion, Bernie infused his vision with his concern for everyday people and their fundamental rights: "In my view, every person on this planet shares a common humanity. We all want our children to grow up healthy, to have a good education, have decent jobs, drink clean water and breathe clean air, and to live in peace. That's what being human is about. Our job is to build on that common humanity and do everything that we can to oppose all of the forces, whether unaccountable government power or unaccountable corporate power, who try to divide us up and set us against each other. As Eleanor Roosevelt reminded us, 'The world of the future is in our making. Tomorrow is now.'"

Bernie often comes off to those who don't know him as a grump, but he is the most profoundly optimistic and idealistic politician I've ever encountered, and it is this quality that drew so many of us to join him. At the same time, though, we were on a mission—fighting a war, Bernie would say, to build a more just world. Though the war would be nonviolent, Bernie did not play down that it would be a struggle, or that we would come into conflict with other powerful forces. When his speech was over, we headed to the airport, to fly to the Bay Area. We had completed the first step in creating the Bernie Doctrine.

* * * *

THE MORE BERNIE LEARNED about the world, the angrier he became with the foreign policy establishment. But he also became more hopeful, believing he could create real change. The potential for a drastic shift—and for saving countless lives—was why he made ending US involvement in the Saudi war in Yemen one of his principal foreign policy goals.

The humanitarian disaster in Yemen had a staggering death toll, and the human rights violations were adding up on both sides. The Saudi regime was our ally in the region. Yet, to Bernie, it was clearly a malevolent force. The rulers of Saudi Arabia were anti-Semites, sexists, homophobic, and funded radical Islamic terror that made our country less safe. Bernie had met with Saudi officials years earlier as part of a congressional delegation to the Middle East, and his discomfort with them had not abated. He described that visit as "a strange experience."

The United States was not simply backing Saudi interests. We were Saudi Arabia's number one arms dealer. American-made bombs were killing civilians in the region, and our country was supplying the necessary intelligence and helping the Saudis pick targets. Our planes were flying refueling missions that allowed the Saudi air force to complete their bombing runs. Bernie wanted to put a stop to it.

Matt Duss proposed partnering with Republican senators Mike

Lee of Utah and Rand Paul of Kentucky on legislation to end US involvement in the conflict. Their interest in the issue came from a different place than Bernie's. While they both opposed foreign wars, they did not do so primarily out of concern for foreign peoples; to them, it was an unauthorized war, and Congress needed to reassert its power over war making. But the agreed-upon strategy was simple: use the War Powers Act to reestablish Congress's constitutional role in foreign policy.

The War Powers Act passed in the wake of the Vietnam War. It limited the president to deploying forces overseas for sixteen days and a thirty-day extension absent congressional approval. In the case of the war in Yemen, the Trump administration claimed the authorization for the War on Terror was enough for them to proceed. Congress would have to act to specifically stop the war in Yemen. But no Congress had ever passed a war powers resolution with the goal of stopping a war through the US Senate. This particular legislative maneuver came with a significant advantage over others, however. War powers resolutions are one of the few items any senator can bring to the floor and force a vote on with no opportunity for opponents to filibuster.

The first time Bernie's bill came up for a vote, in March 2018, it was more of a symbolic effort. But Bernie kept pressing. To him, this was a moral crusade. He found it remarkable that conversations with colleagues kept returning to the fact that the Saudis were our allies in the region. Yet the Saudis were committing the very same crimes that made the Iranians our enemies. Bernie understood, of course, that the main reason for this was the amount of money the Saudis and their allies in the United Arab Emirates spent on influencing the policymaking process in Washington, DC. They funded think tanks and organizations on both the left and the right, and this had a profound effect on the city. Even some progressives were scared of speaking out, and would ask Bernie to moderate the tone of his campaign. But he would not relent.

In October, *Washington Post* journalist Jamal Khashoggi was murdered in the Saudi Arabian consulate in Istanbul, Turkey, and opinion in our nation's capital quickly shifted. Suddenly, almost overnight, the Saudi regime was seen as morally bankrupt. It was the time to strike again. Bernie would bring his Yemen War Powers Act back to the Senate floor.

Chuck Schumer's staff was nervous. It was now December 2018. In the November midterm elections, Democrats had taken back the House, while Republicans still controlled the Senate. Before the new House was sworn in, Trump would have a final, short window with unified GOP control of the federal government.

No one had ever brought a war powers resolution to the floor that was likely to pass. This one was. How would amendments to it be handled? In a meeting a week before the bill came to the floor, Schumer expressed his fears. If there was an open process, any amendment could pass with a fifty-vote threshold. This would be procedurally dangerous with a Republican-controlled House.

In that case, we made the point that Democrats could tank the bill. Our recommendation was to set a precedent on the floor stating that amendments to war powers resolutions had to be germane. Schumer was skeptical but ultimately acquiesced when he saw that Bernie wasn't backing down. McConnell agreed to the precedent. Allowing for an open amendment process might have led to some immediate Republican legislative victories, but he would completely lose control of the Senate and his caucus. That was too high a price to pay. With support from McConnell and Schumer, the overwhelming majority of senators voted to limit the process to only germane amendments.

The night before the vote, Matt and I were in the Senate Cloakroom—a narrow area located just off the Senate floor with a cushioned bench running down the side, several desks at one end, and phone booths for private conversations—figuring out what amendments would come to the floor. As we spoke to staff from

Schumer's office, the Democratic floor team, and the Foreign Relations Committee staff, Bernie was pacing slowly at the other end
of the room.

Bernie was already a bit on edge that day. Elizabeth Warren
had invited him over to her house for a lasagna dinner. There they
were supposed to discuss their potential runs for president in 2020.
Bernie was still undecided at this point. Since the invitation came
from Warren, we anticipated she had made the decision to run for
president, and that she planned on entering the race in short order.

As the cloakroom conversations progressed, there was a clear
moment of tension around an amendment Republicans would propose to force a vote on Israel that could potentially be embarrassing to Democrats. After I made a strategic suggestion on how to
deal with the likely move by the GOP, a senior Democratic leadership staffer asked if I had gotten the approval of AIPAC, the pre-
eminent Israel lobby in Washington, for my idea. Bernie appeared
next to us with such speed, it was as if he had apparated into the
conversation.

"No one on my staff will get permission from AIPAC for *anything*," he bellowed.

The irony, of the most prominent Jewish lawmaker in the United
States angrily objecting to his team consulting with the country's
leading Israel lobby, was not lost on anyone, except perhaps Bernie. But he simply didn't care about a powerful lobby when tens if
not hundreds of thousands of lives were at stake. For their part,
that staff member was just doing their job, posing the question one
would always raise in such moments.

The next day, we won the vote, 56–41. It was a highlight of
Bernie's career. He often talks about the actions of his movement
as "historic." Usually this is an exaggeration, but it shows the
scale of his ambition: Bernie wants to believe that he is creating
radical change.

In the case of his Yemen bill, he had done exactly that. Bernie correctly saw that in Washington, DC, the influence of the Saudis was a mile wide, fueled by hundreds of millions of dollars in donations, but an inch deep. He also saw that there were Republican senators, such as Mike Lee and Rand Paul, who, though Trump supporters, were willing to abandon the president on this issue. In part, Bernie could organize in a trans-partisan way because these members understood that his position, like theirs, was a consistent one. Regardless of who was president, Bernie Sanders would oppose the war in Yemen.

CHAPTER 10

"I didn't say it."

THE MORNING OF THE IOWA DEBATE ON JANUARY 14, 2020, I walked into our prep room, just off the DoubleTree Des Moines Airport Hotel lobby. Arianna Jones was already there on the phone with Mike Casca, the campaign's communications director, looking like someone had died. Casca had heard from CNN. They were about to release a story that during Bernie Sanders's dinner with Elizabeth Warren a year prior—the lasagna dinner before the vote over Bernie's Yemen bill—he told her that he did not believe a woman could beat Donald Trump. We understood it would be the central topic of the debate. We waited for Bernie to come downstairs.

Meanwhile, I tried to piece together for everyone what I remembered about that dinner.

In December 2018, Bernie and Warren met for a late dinner at her apartment in the Chinatown neighborhood of Washington, DC. Early the following morning, Jonathan Martin of the *New York Times* began haranguing our staff for details of the supposedly secret meeting with Warren. Martin became more and more aggressive throughout the day. Following the historic vote on the Yemen War Powers Resolution, Bernie, Mike Lee, and Rand Paul walked up the stairs to the Senate Press Gallery on the third floor of the Capitol, where reporters surrounded them. I saw JMart, as he is known in DC, running up the stairs behind the senators. At the top, he charged through the crowd and started asking Bernie what he had said to Warren over dinner. Bernie looked him in the eye and replied they had talked about the 80,000 children who have died in Yemen.

Martin pressed on, effectively cornering Bernie against the glass of the press gallery. A typical politician would have said something trite to defuse the conversation and move on, but Bernie is incapable of doing anything like that. He started pressing JMart on the lack of coverage in the US media on the war in Yemen, which quickly became a debate about the coverage in the *Times* in particular.

At this point Mike Lee turned to me and said, "Is that a liberal or a conservative protester?"

"*New York Times*," I replied.

"So, a liberal," he joked.

Ultimately JMart was asked to leave. He muttered "asshole" as he strode away. Bernie seemed oblivious to Martin's outburst and proceeded with the press conference.

While the *New York Times* got no information on what happened in the meeting, Bernie had told us that Warren had said that she had decided to run for president and would enter the race soon. In turn, Bernie told her that he had yet to make up his mind. JMart's aggressive attempt to get the story foreshadowed just how critical that meeting—and the dispute about what else was said during it—would prove to be in the race. Warren herself apparently would tell her version of the dinner weeks later, in early 2019, during an off-the-record gathering with reporters.

In Des Moines more than a year later, senior staff informed Bernie about the impending story. None of us believed it to be true—Bernie can say things that are intemperate and not politically correct, but this did not sound like him. In all my time traveling with him, he had never made a similar remark—in fact, he regularly suggested the opposite.

Bernie not only challenged the truth of the story, but he also expressed disbelief that Warren herself had approved the then-anonymously sourced story. Through the description of their sourcing, CNN made it clear to us that one of their four sources would have had to be either Elizabeth Warren or her husband. They were the only people in the apartment that night with Bernie.

We were confident the claim was false. Faiz felt so sure that he went out and called it a lie on camera. I think the Warren team expected us to have Bernie issue a weak apology, and move on. But Bernie was insistent that he never made such a remark. Furthermore, he had always viewed Warren as a friend and ally in the Senate. Both sides had been campaigning for over a year, and while there was no formal "truce" between our camps, we hadn't attacked each other. His relationship with Warren, much like his relationship with Biden, was always friendly, no matter where they ran into each other, whether on Capitol Hill or at the O'Hare Airport Macaroni Grill. The latter had actually happened, at the end of a weekend in 2018 that Bernie and I spent in Chicago campaigning for Chuy Garcia, an ally who was running for Congress. As we finished our dinner and got up to leave, the other patrons erupted in cheers. As people lined up for selfies with Bernie, we walked Warren out of the restaurant. They greeted each other as a man in the selfie line shouted, "This is my political and culinary fantasy." They both laughed as they snapped some selfies together. Bernie had few friends in DC, and he thought Elizabeth Warren was one of them.

Onstage at the debate, Bernie denied Warren's accusation directly, saying, "Well, as a matter of fact, I didn't say it." He continued, "Anybody that knows me knows that it's incomprehensible that I would think that a woman could not be president of the United States. Go to YouTube today. There's a video of me thirty years ago, talking about how a woman could become president of the United States." He went on to note than in 2015 he only entered the race after she decided not to run.

For her part, Warren said the story was accurate before stating, "I am not here to try to fight with Bernie." After the debate she refused to shake Bernie's hand, saying to him, "I think you called me a liar on national TV."

Bernie left the debate stage upset. He had defended himself in the only way he knew how. He believed he had been falsely accused and simply could not comprehend why this was happening. Immediately after the debate, it was Joe Biden who offered him kind words of support in an otherwise empty hallway as we exited the building. Biden said, "It's gonna be all right, Bernie," while patting him on the shoulder.

Later that evening, Bernie, Jane, their son Dave, Faiz, Jeff Weaver, Nina Turner, Cornel West, and I gathered in that same airport hotel conference room for what was the most difficult meeting of the campaign. Jane and Bernie were furious. They wanted an action plan in place that night, but no one was in the proper frame of mind to do anything productive.

Jane was incensed, believing the campaign wasn't doing enough to defend Bernie and that it needed better outreach to women in general. The mood ranged from angry to depressed as we went back and forth in the room for nearly two hours. Bernie was looking for answers. How do we move forward from this? he wondered. The truth was, there *were* no right answers to be had that night, and when everyone was finally worn out, we headed off to bed.

By this point we were conducting daily tracking polls in Iowa, so we could see the impact on the race in real time. Over the next few days, while our overall position in the polls held steady, we watched our standing among Warren voters, in particular women, who said Bernie was their second choice drop. (Because of Iowa caucus procedures, it was important for campaigns to poll voters on who their second-choice candidate was.) As we saw it, this would ultimately harm our chances of victory on Super Tuesday.

* * * *

AFTER THE DEBATE IN IOWA and a short trip to New Hampshire, the impeachment trial began, on January 22. Recovering our footing in the wake of the Warren accusation, the staff was feeling good. We recognized that so much of the Democratic primary vote was being driven by national media narratives. This meant that while Buttigieg and Biden would be able to continue campaigning during the trial, they wouldn't be able to dominate any media cycle, as the press's attention would be nearly entirely focused on the impeachment trial.

Bernie was unhappy that impeachment would take him off the road—his first love as a politician—but he grasped the threat posed by Donald Trump to the country's very foundations. He knew that both politically and morally, there was no choice other than to focus on the trial.

For some of the other candidates from the Senate, however, the consequences were severe. A senior staffer on Cory Booker's campaign confessed to me that impeachment was their death knell. With the final two weeks of campaigning before the Iowa caucuses taken up in the Senate, they would have no chance to forge a comeback in the first state on the primary schedule. That was why they ultimately left the race in mid-January. For us, we soon found, the impeachment trial did offer a second narrative advantage. Not only was the country's attention on the trial, but like a pace car during a NASCAR race, it froze the field in place, locking us in our positions for the time being.

Still, Bernie was worried. He could almost taste victory and didn't want to leave anything to chance. I managed a nutty schedule that would include a full team of surrogates in Iowa: Michael Moore, AOC, Rashida Tlaib, Ilhan Omar, and bands such as

Vampire Weekend, Portugal the Man, and Bon Iver. The events were designed to go on with or without Bernie. If he couldn't make an event, others would take his place onstage. We became obsessed with getting Bernie to Iowa quickly, and we changed our jet provider to one that had experience with takeoffs and landings at Washington National Airport. Because of its proximity to the Capitol and the Pentagon, since September 11 operating private jets from the airport was difficult. We were exempt from some of the rules because Bernie was a sitting member of Congress, allowing us, with the right paperwork, to quickly fly in and out of the airport. We left no detail to chance. If there was a means of getting Bernie on the campaign trail in Iowa, he would. Even if only for a single day, he would get on a plane and go.

As the impeachment trial began in DC, I decided to effectively move into the DoubleTree in Des Moines so I could more closely supervise events in the state. Often Bernie would come off the Senate floor and join a rally by phone. Things could go wrong, and at one event, they did. With an audience of over 1,500 in Clive, Nina Turner tried to introduce Bernie—except cell service was terrible, and they couldn't connect. Nina ended up calling me out, in a joking way, from the stage. Finally, Bernie did connect, and the audience was excited to hear him, but these phone calls could not replace an in-person appearance by Bernie.

Every day I would talk to Bernie multiple times, during breaks in the trial and after the day's business had concluded. I could hear the stress in his voice as he asked me what was happening at his events in Iowa. I told him, truthfully, that things were going well. Our surrogates were drawing larger crowds than most of the other candidates. Our events were not quite as energetic as usual, but we were coming close enough, and the necessary organizing was getting done. Three days before the caucuses, on January 31, the Senate adjourned; it would return the next week to vote. In the meantime, Bernie flew out to Iowa immediately. That night, Cedar

Rapids witnessed our biggest event of the entire cycle in Iowa. Vampire Weekend would perform. Bernie would be there. The logistics of such an event cannot be understood by anyone who has never put one on. It cost upward of $100,000, on top of a typical cost for a rally, for the extra stage, sound, and lighting, plus additional money to pay for transportation, lodging, and other expenses for bands and their crews. Venues also require you to have additional security when the crowd reaches a certain size. But all of it is worth the cost and the toil, for the energy such rallies would bring and that would linger well after everyone had gone home.

We traveled the state in the Bernie bus, stopping in Grinnell for a town hall before getting to Cedar Rapids. At a small coffee shop near the venue, Vampire Weekend performed an acoustic set for our volunteers. Bernie was tired from the trial, but every hour in Iowa he seemed to perk up a bit more.

When we first got to the venue, we parked the bus right behind the stage. Our beat reporters joined us in the room at the back of the campaign bus for an off-the-record conversation. While Bernie rarely engaged in such conversations during the campaign, we convinced him it would be to our strategic advantage, especially if we won Iowa.

We again found ourselves, that night, waiting for the results of the *Des Moines Register* poll. This Saturday night release has become a tradition in the lead-up to the Iowa caucuses. Its results are highly predictive of the final results of caucus night. I trolled the press area, pressing those who might know the results. Finally, we started getting some leaked numbers. It was tight, but Bernie was still in the lead. All indications were that we would win. Then rumors started to swirl. The Buttigieg campaign complained that they were left off some of the survey questionnaires. They waited to get the leak, decided it was to their advantage, and went to complain to the *Register*. This kind of political gamesmanship is expected, but it's also highly annoying. With no time to put the poll back in the field before the Monday caucuses, the *Register* decided not to publicly announce the results. The decision foreshadowed what was to come.

For Bernie, it didn't make a lick of difference. "I don't understand why you guys care so much about a stupid poll," he said to Jeff Weaver and me. He was focused on the thousands of people who had come out to hear from him and were then waiting eagerly. Onstage, he was fired up. Bernie's group picture with our surrogates facing the audience was one of the best of the campaign: Bernie and Jane, their son Dave and his kids; a grinning Michael Moore; Progressive Caucus chairs Pramila Jayapal and Mark Pocan, also with huge smiles; Nina Turner and Susan Sarandon clapping in excitement; and Cornel West looking as though he was going to pop out of his shoes.

On the day before the Iowa caucuses, we were on the bus for one last round of events: town halls and canvas launches as our organizing staff prepared to get people out to caucus.

In the evening, campaign senior advisor Chuck Rocha and I participated in our own Iowa caucus tradition. Four years earlier, we had gone out for lobster corn dogs at the 801 Chophouse, the fanciest steak house in Des Moines. It was time. The election was here.

*   *   *   *

ELECTION DAYS ARE STRANGE when you're part of a campaign but you aren't an organizer. If you aren't making phone calls or knocking on doors, the day of a state's primary or caucus election can actually be the slowest of the campaign. It is haphazardly structured by calls from other campaign staff, the candidate, and reporters asking what you know. And the truth is, nobody knows anything useful. There is a ton of information coming in and swirling about—turnout numbers, modeling, and field data. None of it tells you anything particularly important. But you take it all in, almost as a mental exercise, or an attempt to exert control over something that, at this point, you cannot influence in the slightest, unless you are knocking on doors or doing other activities to bring out voters.

Those members of the campaign who work to nudge voters to the polls obviously have some control on election day. But if you are at the candidate's or the media's beck and call, you sit around. You fidget with your phone. The problem becomes that, other than some appearances to keep the candidate's face on TV, it's best for the candidate to lie low, too. Let the organizers bring people out to vote, and do not let the candidate get in the way.

This was why, other than in Iowa and New Hampshire, we would flee states on election day. The entirety of the press corps were in those two states for post-caucus/primary coverage; therefore, we needed to be present. In Des Moines, I went back and forth from the hotel to a Holiday Inn a few blocks away that would serve as the venue for Bernie's speech later that night.

It was a strange day. I had been through election nights before, but this one was different. Typically, campaigns were quick exercises, intense work over a few months. The Iowa caucuses had been my project for three years. What happened could decide the remainder of the primary. It felt final, even though it wasn't. Bernie, as usual, was more circumspect. "Guys," he said once again to Jeff and me, "you are putting too much importance into this. We have a long way to go."

I and other staffers were worried that we didn't. If the night turned out badly, if our voters didn't show up, if Elizabeth Warren ended up winning, if another candidate ran away with it—our campaign could be over. Bernie had freaked out back in the summer when we told him we thought it would take more than $10 million in paid advertising to win Iowa. But that is what it ended up costing. We had more than 300 staff on the ground organizing. We had thrown everything at this one night.

The caucuses began. The voting process in Iowa is unlike any other in the world. The caucuses are public events in which people stand in corners to signify their support for candidates. If their choice does not have at least 15 percent of the vote, they can switch to the corner of a candidate who has.

The process had changed since 2016. As part of the "Unity Reform Commission" process, Iowa agreed to release the caucuses' publicly tabulated vote counts. In prior cycles the only number that was released was State Delegate Equivalents. This was an arcane mathematical formula that converted votes into the number of delegates you would receive at the state party convention and, ultimately, the number of delegates you would receive at the national convention.

In 2016 most observers thought that while Hillary had won SDEs, there was a significant chance that Bernie had won the popular vote. The Republicans released their totals, but the Democratic Party never did. The lack of transparency bred conspiracy theories and bad feelings. Because of the state Democratic Party's rules, you could easily win the popular vote but trail in SDEs. This is partly what led to the disaster in 2020.

Bernie planned to stay at our hotel for as long as possible, only going over to the Holiday Inn to give his speech. We started watching live coverage as soon as the caucuses began. It seemed to be going well for us, but we couldn't truly know. Jeff Weaver sat in the campaign war room across town, trying to tabulate figures from our precinct captains as quickly as possible. After the caucuses ended, we waited for the state party to deliver the results.

And we waited.

It soon became clear that something was wrong. Rumors started to circulate. The app created to tabulate results was failing. The party could not report accurate counts. This interim period seemed to stretch on endlessly.

The senior team got on the phone with Bernie. I paced in the

back corridor of the Holiday Inn. We learned that Pete Buttigieg would be declaring victory. On what basis, we couldn't tell,
though he had displayed real strength in the state, which was one
of the surprises of the campaign. Our internal numbers showed we
would win the popular vote in the state. We came up with a plan.
Jeff would tabulate our numbers and release them to the press. To
interrupt Buttigieg's media strategy, I would walk into the press
area and brief reporters, letting them know we believed we had
won the Iowa caucuses and would be putting out evidence that
said as much. Bernie, who was still not at the hotel, would arrive
and give his speech.

In the press area, I was instantly mobbed by reporters. I gathered them in a circle, telling them this conversation was on background. I said that momentarily we would be releasing internal
data showing we would win the caucuses. I started to answer questions, but I had nothing to give them.

Bernie was on his way, and he wanted to go right onstage. I had
to physically stop him. "Senator, I don't have the head-on loaded
in." The head-on is the straight camera angle during a rally. In this
case, we wanted people standing on risers behind Bernie waving
signs, signaling the support in Iowa for him. It would take me ten
minutes to finish preparation.

"Ari, does that matter?"

"Yes, it does. Plus, I need to cue the networks when you are
speaking. Give me five minutes."

"You have five."

I queued the network producers via text message, inform-
ing them that they were on a five-minute clock for Bernie. I then
told the advance team that they had two minutes to get the stage
loaded. Bernie was ready.

After navigating a maze of kitchens and back corridors, he hit
the stage to the cheering crowd. It was not the victory speech he
wanted to deliver, but he wasn't defeated, either. Though we were

still confident that we would win the state's popular vote, Bernie was always insistent on never getting out in front of facts, so he led off. "Let me begin by stating that I imagine, have a strong feeling that at some point, the results will be announced. When those results are announced, I have a good feeling we're going to be doing very, very well here in Iowa."

With that, the night was over. The next morning we flew to New Hampshire to continue the race. Bernie and I walked off the plane together. Bernie does not have a public reputation as the warmest person. But in this moment, he could tell I was a little down. As we crossed the tarmac, he put his arm around my shoulder and said, "Don't worry, we're going to win this thing."

A few hours later, sitting on the first floor of our hotel, we watched on TV as the votes in Iowa were finally announced. It was clear we led the popular vote, as expected, but that we were trailing in State Delegate Equivalents. Over the next few days, the count would get sorted out. While we ended up winning the popular vote tally by nearly 3,000 votes, we trailed Pete Buttigieg by less than one SDE. Both campaigns would declare victory (again, in Buttigieg's case). Now, facing a Buttigieg campaign on the rise, we had to do something to blunt his momentum.

CHAPTER 11

The Magic Returns

NEW HAMPSHIRE, LIKE IOWA, HAS ITS SHARE OF HOKEY political events that candidates are required to attend. The morning of the New Hampshire debate, Bernie participated in a state political tradition known as "politics and eggs." The candidates would speak to a room of New Hampshire political insiders in the morning and sign dozens of wooden eggs as souvenirs for the crowd.

Following the Iowa caucuses, our campaign's internal tracking polls showed Buttigieg on the rise. The media loved his story—a gay military veteran with uncommon political talent that belied his job as mayor of South Bend, Indiana—and, based on his strong performance in Iowa, he was drawing media attention away from the rest of the field. While there were almost no Mayor Pete–Bernie crossover voters, we had to do what we could to prevent him from winning New Hampshire.

The debate was set for Friday night, February 7, with the primary the following Tuesday, but Bernie needed to do something to put himself at the center of the conversation before the debate. While hesitant to attack Joe Biden by name, Bernie had no similar reservations regarding the South Bend mayor.

The campaign team was in agreement. Bernie should use the Politics and Eggs breakfast where the entire press corps would be in attendance to launch an assault on Buttigieg. The line of attack was obvious to us. It had been advocated by speechwriter David

Sirota and others for some time. Pete Buttigieg was a candidate of the wealthy elite whose lives were pretty good and had only financially improved under Donald Trump, not of ordinary Americans who were struggling.

"I'm reading some headlines from newspapers about Pete Buttigieg: 'Pete Buttigieg Has Most Exclusive Billionaire Donors of Any Democrat.' That was from *Forbes*. *The Hill*: 'Pete Buttigieg Tops Billionaire Donor List.' *Fortune*: 'Pete Buttigieg Takes Lead as Big Business Candidate in 2020 Field,' *Washington Post*: 'Pete Buttigieg lures even closer look from Wall Street donors following strong Iowa Caucus performance.' *Forbes Magazine*: 'Here Are The Billionaires Backing Pete Buttigieg's Presidential Campaign.'" Bernie told the audience that morning. "I like Pete Buttigieg, nice guy, but we are in a moment where billionaires control not only our economy but our political process.

The question Bernie was asking New Hampshire voters was, "Which side are you on?" Roger Ailes's maxim was once again proven true. The media is biased toward only covering three things: pictures, mistakes, and attacks. Bernie's attack worked. The media was all too anxious to cover a fight. It was too easy and predictable. That night the New Hampshire debate became a pile-on, with other candidates going after Pete as well. Public polling appearing over the weekend showed Buttigieg falling and his support drifting to Amy Klobuchar.

We continued campaigning throughout the weekend, leading up to our largest New Hampshire event of the cycle. The Strokes joined Bernie Sanders and AOC for a concert at the University of New Hampshire the night before the primary. More than 7,000 people packed into the arena.

Bernie introduced the band, who proceeded to play a full set. The audience became a mosh pit, and people kept jumping onstage. We ended up having to pull the barricades out during the show to prevent people from being crushed. Shockingly, one potentially problematic moment for us was missed by the media. At the close of the show, dozens of college students were dancing onstage, ignoring the police while the band performed their song "New York City Cops," the chorus of which includes the refrain, "New York City cops, but they ain't too smart." This moment could have been used against Bernie, in particular in a state like New Hampshire, if anyone in the media had covered it.

In a primary race, every election day is the most important night of the campaign thus far. In New Hampshire, we needed to win cleanly. We knew victory in New Hampshire would likely lead to a blowout in Nevada, given our strengths in that state. We would then have won the plurality of the vote in the first three primaries, hopefully achieving the momentum we needed to get through Super Tuesday.

Our election night event was in the same gym where Hillary Clinton had held hers four years earlier. Unlike in Iowa, results started coming in on time. We were ahead but could see it was going to be close. Standing in the media area, I got word the race was going to be called. I let out a scream and gave Felix Biederman, one of the hosts of the Bernie-supporting podcast *Chapo Trap House*, a high five. I ran to Bernie's hold room, a second gymnasium next door.

"So, any news?"

"You won New Hampshire, Senator."

"Not yet."

"It's about to be called. The networks want timing for your speech."

"Are you sure?"

Bernie turned to the TV as the race was being called by one of the networks. A big smile crept across his face. He had won New Hampshire. Jane came over from across the room, and they kissed.

The next moments are a blur. Bernie was on the stage, and I

was standing behind it with most of the senior campaign staff. We had done it. A few months before, our candidate was in the hospital. We were in fourth place in Iowa and the *New York Times* ran a piece headlined, "Did New Hampshire Fall out of Love with Bernie Sanders?" As the piece put it, "the magic of his 2016 New Hampshire effort hasn't fully returned. The crowds here are smaller, key endorsers remain on the sidelines and his supporters, after three years of stewing about what many believed to have been a rigged primary contest, are wondering why he's not doing better."[26]

Bernie was onstage with his family delivering his victory speech, and I was with my comrades in arms. The feeling was indescribable.

We returned to Bernie's hold room and shot baskets for a while to come down off the high. We went back to the stage and snapped a few photos, taking a moment to savor the win, even as we knew the campaign's most challenging work was yet to come. Bernie told me, as he left the venue, "Get some rest. There's not going to be much of it for the next few weeks." He was right. We would have debates and primaries in Nevada and South Carolina, and then Super Tuesday. The campaign would likely be decided by March. We had surged at the right time, but now we knew the real attacks would start.

*   *   *   *

ON FEBRUARY 14, we started in Washington, DC. We headed first to Durham and Charlotte, North Carolina, for rallies, then on to Mesquite, Texas, finally arriving in Las Vegas. At those stops, Bernie held three rallies and three group meetings, conducted eleven media interviews, and took four plane rides, traveling a total of 2,700 miles. It was the campaign's longest day thus far. We used the time zones, going east to west, to extend the day to twenty-seven hours.

Winning the popular vote in Iowa and the New Hampshire primary made Bernie the clear front-runner and even more of a target for other campaigns. We had spent much of the year not as the front-runner, and thus had drawn less attention, especially from the media. Beat reporters who covered Bernie could not get permission to travel to our events because their editors felt it was not worth the money. But now, we could not be ignored.

The next contest after New Hampshire was Nevada, where the Culinary Workers Union plays an outsized role in the state's Democratic politics. Bernie loves the workers in the union. He would constantly talk about how the union's successful efforts to organize low-income workers in the hospitality industry were revolutionary and a model for other unions. Culinary turned Las Vegas into a city where a maid with a high school education could earn a decent living; they made service jobs something admirable and desirable, proving unions were not just for industrial workers, as the stereotypes often suggested, but for service employees as well.

The Culinary health plan is one of the best in the country. Not only do workers receive top-quality care, but they receive care at excellent health clinics owned by the union. On the day of the New Hampshire primary, Culinary sent a flyer to all their members telling them that Bernie's Medicare for All plan would mean the end of their vaunted health coverage.

Early in the campaign, we toured one of the clinics. I had misplaced some medication and needed to pick up a new prescription. I couldn't get in touch with my doctor and asked during the visit if they could write me a replacement. I was seen by a doctor, given a checkup, and then received a prescription. The level of care was outstanding. The union's problem with Medicare for All was that by eliminating the link between health care and work, Bernie's plan would end this preferential treatment for their workers, and they were prepared to fight it as a result. Oddly, though, the union never seemed to be willing to engage with us directly on the issue.

Our first interaction of the cycle with the Culinary Workers Union took place before the campaign began, in late 2018 in Nevada, when we met with the head of the union, Geoconda Argüello-Kline. Geoconda came to this country as a refugee from Central America, and worked her way up from hotel maid to the head of one of the most powerful unions in the country. She did not raise concerns about Medicare. She spoke mainly about how the Democratic Party was letting identity trump economics. She told Bernie that the one matter she cared about above all others was raising workers' wages. Every other priority, in her view, was often an excuse for inaction by politicians.

On one of our first trips of the campaign to Nevada, we met with Geoconda and D. Taylor, who was international president of UNITE HERE, of which Culinary was a local, during a visit to a health clinic. D. was a legendary organizer who, during his tenure as head of Culinary, had nearly tripled the size of the union, and had led a successful seven-year strike against Frontier Casino. This, too, struck us as a positive meeting. They spoke about the need for Medicare for All to preserve some rights for unions, but most of the conversation focused, again, on wages. What later became clear is they were silent about their criticism because they didn't think Bernie would win the nomination.

In mid-December 2019, the Culinary Workers held a candidate forum. Beforehand, Bernie, D., Geoconda, our Nevada state director, and I sat down in a kitchen at a worker training center. Once again, the conversation centered primarily on wages and workers' rights. When we got up to leave for the forum, Geoconda came up to me to express concern about Medicare for All. As I began to explain our position, she looked me in the eye and said, "We were on the picket line for six years, four months, and ten days to protect our health care, and you aren't going to take it away." Before I could respond, she turned around and walked out.

At the forum, which took place in a union hall, Bernie was generally well received. When health care came up, some members of the crowd started chanting, "Union health care." We noticed that this chant wasn't organic, and seemed to be started by an organizer—not a worker—in a far corner of the room. At that point, we knew the attack was coming, but we didn't know when.

Bernie had spent months building support in the Latino community in Nevada, which is tied directly into Culinary. Now, in the lead-up to the Nevada caucuses, we saw we would never get the union's endorsement—but we still needed their workers to vote for us. Would the attacks harm our efforts? We had poured a massive amount of resources into our field campaign, led by state director Sarah Michelsen, probably the best organizer I have ever encountered, and into a paid media campaign designed by Chuck Rocha. One of Chuck's smartest strategies involved targeting the Latino radio stations hotel maids listened to as they worked. For months we had been on their radios and in their communities, organizing and knocking on doors.

The Nevada caucuses are unique. While in most states people vote in the precincts where they live, on the Strip in Las Vegas, people could vote at their casino workplaces. Those particular caucuses were heavily attended by Culinary members, with organizers helping to steer them to the proper, union-supported candidates. As in Iowa, their votes were public.

In response to Culinary's attack, we released a measured statement: "Bernie has been clear that under Medicare for All, we will guarantee that coverage is as comprehensive or more so than the health care benefits union workers currently receive, and union health clinics, including the Culinary's health clinic, will remain open to serve their members. With health care as a human right, unions will have more leverage to negotiate better wages and benefits."

Culinary retorted that some of our supporters had attacked the union and Geoconda on Twitter. As their statement put it, "It's disappointing Senator Sanders's supporters have viciously attacked the Culinary Union & working families in NV simply because we provided facts on proposals that might take away what we have built over eight decades."

Elizabeth Warren jumped in to support Culinary, tweeting, "No one should attack @Culinary226 and its members for fighting hard for themselves and their families. Like them, I want to see every American get high-quality and affordable health care—and I'm committed to working with them to achieve that goal."

The conflict was no longer about health care, though; it was now about the "Bernie bro" narrative that had started during the 2016 campaign. Earlier in the week, *Meet the Press* anchor Chuck Todd read a quote on-air effectively comparing our supporters to Nazi street thugs, calling them a "digital brownshirt brigade." This was particularly offensive, given Bernie is Jewish and had lost many family members in the Holocaust. But it was just another example of the invective we faced from the mainstream media. Beginning in 2016, the "Bernie bro" narrative, the idea that our campaign's online supporters were in general misogynistic, mean, and uncouth was a significant attack often taken as a point of fact in the media. Bernie hated this. First, he did not believe that these online trolls were representative of his supporters. He had met thousands of them between 2015 and 2020 and found them uniformly warm and thoughtful. He had also seen members of our campaign and surrogates, particularly women of color, subjected to bigoted attacks. He had seen racist and anti-Semitic attacks hurled at our staff and had experienced them himself. Yet no other Democratic campaign faced similar attacks based on the behavior of their supporters. Furthermore, Bernie did not want any heated or insulting language in our campaign. When he found out a staff member went too far, he often personally reined them in.

One of the most personally painful moments of Bernie's

career was in 2017, when a supporter committed a horrific act of violence. Early in the morning of June 14, rumors began to spread around Capitol Hill that there had been a shooting at the Republican baseball team's practice. The Congressional Baseball Game is one of those bipartisan activities that everyone on Capitol Hill loves. Republican and Democratic lawmakers face off against each other at National Park, with the proceeds of the event donated to charity, and with bragging rights at stake for the participants.

The members take the game fairly seriously. Even though it only takes place once a year, the two squads practice for the big night. Because of legislative schedules, these practices, which involve dozens of lawmakers, occur early in the morning.

Most members of Congress, even while in DC, enjoy a level of anonymity. Other than a few who are consistently seen on cable news or are members of party leadership, almost none are recognized when they are away from Capitol Hill. Furthermore, contrary to popular assumptions, only a handful have security. The majority and minority leaders, the speaker of the House, and the whips all receive a detail from the Capitol Police. A few other members are granted protection on an as-needed basis.

After the 2016 campaign, during which Bernie had Secret Service protection, he never received that level of protection while on the road. At no point during the 2020 primary was any candidate provided with Secret Service protection. In fact, we were the only campaign that used metal detectors to screen the attendees at nearly every event. In specific circumstances, in particular later in the campaign, we would hire private security to protect Bernie, but overall, he rarely traveled with security.

Steve Scalise, the House minority whip, was a member of the Republican baseball team, so thankfully, his small Capitol Police detail was at the practice that morning when a gunman opened fire.

Scalise was seriously injured in the shooting and flown to Wash-

ington Hospital Center for surgery. It wasn't long before the shooter's name was broadcast on cable news channels. Tim Tagaris,
who ran Bernie's online strategy, called me as soon as the shooter's
identity began circulating. He searched our database of supporters, and the shooter was among them. He had volunteered for the
2016 campaign. We knew this would inevitably become public as
people scoured his social media profiles and dug into this latest
shocking act of violence in the United States.

As we were absorbing these facts, Bernie arrived at the office.
As often was the case, I was assigned to give him the bad news.
I walked into his office and told him about the shooter. He gri-
maced, as though in physical pain.

The idea that someone who was a part of his movement would
engage in violence, and political violence in particular, was not
upsetting to him from a public relations perspective, though he
certainly understood the ramifications of the event. It was upsetting on a personal level. That he and his cause would be used in
this way was anathema to him and his vision for politics. Our
ideas were powerful enough to win at the ballot box. They did not
require violence.

Bernie asked a few other staff members to come into the office.
He said that he would immediately request time on the Senate floor
to make a statement. But what, exactly, would he say? Tensions
within the small group ran high, and it quickly became apparent that writing this statement by committee would not work. He
kicked everyone out. As soon as I got back to my desk, my phone
rang. It was Bernie asking me to come back in to write the statement with him. Bernie was horrified that Steve Scalise was fighting
for his life in the hospital, and one of his supporters was responsible. This would need to be addressed directly.

In the most difficult moments, my belief was that Bernie should
let his humanity, and his core values, shine through. Unlike Donald Trump or, in truth, most other politicians, Bernie has no prob-

lem condemning action he finds objectionable even when it comes
from his supporters.

We knew the remarks would have to be short and leave no
question as to what he was saying. Bernie and I worked on the
statement, and in fifteen minutes it was done. I emailed it to press
secretary John Miller-Lewis and asked him to print twenty copies. He would walk down to the Senate floor with them. The office
would email out the remarks as soon as Bernie gave them on the
Senate floor, but if a reporter stopped him on the way into the
chamber, Bernie could hand them his remarks.

Bernie took off for the floor with Miller-Lewis in tow. The rest
of us remained in the office, monitoring C-SPAN. Bernie read his
statement. "I have just been informed that the alleged shooter at
the Republican baseball practice is someone who apparently volunteered on my presidential campaign. I am sickened by this despi-
cable act. Let me be as clear as I can be. Violence of any kind is
unacceptable in our society and I condemn this action in the stron-
gest possible terms. Real change can only come about through
nonviolent action, and anything else runs against our most deeply
held American values." He wished Scalise and the other people
injured a speedy recovery and thanked the Capitol Police for their
heroic efforts.

*　*　*　*

IN HIS INTERACTIONS with Culinary on the eve of the Nevada
caucuses, Bernie would again rely on his core values. He never
attacked or even criticized Culinary in response to the claims
about his abusive supporters. We could stand by our vision for
Medicare for All without doing either.

Later in the week before the caucuses, we conducted what is
known as a "back of house visit." In this case, it consisted of a
walkthrough of the workers' area of the casino to meet workers.
At the MGM Grand, Bernie was greeted like a hero. Worker after

worker cheered him on and asked for selfies. None of the animosity surrounding the health care debate surfaced. We turned into the dining hall, where hundreds of workers were eating. In the front part of the hall, we were again greeted by cheers. Around a corner, we could see a union organizer gathering workers in red culinary worker T-shirts. As Bernie walked toward the group, the organizer started sending workers up to Bernie. Each one would tell a health care story and ask Bernie not to take away their insurance. He told them he wasn't going to. It was an organized ambush. We couldn't film during a back of house visit, but the organizer had his phone out recording as Bernie talked to the workers. I guess they didn't get the footage they wanted, because we never saw it online.

None of this seemed to register in our polling. The media was covering the attacks, whether from our "supporters" (a least a portion of whom we believed were bots or sock puppets) on the Culinary or from the Culinary on us, but this did not seem to be having an impact. We just seemed to keep gaining momentum.

One thousand people attended our rally in Carson City on February 16. The event was interrupted by topless vegan protesters—angry at Bernie's advocacy for Vermont's milk industry—who stormed the stage, pouring fake pink milk everywhere, including on me as I tried to usher them offstage. But the crowds at our rallies felt even more enthusiastic than ever, and they were immense. Over a span of the next twenty-four hours, over 11,000 people came out in Denver, 10,000 in Richmond, California, and 17,000 filled the Tacoma Dome in Washington State. Eddie Vedder was in attendance. Bernie had never listened to Pearl Jam, but they were my favorite band growing up, so I was particularly excited to spend a few moments with one of my musical heroes.

At this stage of the campaign, we were moving as fast as we could—putting on event after event after event. We believed we could win. Bernie believed it, too. Conversations on plane rides shifted from planning events to his finally starting to talk about what his White House could be like. What issues would we tackle first? There were a variety of opinions on this subject. What he was most focused on was the need to move quickly—that his White House would be defined by action. Additionally, he would want to spend as much time on the road as possible in personal conversations with ordinary people.

Two days before the caucuses, we held a critical meeting. In the conference room in our hotel in Las Vegas, the senior team gathered. We would decide the final ad buys for Super Tuesday. Before the meeting, Faiz, Bernie, and I headed to another hotel so Bernie could sit down with Anderson Cooper for an interview for *60 Minutes*. The hour-long conversation would be edited into a shorter piece that would air the Sunday after the Nevada caucuses. One answer Bernie gave about Cuba would end up dominating a week of media coverage.

I left the interview before it ended to attend the ad buy meeting. We sat down and went through the Super Tuesday states. We would spend more money and buy more ads than anyone except Michael Bloomberg, who was on a quest to burn a billion dollars as quickly as possible (it would take him about a month). We set a strategy, locked in the final totals, and went back on the campaign trail.

We swung through California and held a final Las Vegas rally, where there was one last good omen before caucus day: when I looked at the final electronic door counters tabulating crowd size, they totaled 2020.

*   *   *   *

THE MORNING OF THE NEVADA CAUCUSES, we were flying to El Paso for a rally before heading to San Antonio. On the plane, we started searching for early results. As we arrived at the giant dance hall where we would hold the El Paso event, the race was called.

Bernie not only had won Nevada but received over 40 percent of the vote, capturing two-thirds of the state's delegates.

When Bernie took the stage that night, we timed his appearance in coordination with the control rooms of the news networks. I was texting executives, counting them down to the moment I yelled into an offstage mic, "Ladies and Gentlemen, the next President of the United States, Bernie Sanders."

What made the win even more remarkable was that despite the weeks of attacks from the Culinary Workers Union, we won five of the seven caucuses held at Strip casinos, tied another, and only lost the one at the Paris Hotel. In the locations where Culinary workers voted, we won nearly 60 percent of the county delegates.

Bernie's campaign was based on the idea that we could go directly to workers and talk to them and win their votes. Even if the union leadership did not like our message, it was the workers who counted. That was why we walked picket lines every chance we got. It wasn't for show or to pick up chits. It was because we were on the side of the workers. In Nevada, we had spent months talking to the Latino community and Culinary members, explaining why Bernie's policy programs were right for them and their communities. In the end, this organizing worked.

Now we would enter what we knew would be the most difficult stage of the campaign. While winning a plurality of votes in the first three states had made us the favorite, South Carolina would likely not go our way. We had taken the lead in the polling average after New Hampshire. After Nevada, we jumped out in front of Joe Biden by 12 points. Other than Elizabeth Warren, who only led Joe Biden by a single day, and that by less than two-tenths of a point, we were the only candidate so far to overtake the former vice president in the national polling average. One of our central theories of the campaign was that we would prove that Bernie could win against Donald Trump by doing just that—winning. The polls suggested Democratic voters were growing more comfortable with the idea of nominating Bernie Sanders. Now the attacks from other candidates would grow even more vicious. Memos went out from centrist Democratic groups and campaigns warning that Bernie needed to be stopped on Super Tuesday. They begged candidates to join forces against us. Media commentary shifted to indignant opposition to Bernie's campaign.

As Bernie ran away with the Nevada caucuses, Brian Williams turned to Chris Matthews on MSNBC and asked, "Is this any way to pick a nominee?" Williams's biased question did not go unnoticed by our campaign. Matthews responded, "Well, I don't think so. But it is the way we are picking this one and it looks like Bernie Sanders is hard to beat right now. I'm with [James] Carville all the way in terms of what lies ahead in November." Matthews had concluded that Bernie was on track to win the nomination. And he was terrified. As he said: "Brian, I know you are a history guy too. I'm reading last night about the fall of France in the summer of 1940. And the general calls up Churchill and says it's over. And Churchill says, how can it be? You've got the greatest army in Europe. How can it be? He says it's over."

Here was yet another implicit comparison of Bernie Sanders to Nazis, in this case to the Nazi invasion of France. Faiz called up network executives, and I spoke privately to our traveling MSNBC reporters to express our anger. Matthews would apologize for the remarks.

Three days after Matthews's comment, I would appear with him on set, in the media filing center in the lead-up to the South Carolina debate. Before we went on air, he pulled me aside, apologizing again and saying he understood the pain he had caused. Then he said, "Ari, I just fucking love being on TV." A week later, he would "retire" after a report about inappropriate comments he made to a female guest off-air along with inappropriate behavior toward other women.

Chris Matthews's attack was only the start. The media seemed to divide themselves between taking Bernie Sanders's nomination as a fait accompli on the one hand, and expressing the need for the party to consolidate against him on the other.

Bernie himself ignored most of the noise. The campaign was working. The polling looked better and better, our rallies were growing, and Bernie was feeding off their energy. Nearly 7,000 people came out in Houston and 12,000 in Austin. The latter rally led to one of the worst security scares of the campaign. While Bernie was onstage, we got word that a death threat had been made on Twitter. We consulted with local police and decided to rush Bernie off the stage. I walked to the front of the stage and signaled him. Bernie ended the speech. As he walked down the stairs, I told him, no rope line, and we moved as quickly as possible to the cars and raced away.

We took off from Texas with the wind at our backs. That Sunday, the *60 Minutes* interview aired.

CHAPTER 12

"Not good."

IN IOWA, ONE SUPER PAC, DEMOCRATIC MAJORITY FOR ISRAEL, ran ads against Bernie. Now, as the front-runner, we were facing a second dark money group, run by staffers affiliated with West Virginia senator Joe Manchin. Choosing not to buy television ads, they spent millions online and on direct-mail attack pieces that were more difficult to track.

Worse than the super PAC activity was the impact the media narrative had on our campaign. Cable news coverage reflected, at best, a reluctant acceptance that Bernie Sanders might be the nominee, and at worst (aside from the comparisons of our movement to the Nazi conquest of France), predictions by establishment mouthpieces such as James Carville that Bernie's ascension meant sweeping losses for Democrats in the fall. We responded by continuing to campaign at a rapid pace, with Bernie continuing to make the case he had been making from the start.

In the wake of his win in Nevada, there were suggestions that Bernie should have embraced the Democratic establishment, attempting to win at least their tacit support. This ignores the reality that his policy platform was in part designed to disempower these individuals and institutions, and that is why they had to defeat him. Furthermore, if he had suddenly changed his rhetoric, it wouldn't have made much of a difference.

Even if there had been agreement at a staff level to moderate

Bernie's message and embrace the establishment wing of the Democratic party (there was not), we would never have convinced him to alter his message. The Monday-morning quarterbacks who proposed, after the campaign, that our failure to moderate Bernie's message after the Iowa caucuses was the reason he ultimately lost, were ignoring the reality that Bernie simply would not have done so. He is who he is, and his authenticity, stubbornness, and anti-establishment ethos are in part why his supporters flocked to him.

One comment during Bernie's *60 Minutes* interview gave our opponents a new line of attack. Asked by Anderson Cooper about his previous statements about Fidel Castro's regime in Cuba, Bernie said, "We're very opposed to the authoritarian nature of Cuba, but, you know, it's unfair to simply say everything is bad." He continued, "When Castro came into office, you know what he did? He had a massive literacy program. Is that a bad thing, even though Fidel Castro did it?"

Aside from a small number of voters, primarily Cuban Americans in Florida, I don't believe anyone truly cared about Bernie Sanders's comments on Castro's literacy program. Yet it became the focus of intense media scrutiny. I did television interviews on CNN and MSNBC that were devoted to the remark and nothing else. As we saw it, the media was obsessed with talking about a dead dictator but refused to acknowledge other Democratic candidates' support for living dictators. Michael Bloomberg had a close relationship with the Chinese government and refused to criticize them over the ethnic cleansing of the Uyghurs. Other candidates and figures within the Democratic Party had supported permanent normal trade relations with China in 2000 as well as the country's entry into the World Trade Organization in 2001. These were financial boons to that country's authoritarian regime. Bernie had opposed both policies.

Then there was Saudi Arabia. Most of the Washington establishment had spent years fawning over Mohammed bin Salman, who had ordered the murder of Jamal Khashoggi. Bernie was one of the first to call him what he is—an authoritarian thug—and led the opposition to US involvement in his war in Yemen.

The media and our opponents used the Castro answer to again intone that there was a secret opposition research book on Bernie that nobody had used yet. These rumors had been spreading since 2016, and back then, I believed them. But there was no secret book. We know this because our campaign had hired Tyson Brody, the researcher hired to conduct opposition research against Bernie by Hillary Clinton's campaign in 2016. Hillary had thrown everything against Bernie, and nothing stuck.

Yet the Castro answer did damage our campaign, in that it became a distraction from our main arguments, allowing the media to paint Bernie as radical, arguing that a general election campaign against Trump could get bogged down in similar controversies. The message was simple: this is the risk you are taking if Democrats nominate Bernie Sanders.

We knew our winning streak would come to an end in South Carolina, whose primary would take place three days before Super Tuesday. But would this change our position in the race? As we had in Nevada, we used the state as a base from which to travel to nearby Super Tuesday states for events. We believed Elizabeth Warren was likely to do poorly in her home state of Massachusetts, and saw an opportunity to use our momentum to win there. More than 10,000 people attended our rally on the Boston Common on February 29.

Michael Bloomberg had been the target of attacks from many candidates at the Nevada debate, with Elizabeth Warren launching a blistering assault on his credibility. We knew that Bernie would be the primary target onstage in South Carolina. He stood up and defended himself and did all he could to fend off the onslaught. The attacks were largely unremarkable, and therefore we assumed they would have little effect on the overall narrative. The pace of the campaign had only increased, if that was possible. Bernie was going from speech to speech, interview to interview. There was no time now to stop or think or strategize. Our field staff was in place; our final TV ads had been bought; our final series of rallies were scheduled through Super Tuesday. We just charged ahead.

The day after the South Carolina debate, Jim Clyburn endorsed Joe Biden. We expected this. Questions were raised about whether Bernie had met with him and asked for his endorsement. In fact, Bernie had met with him several times the previous year to work with Clyburn on increasing funding for Community Health Centers, a policy priority for both men. Bernie never asked for an endorsement, primarily because he viewed it as a waste of time. Clyburn had publicly expressed concerns about socialism and was unlikely to be swayed by a personal plea from Bernie. Once we took the lead in the race, we knew his endorsement of Biden was likely inevitable.

For weeks, we had been aggressively trying to win two other endorsements we felt were within reach, that would boost our standing with both progressives and African Americans. The campaign was having conversations with both Al Sharpton and Jesse Jackson about their potential support for us. It was an arduous back-and-forth. Jackson did not want to endorse while Elizabeth Warren was still in the race. At one point, we thought Sharpton was ready to endorse. He said he would support Bernie but just had to make one phone call, and we should plan for an event with him. We set our schedule to accommodate the endorsement, but it never came. Jackson, meanwhile, was still undecided.

Clyburn's support would help Biden consolidate the field. By the time we landed in Virginia Beach for Bernie's nighttime rally, the South Carolina primary had been called. Biden had won his first victory, and we had come in second. The rally would be Bernie's first concession speech of the campaign. The question was, could Biden turn around the media narrative in forty-eight hours, the time between the race being called in South Carolina and Super

Tuesday? He had no field program, limited television advertising, and, until the moment he won South Carolina, seemingly limited enthusiasm, after shaky performances in the debates to this point.

Bernie watched the results on the TV in the greenroom in Virginia Beach before going onstage and said, "Not good." He called Nina Turner and told her she had done an excellent job as our head of operations in South Carolina and had worked harder than anyone on the campaign. We had come in second in South Carolina, with 20 percent of the vote. A year earlier political observers would have likely stated this was a better than expected performance for Bernie in a crowded Democratic field. But with Joe Biden receiving nearly 50 percent of the vote, would it be enough?

*   *   *   *

THE SUNDAY BEFORE SUPER TUESDAY was the longest day of the campaign, not only because we had just lost the South Carolina primary, but because it was another day of nonstop appearances and travel. Bernie would begin with two Sunday show interviews. We would then get on the plane and fly to an event in San Jose, California, attended by 9,500 people. This would be followed by a rally in Los Angeles that included a concert by Public Enemy; at that event, two comedians, Sarah Silverman and Dick Van Dyke, would also speak. There is a photograph from that night of all these celebrities alongside Bernie, perhaps the most random assortment of public figures we assembled during the course of the campaign.

We had made news in the hip-hop world because Chuck D and Flavor Flav of Public Enemy had a public argument about the group's Bernie Sanders endorsement. Because Flavor Flav was not part of the LA performance, we had to promote the band as Public Enemy Radio. He was apparently so upset by the decision to appear at a Bernie rally that it broke up the group. This all had to be explained to Bernie, naturally. (The breakup turned out to be a media stunt by the group to garner attention as they promoted a new album.)

On March 1, the same day as the Public Enemy rally, Pete Buttigieg would end his presidential campaign. It came as a bit of a surprise that someone who ran such an impressive and unlikely campaign, winning the most delegates in Iowa and coming in a close second in New Hampshire, would bow out before the most significant election day on the primary calendar. In 2016, Donald Trump won the Republican nomination because the field did not unite against him, with Ted Cruz and John Kasich continuing to fight it out with each other. This divided the Trump opposition, allowing him to build an insurmountable delegate lead. Buttigieg's withdrawal from the race was the first sign that the Democratic Party would not make the same mistake.

The second sign came soon enough. In the weeks leading up to Super Tuesday, two planes had shuttled Bernie and the press back and forth across the country to campaign events. Most of the time Bernie sat in the back of his plane, engaging in conversations with Jane, Faiz, Jesse, or me. During one of these flights, Faiz and I talked about what would happen if Amy Klobuchar dropped out and endorsed Biden. Bernie suggested that this was ludicrous— with her better than expected performance up to that point, she would want to at least compete and likely win her home state primary on Super Tuesday. Unlike the other candidates in the race, Bernie knew Amy well from their time in the Senate.

I was on the press bus headed to our rally in Salt Lake City on March 2, the day before Super Tuesday, when news broke of Klobuchar's endorsement of Biden. The media on the bus was in a frenzy and tried to hold an immediate "gaggle" with me to get the campaign's response. I did my best to avoid that discussion; when we arrived at the rally site, I ducked backstage.

Bernie arrived at the event site about ten minutes later. I went to his hold room, and he looked at me and said his now typical "Not good." He had heard the news from Amy Klobuchar herself. Nothing more needed to be said. Voting on Super Tuesday

would start in less than twenty hours. We couldn't shift his schedule; we couldn't buy more ads; we couldn't move field staff around.
Within the hour, the success of the effort to consolidate around
Joe Biden in order to prevent Bernie from winning the nomination
became clear. Buttigieg and Klobuchar would endorse the former
vice president in Dallas. Other members of the party's elite would
also be joining Biden's campaign. Harry Reid called Faiz to let
him know that he would be endorsing as well. Additionally, news
broke that former presidential candidate Beto O'Rourke would
also endorse Joe Biden, joining him onstage in Dallas. And though
I did not realize it at the time, *this* was the moment we lost the election. Buttigieg and Klobuchar's exit from the race and combined
endorsement of Biden was likely what led to our defeat in Texas,
Maine, Massachusetts, and Minnesota on Super Tuesday.

Bernie had often predicted that if our campaign truly took off,
the Democratic establishment would unite like never before, to
defeat us. Yet our strategy was premised, in part, on this not happening—that like the 2016 Republican field, Democrats, normally
disorganized and prone to infighting, would remain divided in
their opposition to Bernie. Instead, they united like never before
around Joe Biden.

Thus far we had matched our best expectations: Entering Super
Tuesday with a delegate lead. Winning the plurality of votes in the
first three contests, coming in second with 20 percent of the vote in
South Carolina. Denying Joe Biden any victories before that date.
Elizabeth Warren failing to finish higher than third. Two candidates,
Pete Buttigieg and Amy Klobuchar, who could not win the nomina-
tion, garnering enough support that dropping out on the day before
Super Tuesday would have seemed ludicrous in any other year. The
Democratic Party is a disorganized institution, but it would organize against Bernie Sanders in a way they had not against any other
candidate—Democratic or Republican. Bernie's premonition that
the establishment would never let us win was coming to pass.

At the same time, other former candidates who might have endorsed Bernie declined to do so. Andrew Yang, whose emergence as a serious candidate had impressed Bernie, was always a bit of a danger to us, because a group of his supporters were similar to a group of ours: young independent men who disliked both parties and the two-party system itself. Yang also craved Bernie's attention. Early in the fall, one of his staffers asked us backstage at a debate if Bernie liked Andrew, because Andrew was *really* concerned that he didn't. Bernie, though he did not personally interact that much with Yang, respected that he had built a grassroots following around an issue-focused campaign. The overlap between our supporters did not matter. Yang did not endorse Bernie.

Tom Steyer was another candidate whose support might have helped. There was a popular meme on Twitter about Steyer's unrequited love for Bernie based on awkward pictures of them from a Martin Luther King Day celebration in South Carolina. Bernie and Steyer did share a mutual affection. In 2018, Bernie, Jane, and I had breakfast with Tom and his wife, Kat, at their office in San Francisco. The conversation focused on climate policy and how to bring young people into politics. Even though Steyer was a Democratic megadonor, fundraising was never discussed—just ideas.

Finally, Warren remained in the race. Supported by a super PAC that had received an eight-figure donation from a single person, she continued to fight through Super Tuesday. If she had dropped out and endorsed, it would likely have not made the difference, but the fact that she didn't simply added to the momentum moving against our campaign, with no positive stories to push back against the media narrative.

On the day of the South Carolina primary, the national public polling average had us at 30 percent, which was our peak of the entire campaign. We were leading Joe Biden by 11 points. By Super Tuesday, March 3, three days later, Joe Biden was leading us by half a point. Two days after that, he was up by almost 8. Something unprecedented had happened. The Democratic Party establishment, the other candidates in the race, and the media were convinced that Joe Biden was the best candidate to take on Donald Trump. Nominating Bernie Sanders was simply too risky, in their view.

It is not a surprise that in those same three days from South Carolina to Super Tuesday, according to Critical Mention, a service that monitors media impressions, Joe Biden received more than $70 million in positive national media coverage. When local media coverage was included, some estimates topped $100 million. Ultimately it was an "earned-media tsunami" that swept our campaign away.[27]

On March 2, we flew from Salt Lake City to our final pre–Super Tuesday rally, in Minneapolis. With 8,500 people in attendance, Bernie Sanders and Ilhan Omar spoke to the crowd about the possibility of victory the following day, and in the primary overall. We boarded our planes and flew to Burlington.

Another story, unrelated to the primary, was bubbling up. We had heard about the coronavirus but were so focused on the campaign that it did not draw our attention. Former Bernie staffer Matt Stoller was tweeting about how seriously everyone should be taking the virus. Winnie Wong, a campaign senior advisor, had been texting Palestinian activist Linda Sarsour and me about it since January, suggesting it would be the worst global pandemic we had ever seen.

A few days earlier, as we planned for the rallies in California, where a few cases had been publicly reported, we decided to eliminate rope lines to prevent Bernie from shaking hands with rally attendees. We did consult with public health departments in the states where we were scheduled to appear, and we were told that there was no reason to cancel. When we arrived in Burlington on Monday night, we began preparing ourselves for Super Tuesday itself.

At around 6:30 PM on Tuesday, Faiz Shakir, Arianna Jones, and I went over to Bernie's house to watch the returns with his family. But I was too nervous to stay there. Knowing what was likely coming, I decided to decamp to the Champlain Valley Expo Center, where we would hold our election night event, with Bernie and Jane's son Dave. I wanted to get away from Bernie's living room, and to see the two members of Phish who would be performing that night. I was watching TV in the greenroom as Virginia and North Carolina were quickly called for Biden. We knew that California, Colorado, and Utah would be good for us, while Alabama, Arkansas, and Tennessee would be Biden states. The race would be decided by Maine, Massachusetts, Oklahoma, Minnesota, and Texas. If we could win the majority of those states, we would likely leave Super Tuesday with a delegate lead and could fight for the nomination. But as the results came in, it wasn't to be.

The next morning Bernie held a press conference. California was still counting, and we could still come out of Super Tuesday with a lead in the overall delegate count. Yet the media was declaring our campaign dead. They began to ask when we would be dropping out. The momentum had definitively shifted. The race technically wasn't over, but in the minds of the Democratic electorate, it had ended after South Carolina. They had found their candidate, and it was Joe Biden.

* * * *

THAT THURSDAY, MARCH 5, the campaign was in Arizona for a rally. The large crowd that turned out was a sign that our supporters still believed in us. The rally was also where one of the darkest moments of the campaign occurred. In the arena, a swastika was flown behind Bernie by a supporter of Donald Trump. This was the first explicit act of anti-Semitism we had faced. The gross display of bigotry disgusted Bernie. The horrors of the Holocaust are foundational to his political beliefs. As Bernie had explained at a CNN town hall in February, "I remember as a kid looking at these big picture books of World War II, and tears would roll down my cheeks when I saw what happened to the Jewish people. Six million people were killed by Hitler." He continued, "And I think, at a very early age, even before my political thoughts were developed, I was aware of the horrible things that human beings can do to other people in the name of racism or white nationalism or, in this case, Nazism. And in the community that I lived in, there were people— when you go downtown and you shop, people had their tattoos from the concentration camps on their arm. A few years ago, my wife and I and my brother and his wife went back to the town in Poland where my father was born. And we were shown—people were very, very nice, and we were shown an area where the Nazis had put some 300 people and just mowed them down in a ditch."

He concluded, "The pain that my family, my father's family suffered in Poland is something that has impacted my life, absolutely."

Before the incident at the Arizona rally, more subtle examples of anti-Semitism had occurred during the campaign, including a *Politico* story about Bernie's wealth. The piece attacked Bernie for being a socialist who owned three houses. But the headline was "The Secret of Bernie's Millions" and displayed a graphic of a house with a money tree in the front yard. Bernie immediately saw the graphic for what it was, an anti-Semitic trope about Jews and money. I spoke to several reporters and editors at *Politico*. No apology or retraction for the headline or graphic ever came. The morning of the South Carolina primary on CNN, weekend host Michael Smerconish's chyron read, "Can either coronavirus or Bernie Sanders be stopped?" It is an old anti-Semitic trope to compare Jews to a disease. While discussed on social media, these instances of anti-Semitism never drew widespread condemnation.

Bernie is not religious, and he never wanted to point to these affronts in public for fear that he would be seen as using his Judaism only when convenient. In truth, though, his ties to Judaism and the Jewish community run deep. While mayor of Burlington, he allowed Chabad, a religious Jewish sect, to erect a giant menorah at city hall to celebrate Hanukkah, fighting an ACLU lawsuits in defense of the display. He wore a yarmulke and joined Chabad to lead prayers over the candle lighting. He would repeat this act during the campaign, participating in Chabad's menorah lighting in Des Moines.

Several times during his mayoralty, he issued proclamations declaring that the birthday of the spiritual head of Chabad—Rabbi Menachem Schneerson, who is revered by some of his followers as the messiah—a "day of education." Schneerson was so touched he wrote Bernie a personal note, ending with the sign-off, "With prayerful wishes for success in your important and responsible position, for the prosperity of all your citizens, both materially and spiritually."

One of Bernie's closest friends is an Orthodox Jew named Richard Sugarman. He once recalled the pride Bernie took in the letter: "He says, 'I got a letter you might be interested in seeing.' I went over there and read it, and then I asked if he minded if I keep the original letter. I was surprised when he told me, 'No, this letter is for me, I want to keep it.'"[28] While Jane is a collector of Bernie's documents, Bernie himself is unsentimental about most correspondence.

I once asked Bernie when he had last attended synagogue. He brushed off the question, never answering. Yet he knows more than he lets on. When we were in Pittsburgh in April 2019, during our first campaign swing through the rust belt, he wanted to meet with the rabbi at the Tree of Life Synagogue, the site of a horrific mass shooting the previous fall by a sworn anti-Semite. He insisted that the meeting not be publicized and that the campaign not even shoot video for our own purposes. He would see the rabbi alone and in private. On the way to the temple, I told him the rabbi might want to say a mourner's Kaddish, the traditional Jewish prayer intoned in honor of the deceased. Did he know the prayer?

"Ari," he said in an annoyed tone, "Yitgadal veyitkadash shmay rabba," reciting the first line of the prayer with perfect pronunciation. "I *am* Jewish," he reminded me, punctuating the statement.

A little-known fact about Bernie is that he spent time living in

Israel, on Kibbutz Shaar HaAmakim, in the 1960s. Kibbutzim, or collective farming communities, were a significant part of early Israeli history and culture and still play a role in the country today. The experience, rooted in the socialist-Zionist tradition, helped shape his progressive values, though it is not easy to get him to speak about that period of his life. As he wrote in his book *Our Revolution*, "It was a unique experience and a very different type of culture than I was used to. I enjoyed picking grapefruits, netting fish on the 'fish farm,' and doing other agricultural work."

Most important to Bernie was how the people on the kibbutz organized their collective life. "It was the structure of the community that impressed me. People there were living their democratic values. The kibbutz was owned by the people who lived there, the 'bosses' were elected by the workers, and overall decisions for the community were made democratically. I recall being impressed by how young-looking and alive the older people there were. Democracy, it seemed, was good for one's health."[29]

Still, during the 2020 campaign, even Jewish organizations would attack Bernie as not Jewish enough. Mark Mellman, the head of Democratic Majority for Israel, came to our campaign headquarters to meet with Faiz, Matt Duss, and me. He lamented that Bernie said his father came from Poland, saying this was a mockery of his heritage and evidence to some that Bernie was a self-hating Jew. Mark's true complaint about Bernie was rooted in his failure to adopt a hard-line pro-Israel stand. Throughout the campaign, Mellman would write us letters asking that we distance ourselves from prominent Muslim campaign surrogates. It became clear that any affiliation with the Muslim community was too much for Mellman, so it was no surprise that his organization's super PAC was the first to attack us, running nearly seven figures' worth of television ads in Iowa. Of course, the ads never mentioned Israel and instead focused on issues such as Bernie's heart attack as evidence he wasn't fit to be president.

While Mellman's barbs were expected, the anti-Semitism directed at our campaign deeply saddened Bernie, in part because he did not recall the 2016 campaign being marred as frequently by similar incidents. But he was not surprised. Despite his optimism, he understood there was an underbelly to American politics, and he hoped our campaign would avoid any kind of ugliness of our own.

*　*　*　*

FOLLOWING THE ARIZONA RALLY, THE CAMPAIGN PRESSED ON. Checking with local health departments every day, we still were holding rallies, unclear when we would have to stop. Our new strategy was to hunker down in Michigan, adding events in the state and fighting for every vote in advance of the primary on March 10.

Other than a rally in Chicago and one in St. Louis, Michigan would be our last stand. Bernie was scheduled to deliver a speech on African American issues at the Civil Rights Museum in Jackson, Mississippi. Campaign pollster Ben Tulchin and Jeff Weaver insisted we needed to narrow things to Michigan and should cancel the speech. We would instead hold a town hall on racial and economic justice in Flint.

On the flight from Chicago to Detroit, Bernie worked on his remarks for the town hall. He left the plane with a full speech ready to go, handwritten on his yellow legal pad. We had promoted the event as a speech on racial justice. He would be joined onstage by several prominent African American surrogates, including Cornel West and Nina Turner. Yet instead of delivering his prepared remarks, Bernie gave his standard stump speech and then turned to the African American panel to engage in a conversation about race.

The reaction from the press was immediate and severe. Bernie, for his part, wholly rejected the notion he had done anything wrong. "I had some of the best experts in the world on African

American issues. It was more important to hear what they had to say and learn from them, then hear me spout political talking points for the press."

With two days left before a critical primary, Bernie was still Bernie.

Then a miracle happened. We had been chasing the endorsement of Jesse Jackson for months. Congressman Ro Khanna and Nina Turner were on the phone with Reverend Jackson as we were headed to Michigan for the Flint event. After the event, Faiz and I left the hall in a sour mood over Bernie's refusal to deliver the speech on racial justice. But then we learned Jackson would be endorsing Bernie, and would drive from Chicago to Grand Rapids, Michigan, to appear with him at a rally. Bernie often spoke about how he wanted to model his campaign and his movement after Jackson's Rainbow Coalition—building another working-class coalition of all races fighting for economic, racial, social, and environmental justice. As mayor of Burlington, he endorsed Jackson for president in 1988, Bernie's first real foray into Democratic Party politics. It was an incredibly risky move. Burlington is nearly all white, and his decision was not without detractors in the city. In fact, Bernie was slapped in the face at a Democratic Party gathering by a voter angered by his support for Jackson.

When Jackson arrived in Grand Rapids, he and Bernie sat in a small, curtained-off space. I watched Bernie do something I had never seen him do before: he prayed. Here were two men who had spent their lives fighting for change, who had worked together for more than thirty years and were united once more.

Then Jackson, his body and voice frail from Parkinson's disease, spoke to a crowd of more than 7,000 who listened, rapt, in silence.

"With the exception of Native Americans, African Americans are the people who are most behind socially and economically in the United States and our needs are not moderate," Jackson said. "A people far behind cannot catch up choosing the most moderate path. The most progressive social and economic path gives us the best chance to catch up, and Senator Bernie Sanders represents the most progressive path. That's why I choose to endorse him today." It was a remarkable speech, and it restored some of our confidence after a difficult week for the campaign.

Later that day, in Ann Arbor, Michigan, in front of 10,000 students, with the campus beginning to implement restrictions surrounding COVID-19, Bernie and AOC made their final case before the primary. Though we understood the significance of the day at the time, in retrospect it appears to be a capstone of sorts. Bernie had taken the progressive torch from Jesse Jackson in the morning and passed it to AOC as the sun set.

Bernie, Faiz, and I celebrated the birthday of AOC's partner at a tapas restaurant in Ann Arbor before we took off for a rally in St. Louis. At dinner, Bernie was feeling optimistic, despite it all. There was one problem. He didn't know what tapas were. "Ari, you just order for me. You know what I like."

The St. Louis rally would end up being our last, due to COVID-19. And March 10 would be our final day of campaigning. We were scheduled to visit polling sites before going to Cleveland, Ohio, for a rally the night of what some have called Super Tuesday II. Bernie's mood was Zen-like. It was as if he knew this was not going to be a good day—all the polling was headed in the wrong direction, and barring an act of God, it was clear we would lose both Michigan and Missouri, two critical states voting that day, by wide margins.

After our last polling location visit, we had some down time before the flight to Cleveland. Instead of returning to his hotel, Bernie suggested we visit the Henry Ford Museum in Dearborn. Bernie, Faiz, Mike Casca, and I were taken on a tour by the museum's staff. It was as if the election wasn't happening. He was transfixed by the artifacts on display. "Ari, isn't this cool," he said, pointing at George Washington's camp bed, which he used in the field during the Revolutionary War. "Look how it folds up."

"I don't think that looks very comfortable," I said.

"More comfortable than the ground," Bernie said, scoffing at me.

After the museum, still not due at the airport, I said that we could always go to the Motown Museum. Bernie loves Motown; it was the music of his youth.

Bernie lost himself again at this second museum of the day. He eagerly talked about Motown artists, humming their tunes. When we reached the recording studio, he was as happy as I have ever seen him. "Ari, make sure you take a picture of me in here," he said. Bernie had never asked me for a photo before. Our tour guide began to sing "My Girl," which The Temptations had recorded in that very room. Bernie joined in the chorus, smiling the entire time.

In the car driving to the airport, we heard the news that Ohio was canceling public events due to the pandemic. The state's governor, Mike DeWine, had exempted political rallies from his cancellation order because of First Amendment concerns, but when I told Bernie what was going on, his instructions were clear: cancel the rally in Ohio. We would fly back to Burlington. Public health had to take priority over the campaign.

As the results from Idaho, Michigan, Mississippi, Missouri, North Dakota, and Washington came in that night, Bernie and Jane were at home alone. Faiz, Mike Casca, Josh Orton, and I went for dinner at Hen of the Woods, a restaurant next door to our hotel in Burlington, avoiding the media. The restaurant did not have a TV; this, too, was by design.

* * * *

BEFORE THE MARCH 10 PRIMARIES, reporters were on death watch. Afterward, they were actively trying to push the campaign over the cliff edge. Walking through the lobby of the Hotel Vermont meant walking a gauntlet of jeers. "When is he dropping out?" "Why is Bernie still in the race?" "What are you guys doing?"

For Bernie, none of this mattered. He still had the opportunity to talk to the American people, plus there was one more debate. Why would he drop out before then? For Bernie, though, the upcoming debate, on CNN, was secondary to the pandemic. Debate prep sessions became conversations about what the government needed to do as the world began shutting down.

Also on Bernie's mind was how the campaign would function during a pandemic. We could no longer hold rallies. Even smaller town halls would be impossible. If the campaign were to continue, it would have to become more online than ever. We had the experience to make this transition, as we had been successfully putting on livestreams for years. That knowledge would now be put to use as never before.

Before the final debate between Bernie Sanders and Joe Biden, the two remaining candidates, we would do a stream from Bernie's house. The twenty-first-century "fireside chat" featured Bernie and Faiz in conversation in front of the woodstove in his living room. We concocted a makeshift set, moving furniture, clearing random artwork, and lighting Bernie and Faiz with table lamps strategically placed on the floor in front of them. More than one million people watched the stream, which gave Bernie some hope that he could still communicate his message to a broad audience despite the unprecedented crisis.

Our conversations with CNN about the debate took a unique turn. The network moved the debate from its scheduled location of Arizona back to its studio in Washington, DC. Instead of questions from a live audience, they would air questions via video. To suggest the seriousness of the moment, CNN wanted to have the candidates seated behind desks.

That third change was a nonstarter for us, and Bernie was inflexible. They could have everyone else onstage seated, but he would stand up to address the camera. It wasn't a slight at Biden, as some at the network interpreted this demand. It was about his own comfort. He did not like speaking while sitting down. CNN could not understand this. Network executives pushed me on this over text, to which I simply replied, "Bernie stands." After several days of back and forth, CNN agreed that the candidates would stand during the event.

It was an odd time in Vermont. The state, which as of this writing still has the lowest number of COVID cases in the country, felt utterly unaffected by the pandemic sweeping across the globe. In a retrospectively irresponsible move, campaign staff and reporters in Burlington celebrated my birthday at an arcade and a karaoke bar. It was one final instance of levity pre-lockdown and before the end of the campaign.

After our morning prep session the day of the debate, Bernie seemed hesitant to leave Burlington. Landing windows at National Airport are relatively tightly controlled, but he insisted on moving ours to the last possible slot. He wanted to forgo a walk-through at CNN's studios, arguing that he had been there numerous times before, and to arrive just before the debate was scheduled to start. When we landed, Bernie went right to his townhouse, while staff, myself included, scattered to our homes and hotel rooms. After being on the road almost constantly for nearly three years, we were about to be stuck in our homes for a long time to come.

Arriving at CNN studios that night was an unusual experience. There were few people there, no other networks, no reporters, even from CNN, and blessedly, no spin room. The debate itself was uneventful, certainly not what we needed to turn the campaign around. It began with a friendly elbow tap, and while there were the expected contrasts on many issues, nothing was said that would dramatically change the course of the race.

This reality was reflected in the primary results two days later. Biden swept the Florida, Illinois, and Arizona primaries. Reporters once again began to light up our phones, almost mocking us for not dropping out. Continuing conversations that began in Burlington the week before, we would get on the phone every day with Bernie and discuss whether he should end the campaign and what he should be doing to confront COVID. Bernie had several concerns about the former. What message would dropping out send to our supporters, who had dedicated so much to our campaign? Could we keep them involved in politics? Yes, they would be let down by our loss, but would it chase them from the political process and convince them not to vote in the general election?

Bernie also wanted to make sure that our political platform endured. He and Joe Biden disagreed on so much, but he wanted the issues he cared about to be integrated into Joe Biden's agenda. With no in-person primaries until Wisconsin in early April, he felt no pressure to make an immediate decision.

It was almost a reprise of his indecision before launching his campaign. Every day a group of us, including Jeff, Faiz, Arianna Jones, and me, would discuss our options for continuing the campaign. Bernie was still holding livestreams on various topics related to the pandemic and talking to people about the issues he believed were important. It was still the type of campaigning he loved, minus the live crowds. We took steps to convert his house into a television studio to broadcast whenever he wanted, with the campaign office in DC now serving as a control room. Media coverage shifted away from the race, which most reporters thought was over anyway, and to the pandemic.

At the same time, the campaign was in a precarious position. We had stopped asking for money, instead directing our fundraising toward pandemic relief, raising more than $5 million. We were not running TV ads or doing rallies, and field organizing was impossible. Yet we still had a staff of more than 500 people and a $4 million per month payroll. While we had sufficient money for the short term, it would not last much longer.

There was also the hard fact that Bernie did not want to campaign against Joe Biden. At this point, his hesitancy was not just a result of his relationship with Biden, but of the reality of the global crisis caused by the pandemic. Bernie believed he should be focused on beating the pandemic through policy. His proposals included giving every American $2,000 a month during the crisis and expanding Medicare. These were pressing priorities, and he couldn't imagine launching blistering attacks on a political opponent, given the urgency of the moment.

At one point, Jeff said to Bernie, "Candidates don't fall off a cliff. They need to be pushed." Jeff's point was that if Bernie wasn't willing to campaign against Biden, point out their contrasting proposals and attributes, and run ads against him, then the former vice president would be the party's nominee. And if Bernie wasn't going to be the nominee, there were better avenues for influencing the process: working with Joe Biden to advance our agenda while using the movement to push Biden in more progressive directions.

After repeated discussions over several weeks, Bernie ultimately decided to explore the possibility of leaving the race, and told Jeff and Faiz to let Biden's people know our campaign was nearing its end and Bernie was ready to endorse Biden's candidacy. Biden was amenable to many of our policy demands, including lowering the eligibility age for Medicare, debt relief for student loans, and a list of more than twenty executive orders. Biden also agreed to create policy task forces staffed with experts selected by both campaigns. They would start meeting during the late spring and produce an agenda for the prospective Biden administration.

A story in the *Washington Post* claimed that Faiz and Jeff had been urging Bernie to drop out.[30] This was not true. In fact, they had been suggesting that if we were going to continue the campaign, we needed to campaign. It was not good enough to do nightly livestreams. If Bernie wanted to stay in the race, we needed to start treating it like a campaign again. That meant considering paid media, direct mail, and phone banking in Wisconsin and other upcoming states.

As the weeks progressed in late March, our daily conference calls with Bernie continued. Our payroll alone was costing the campaign nearly $100,000 per day. And most of the staff had little to do. Finally, in early April, Bernie decided to leave the race. We would allow the Wisconsin primary to go forward because of a critical judicial race that day, where high turnout would be to the advantage of Democrats, and then exit the race the following day.

One decision came easy for Bernie. We would not let our staff go without health care in the middle of the pandemic. We would have to investigate the necessary mechanism, but both Bernie and Jane were insistent that the staff continue to have their health care paid for through the end of October—essentially what would have been the end of Bernie's general election campaign. The continuation of staff health care would end up costing almost $3 million.

As the daily phone calls continued, the subject matter shifted from whether and when Bernie would leave the race to how he could remain an influential force in American politics. What was most important to Bernie was that progressives would not lose the momentum created by his two national campaigns.

Finally, on April 8, 2020, Bernie held a call with the entire campaign staff to thank them for their work and to tell them the campaign was ending. One of the things that made me proudest in that moment is that his exit did not leak ahead of time. Our staff heard the news from Bernie directly and not from the media, as so often takes place.

CHAPTER 13

"If Donald Trump is reelected, it's over."

LOCKDOWN ORDERS WERE IN PLACE, AND THE REALITY OF COVID-19 set in. Store shelves were bare, and in New York City, the health care system was stretched to the brink. Bernie was not only concerned about the pandemic, but he had to consider his own health. At seventy-nine, he was at significant risk of serious consequences if he caught the virus. Bernie was soon isolating himself from even his children and grandchildren.

The only staff member who regularly saw Bernie in person was a videographer, Chris Witschy, who remained in Burlington to film web videos and help produce livestreams. Over the next few months, these videos became Bernie's sole means of interacting with the world. But he was not alone in the videos themselves; he would use them to talk to experts, activists, and candidates. He would focus not only on the pandemic but on the issues that had propelled his campaign in the first place, including unlivable wages and student debt. Many people still tuned in, even with the campaign over and everything now mediated through our screens.

Bernie could no longer travel around the country, but loved conducting "local" livestreams, targeting audiences in specific states. These would attract a smaller audience, but in his mind, it was critical work and the closest thing to grassroots campaigning that was possible at this point. There was nothing he wanted to do more than get back out on the road, to interact with people and let them tell their stories. He wanted to speak in person with voters about the danger posed by Donald Trump.

Initially, after the Biden team approached him about a speech at the Democratic National Convention, Bernie hoped that he would give his speech in front of a live audience. Venues in New Hampshire were scouted, but ultimately COVID interfered.

After the campaign I took a break from Bernie and the campaign, needing a few months to recover, but in August, as the convention approached, Bernie called and asked if I could come back to help with a few things.

One was preparing his speech for the convention. As Jeff Weaver and I worked on the draft of his remarks, I was struck by how focused Bernie was on the danger to democracy represented by Donald Trump. It was not a policy disagreement; he truly felt the president's reelection would threaten our very system of government. Far from an abstract prediction, this was personal to Bernie, and he wanted to focus on that element in his speech. "But let us be clear, if Donald Trump is reelected, all the progress we have made will be in jeopardy. At its most basic, this election is about preserving our democracy," he would say, looking into the camera, standing inside Hen of the Woods, the popular restaurant in Burlington. "During this president's term, the unthinkable has become normal. He has tried to prevent people from voting, undermined the US Postal Service, deployed the military and federal agents against peaceful protesters, threatened to delay the election, and suggested that he will not leave office if he loses. This is not normal and we must never treat it like it is. Under this administration, authoritarianism has taken root in our country. I and my family, and many of yours, know the insidious way authoritarianism destroys democracy, decency, and humanity."

Even though I knew the text of the speech intimately, having spent hours on the phone with Bernie drafting it, I was still taken aback by its bluntness as I watched Bernie give it. He had tied Trump's strongman tendencies to his own family's history in the Holocaust. Bernie looked not only at the president but also at groups such as the Proud Boys and saw an emerging fascism here in the United States. Vast policy differences existed between him and Joe Biden, but when it came to preserving our democracy, they were aligned.

Following the speech, Bernie only wanted to engage more directly in the 2020 election. "Guys, we only have a few weeks left to save our democracy. Not the time for a vacation," he would constantly remind us. We went into planning mode, holding sometimes three livestreams a week. Bernie was intent on virtually visiting every swing state at least twice. We also put on issue-based events and livestreams with numerous progressive candidates for Congress whom we were supporting.

Bernie, in a limited sense, would also head back out on the road. With trips to New Hampshire, Michigan, and Pennsylvania, Bernie—with the support of the Biden campaign—held outdoor events and car rallies. While he was eager to do these events, they were so restrictive, and so risky, that they did not present true opportunities for the grassroots campaigning that Bernie excelled at.

But he did not slow down. At one point, I questioned him about the utility of so many events. He was expending a lot of energy on livestreams, not to mention the risk to his own health of traveling during a pandemic. Was the change he would create in this election worth it? Was it worth it to support Joe Biden, a candidate who was against Medicare for All and other policies Bernie had fought for over decades? "Ari, I'm not going to wake up the day after Election Day and think there was anything more I could have done." He punctuated his comment by stating, "If Donald Trump is reelected, it's over."

Bernie had long believed that the Democratic Party had abandoned a certain portion of the American electorate, and he now saw that some disaffected people were turning against democracy. A significant percentage of Trump supporters were simply bigots.

But another group had given up on the system itself. In the short term, our job was to make sure Democrats won in November. But in the long term, Bernie saw the challenge as one of restoring people's faith in democracy.

Bernie would often raise Jesse Jackson's Rainbow Coalition and talk of the notion of working-class people of color, allied with working-class whites, taking on the ruling elite. He saw elements of such a coalition in Reverend William Barber II's Moral Monday movement in North Carolina, where the civil rights leader organized African American churchgoers and rural whites, and believed the Democratic Party should take this approach. Some Democrats would claim Bernie was naive for believing that the party could do more to appeal to lower-class white voters. Others within the Democratic establishment were less charitable and would accuse Bernie of ignoring the history of racism and racially motivated divisions in our country. Yet Bernie thought that the formula was simple. Give people nothing to vote for, and you allow them to retreat to their worst instincts and prejudices. Give them something to support, and you can win them over to a larger cause.

Bernie's other focus during the run-up to the general election proved prescient. Early in the summer, he learned about the problems involved in counting mail-in ballots. Because Democrats were more likely to vote by mail than Republicans, some states could take days, or, in the case of California and New York, weeks, to determine a winner. "It is insane in this country we can't count votes," he would say over and over again.

Trump, Bernie believed, would use the fact that due to COVID, more people than ever before would vote by mail, and then use that fact to cast doubt on Biden's victory. In September and October, Bernie convened a series of phone calls and briefings with experts. He was intensely interested in the outside groups that were conducting planning processes for worst-case scenarios. He also started discussing worst-case scenarios in interviews. He used the platform offered by late-night comedy shows to talk about what could go wrong on election night.

Some Democratic officials and Biden campaign aides called, perturbed by Bernie's remarks. By having this conversation in public, they worried, Bernie was risking giving Trump and the Republicans ideas—as if they needed our help to develop plans to gut democracy. Bernie wanted to prepare our supporters and the media to cover what became the "Stop the Steal" protests. He believed that by getting out in front of things, he could at least help prevent misleading coverage in the media.

Bernie's nightmare was that Donald Trump would lose the election but remain in power, propped up by his supporters and undeterred by a complacent media. He believed this was a real possibility and felt he could play a unique role in preventing it. Joe Biden had to campaign on the issues, but Bernie was under no such constraints. While allied with Joe Biden, he was completely free to speak his mind.

Throughout the fall, our team, led by Faiz, was in touch with the Biden team, and Bernie had developed a good rapport with Biden campaign senior advisor and future White House chief of staff Ron Klain. And while other establishment Democrats grimaced at Bernie's stark warnings, Klain did nothing to dissuade him.

* * * *

WHEN ELECTION DAY FINALLY ARRIVED, Bernie knew he had done everything he could to help Joe Biden win. And his actions had not been simply out of obligation to the nation. He feared Donald Trump but also believed that Biden, despite their disagreements, was a fundamentally decent person and that this would be an important quality in a president.

We knew it would be a long few days before the election was called. Bernie was home in Burlington that week. Many members of our campaign's advance team had come together in DC to help organize street celebrations downtown. It became a version of a campaign reunion. Bernie called repeatedly. "Got any gossip?" "What's going on?" "What are you hearing?"

The answer was, nothing. Or at least nothing worthwhile. There was less information than ever.

When the election was called on Saturday, November 7, Bernie spoke on the phone with the campaign's senior staff. After thanking everyone for their hard work, he got personal—for the first time. "This was the 1932 election in Germany. We prevented that result from taking place. I think about what my family went through and thank God we will not have to go through that here in America."

But he quickly moved on and reminded us we had work to do. There were two runoff elections for Georgia's Senate seats, and if the Democratic candidates won, Bernie would become chairman of the Senate Budget Committee. At the same time, there was a new COVID relief bill making its way through the Senate. When the first bill, the CARES Act, passed in the spring, Bernie had just ended his campaign. Now he wanted to be fully involved from the start of the new administration.

* * * *

BERNIE NOW HAD two priorities. With the second COVID relief bill finally moving through Congress after months of intransigence by Mitch McConnell, Bernie wanted to make sure that the bill included a new round of direct payments for working people. To Bernie, if you're going to help people, be direct about it by putting money in their pockets. More than his support for Medicare for All or even his opposition to American military adventurism, this belief separates Bernie from many of his Democratic colleagues.

Senior Republicans and Democrats came of age during the Reagan and Clinton years, after the end of the era of big government inaugurated by the New Deal. Leading politicians today have long believed that government programs should be smaller and more targeted. This seems sensible on paper. Targeting means more efficiency and less waste. However, targeting has a huge downside. Universal programs such as Social Security and Medicare have substantial public support precisely because everybody pays, and everybody benefits.

Targeted programs are stigmatized and racialized—often as "handouts" to the poor, who are frequently caricatured as lazy and undeserving—and constantly under threat of cuts. But what often gets lost is that many people who need these programs don't take advantage of them because they simply do not know that they qualify or the application process requires cumbersome legal hurdles. Millions of Americans forgo critical benefits every year because they do not understand they are eligible. This is true of essential programs such as food stamps, public housing, and the earned income tax credit.

At the beginning of the pandemic, Bernie joined with Kamala Harris and introduced a bill that would have provided a $2,000 monthly check to all Americans for the remainder of the pandemic. Instead, a smaller relief program was passed, which involved a single $1,200 check as well as federal support for unemployment insurance, which is administered by the states. Bernie decided the compromise position—not his ideal outcome—was a second, similarly sized check in the new relief bill.

The pushback did not come from Republicans, who were mainly frightened of ending up on the wrong side of Donald Trump, but from conservative Democrats such as Mark Warner and Joe Manchin, who wanted the aid to be "more targeted." We found an unlikely ally in Missouri Republican senator Josh Hawley. Bernie was hesitant at first. He didn't know Hawley well and certainly didn't trust him. And Hawley had ulterior motives, clearly using populist rhetoric and dabbling in populist policy to fuel a future run for president as a more capable version of Donald Trump. Ultimately Bernie decided it was worth working with Hawley if we thought it could make a difference for Americans, even as he remained wary of empowering Hawley. "This guy is very dangerous," he told us.

We pressed ahead, with Hawley and Bernie introducing the legislation and giving floor speeches on the subject. The media could not resist a story about strange bedfellows, so we gave them ample access. The notion of direct aid received the support of both the president-elect and Donald Trump's administration. When Bernie and Hawley began working together, moderates had presented direct payments as a nonstarter. Suddenly, as the relief package made its way through the chamber the week before Christmas, the payments became inevitable.

Bernie was uniquely aware, after his own experience running for president twice, that in American politics, what is impossible this morning can become never-in-doubt by the afternoon. This is why he sees it as critical to always be pressing forward and ignoring the conventional wisdom. On Thanksgiving Day, direct payments were never going to happen. By Christmas, we had secured $600 checks.

Donald Trump stalled on signing the relief legislation into law, of all things claiming the direct payments were insufficient, and that he would prefer $2,000 checks every month. After a long back-and-forth, he finally signed the bill the day after Christmas. But Trump's delay had created an opening.

Following the Christmas holiday, the Senate would have to come back into session for one more week to pass the Defense Authorization Bill. This is one of the most significant policy bills Congress passes every year, providing policy and spending directives for the entire defense establishment. While a stalled appropriations bill can shut down the government, the Pentagon won't shut down if the bill doesn't get signed into law, but it is still considered a "must pass" piece of legislation, largely due to tradition.

Democratic leadership sensed an opportunity to gain a political advantage over Republicans, by pitting them against Donald Trump's announced policy preference. With the senate runoffs in Georgia, House Democrats passed a bill adding $1,400 to the $600 checks, meaning that individuals ultimately would receive $2,000 from the federal government: Bernie's number from the start. The legislation would go to the Senate. Chuck Schumer would make a unanimous consent request that the chamber take up the bill. Republicans would, of course, reject the motion. The Senate would pass the defense bill and the members would get to go home a few days before New Year's Eve.

That Monday, December 28, Faiz, Warren Gunnels, and I got on a call. In the Senate, doing anything requires a unanimous consent request or the legislative process grinds to a halt. What if Bernie announced he would publicly object to the Defense Authorization Bill, keeping the Senate in session through New Year's to pass it? All he would have to do is take an early flight the following day and go to the floor to object.

We pitched Bernie on the idea. When confronted with radical proposals, Bernie is thoughtful. He doesn't like to make rash decisions and needs time to think. Bernie told us he liked the idea but would call us back. An hour later, he said, let's go for it.

The plan would require a bit of subterfuge. The polite way to handle an objection such as this would have been to call the Senate Cloakroom and let them know what Bernie planned to do. The worry, though, was that the bill wouldn't pass the House if people found out Bernie was going to try and force a real vote in the Senate. We decided to wait for the House vote and then immediately tell leadership we would be objecting to the Defense Authorization Bill unless the Senate were also to vote on the increased direct payments. If the American people didn't get their checks, then senators should not have a New Year's holiday.

Warren and I were watching on TV and talking with each other on the phone as the direct payment bill narrowly passed the House.

We audibly cheered and then went to work. The cloakroom was informed of our plan, and Bernie also tweeted it out to the world. The reaction was swift. Our phones buzzed with staffers from other offices. What were we doing? What if McConnell decides not to take up the defense bill at all? Bernie had been voting against the defense bill for years. Not passing a $700 billion defense bill might have been the preferred outcome for him. When I told Bernie about these calls, he replied, "They think that's a threat?"

Other senators' staff complained that because of what Bernie was doing, their bosses were going to have to fly in early and cancel their New Year's plans. If they thought that was going to garner sympathy from Bernie, they were wrong. All he was asking for was a vote. What was McConnell scared of?

While there was yelling behind the scenes, by the next day the tune had changed. Biden, Schumer, and the rest of the Democratic establishment realized the political benefit of Bernie's gambit. With a week to go until the Georgia runoffs that would decide control of the Senate, Bernie's maneuver had refocused the media narrative both within that state and nationally on direct payments, which happened to be incredibly popular with voters. It took the Senate the entire week to pass the defense bill, and by the end, some of the same staffers who had panicked on Monday night were now calling to offer their congratulations.

The defense bill passed on January 1. The January 5 election in Georgia was mere days away, and it had the potential to profoundly shape Bernie's future. If both Democrats won, Bernie would be chairman of the Senate Budget Committee, but if they lost, there was something else in the works, which he found that he wanted more and more.

While focused on direct payments, the other thing on Bernie's mind in late 2020 and early 2021 was a conversation he'd had with Biden about the possibility of becoming secretary of labor. After election day, he grew increasingly excited about what the position would allow him to accomplish. To Bernie, it was a platform he could use to stand up for all workers in the United States. Instead of sitting in Washington, he would go back out on the road, to support strikes and expand the labor movement.

Following the election, Bernie had a follow-up conversation with Ron Klain, now officially the incoming White House chief of staff, and they again discussed the position. Klain told Bernie the content of the conversation from the spring was still very much a reality, and Biden would call him the week after Thanksgiving.

That week came and went with no word from Biden, though Bernie did have a friendly conversation with vice president–elect Kamala Harris. Nothing came the week after, either. Bernie accepted that they were likely going in a different direction. He didn't take it personally and instead turned to the pressing work in the Senate. Yet whenever we spoke to the transition team, they would send the opposite message: Bernie was still very much in consideration; in fact, he was a leading candidate.

During the week of Christmas, the call finally came. Bernie and Biden spoke. Bernie laid out what kind of secretary of labor he would be. He would be an active champion of unions. He wouldn't treat it as a desk job, but as a mandate to travel the country in support of the country's workers. To Bernie's surprise, Biden supported this vision. Workers needed a champion. He wanted his administration to create that champion, and he agreed with Bernie's philosophy.

The problem was Georgia. If our Senate candidates won, the Senate would be divided evenly, and Biden would need Bernie's vote. While Vermont's Republican governor had pledged to appoint someone who would vote like Bernie for the interim ninety-day period before a special election, anything could happen. The memory of Scott Brown winning Ted Kennedy's former seat in 2010 was still fresh in people's minds. It would not be worth the risk. But if Democrats did not win both seats in Georgia, which seemed the likely outcome, Biden would appoint Bernie secretary of labor.

Bernie was excited. While we worked on the direct payment legislation, we also researched and briefed Bernie on programs he could implement as secretary of labor. His eyes lit up as he realized the sheer power of the department. There was something to being an executive again—though the difference in scale between mayor of Burlington, Vermont, and cabinet secretary is vast—and not dealing every day with the complexities, and the slowness, of the legislative process.

"I really have no bad options here," he told me.

As the Georgia returns rolled in, there wasn't a glimmer of disappointment on Bernie's face. He would not be secretary of labor. But he was thrilled that the Democrats, with unified control of the government, would have a chance to make real change, starting with the $1,400 checks. Bernie would be chairman of the Budget Committee and a pivotal figure in passing the Biden agenda.

"We have a lot of work to do," he said.

* * * *

BERNIE WAS NOT EXAGGERATING. On January 6, the day after the runoffs, we met in the morning to plot out his priorities for budget reconciliation. Later, Bernie would be on the Senate floor, where Congress would carry out what is the ordinarily routine task of counting Electoral College votes. Yet, urged on by Trump and some GOP members of Congress, thousands of protesters against the election gathered at the Capitol. Bernie was already wary that day. He had only received his first vaccine dose and was exasperated over being on the House floor with anti-mask Republicans.

When the attack on the Capitol reached the Senate floor, Bernie and the other members of Congress were rushed to a secure location in the adjacent office buildings. I spoke with him on the phone, and Bernie was stoic but also anxious, in particular about the potential spread of COVID among members and their staffs. I was in the Rayburn Building, on the House side of the Capitol, when the shelter-in-place order went out. To return to Bernie's office, I entered the tunnel connecting the Rayburn Building and the Capitol, but police officers stopped me and told me it was too dangerous, and I should remain with them at the tunnel entrance. After a few minutes a phalanx of Capitol Police, some plain-clothed, some in uniform, some in riot gear, moved through the area, surrounding Nancy Pelosi.

Soon after that, the radios of the Capitol Police I was standing near spoke up: "Shots fired." Minutes later a second group of police in riot gear came through the tunnel. Some were injured, one was bleeding, others with their faces red and teary, obviously from the effects of chemical irritants. They yelled that it wasn't safe, and that we needed to retreat.

I ran up an escalator that connects Rayburn to the Longworth House Office Building next door. As I moved from Longworth into the tunnel that connects it, in turn, to the Cannon Building, another group of officers in riot gear came running at me. They, too, yelled that it was not safe, telling me to turn around and head in the opposite direction. I ran back toward Rayburn.

It is a cavernous four-story building, and I decided to find a place in it to hide. I took the elevator to the third floor and locked myself in a committee hearing room, barring the door. After spending forty-five minutes, my phone dying, I reached out to a colleague to see if there were any friendly offices nearby. After linking up with Progressive Caucus chairwoman Pramila Jayapal's chief of staff, I made my way to their office and spent the next several hours hunkered down with the congresswoman's husband and chief of staff. Several hours later, when the Capitol was cleared, I made my way back to Bernie's Senate office.

Having been split off from the rest of Bernie's staff when the shelter-in-place order was given, I did not evacuate with them. Therefore he and I were the only people in his office when he finally made it back at around 9:30 PM. We sat together for a while, mainly in silence, both shaken by what had happened. I went and got him some snack food from vending machines downstairs. Finally, after the votes were cast at 1:30 AM, I drove him home. Before we parted ways that night, he said to me, "Our democracy was really at risk here. We were lucky today."

* * * *

A FEW WEEKS LATER, Inauguration Day arrived. Instead of the typical massive crowds, Washington, DC, was empty. A giant security barrier surrounded the Capitol. Jane worried for Bernie's safety and called to discuss security protocols. We were all on edge. The process for attending the inauguration was cumbersome. To drive to the Capitol that day, my car needed three passes just to get through security.

Bernie would have to arrive the day before to take a COVID test from the Capitol physician. Then he was required to undergo a health screening three hours before the inauguration began. I was sitting in our office watching on TV when I saw Bernie walk out wearing his Burton jacket and a pair of mittens he had worn on the campaign trail.

I turned to Terrel, who had walked him over to the Capitol that morning, and said, "You let him go there wearing those mittens?"

"What are you talking about?" he replied. "They must have been in his pocket."

My phone began buzzing, and didn't stop. Nearly two dozen reporters texted to ask what was in the manila envelope Bernie was carrying. "Ari, that's the bullshit they were interested in," he told me that afternoon. The envelope had simply held his tickets to the inauguration.

The photos of Bernie, in his snowboarding jacket and mittens and carrying the envelope, became a viral sensation. Bernie thought the whole thing was nuts but immediately jumped at the idea of selling merchandise that would raise money for Vermont charities. If we could turn the moment into something good, it would be worthwhile. We ended up raising nearly $3 million over the next week. Bernie, for his part, ignored most of the hoopla, though he did enjoy some of the memes. I watched him laugh at the meme of the Mona Lisa wearing his mittens as we walked through the Capitol Tunnel.

* * * *

DOMINATING THE WORLD OF MEMES was fine and good, but Joe Biden was now president, and we would have to get to work on a relief bill that could help rebuild the American economy. It would be passed through the budget reconciliation process, which allows for a fifty-plus-one vote threshold in the Senate. Direct payments of $1,400 would have to be included, which alone amounted to hundreds of billions of dollars. We created a spreadsheet with a list of priorities. The first step would be COVID relief. We priced this section of our spreadsheet at $2.1 trillion.

We presented the spreadsheet to the incoming White House economic team and congressional leadership. We also asked for several funding priorities related to COVID, but that were not precisely relief. For years Bernie had been trying to increase funding for Community Health Centers, which provide free medical care around the country. He also wanted a massive increase in funding for the National Health Service Corps, which pays for medical school for doctors who will go on to work in underserved communities. The big one was increasing the national minimum wage to $15 an hour. We knew it was a stretch to include this provision in the bill and would likely not survive parliamentary challenges, but it was worth the shot.

To Bernie's surprise, nearly our entire program, with slightly adjusted budget numbers, made it into Biden's plan. As the drafting of the bills began, our staff was at the center of the effort. Bernie worked the phones like I had never seen him do before. He met again and again with other committee chairs and now Majority Leader Chuck Schumer, and whenever an obstacle arose, he was willing to do the work to knock it down.

He wasn't engaging in process for process's sake. Bernie hates process. Everything we were working on would result in genuine and significant change for the American people. Never before an inside player, Bernie was relishing the moment. He saw a singular opportunity. As the reconciliation bill progressed, he would occasionally try to determine if there was anything else we could insert in it. After learning that federal spending for after-school programs, through a program called 21st Century Community Learning Centers, only totaled about $1.2 billion, he asked me to work on increasing this funding so as many children as possible could attend summer programs with little to no cost. When the bill was signed into law, the education portion of the bill contained multiple pots of money for these programs, totaling over $12 billion—less than the rounding error in a $1.9 trillion bill.

Bernie wasn't done. Now that after-school and summer programs would be getting more money, he wanted to make sure it was used correctly. He worked the phones in Vermont, talking with the people in the state who ran these programs, school superintendents, and the governor. He got into the details. Support for children is essential to Bernie. Some of it harkens back to his memories as a kid playing punchball in Brooklyn. In Burlington, Jane, who ran youth programs for the city when he was mayor, set up a community center with programming designed by the kids themselves. Bernie would talk about how much that facility meant to the city, its kids, and him. Now he had secured the funding to create similar programs across the nation.

In March, the reconciliation bill finally came to the Senate floor.

What followed was the longest series of votes in Senate history, lasting twenty-seven straight hours. We began at 9:30 AM on March 5 and didn't finish until nearly one o'clock in the afternoon the next day. The final version wasn't perfect. Minimum wage had been stripped out by the parliamentarian, and eight Democrats voted against Bernie's amendment to add it back in. Nonetheless, what he had accomplished was incredible. The direct payments that in November we were told were impossible became $600 in the first bill. Then another $1,400 was added in the reconciliation bill. Nearly every COVID relief item from Bernie's January list was in the bill. Funding for Community Health Centers had doubled, as had funding for the National Health Service Corps. There was an enormous amount of new funding for after-school and summer programs for kids who, due to COVID, spent more than a year away from school and camp.

After the bill passed, Bernie and I walked back through the tunnel from the Capitol to his office in the Dirksen Building. He put his arm over my shoulder and said, "We got something done here, didn't we? This is fun." And as tired as we both were after the all-night session, I could see that Bernie was content.

Epilogue

IN FEBRUARY 2020, A REPORTER ASKED ME WHY I WAS smiling. "Simple," I responded. "I work for a seventy-eight-year-old Jewish socialist, who had a heart attack a few months ago and has won the popular vote in Iowa, New Hampshire, and Nevada. That's fucking remarkable."

Now that the campaign is over, I've spent time mulling the central question it left for everyone who worked for him: could Bernie Sanders have won the presidency?

When considering this question, I think back to a day in March 2018, when Bernie Sanders and I met with President Obama at his Washington, DC, office near Georgetown. Bernie had been interested in meeting with Obama for some time, believing it was appropriate to at least have a conversation with the former president, if he was considering running in 2020. But getting them together had been a challenge due to their travel schedules.

The meeting was supposed to be just the two of them, but as Bernie walked in, the former president put his arm around my shoulder and intentionally—or unintentionally—pushed me through the door and into the office. Obama was dressed casually, in a tan collared shirt and jeans. The office was filled with memorabilia and awards from his time as president.

We sat down on the couches, and I remained silent as the two men spoke. When they turned to Bernie's potential second presidential run, Obama dispensed some advice. "Bernie, you are an Old Testament prophet—a moral voice for our party giving us guidance. Here is the thing, though. Prophets don't get to be king. Kings have to make choices prophets don't. Are you willing to make those choices?"

Obama continued, making the point that to win the Democratic nomination, Bernie would have to widen his appeal and convince the party to back him—which would mean being a different type of politician and a different type of candidate than he wanted to be. Bernie listened to Obama, but it was clear to me he never accepted that premise. He had and still has a fundamental belief that he could lead an uncompromising movement that would challenge those who ran the Democratic Party while also leading that same institution, one he steadfastly refused to join.

If he had listened to Obama in 2018, could he have won in 2020—beating not only Biden, but Trump? I believe that is unlikely, because if he had followed this advice, he would've lost many of the people, especially young people, who made up the core of his movement. Even without giving an inch, he came within twenty hours—the time between Pete Buttigieg's and Amy Klobuchar's endorsements of Joe Biden and Super Tuesday—of winning the Democratic nomination. He only lost the race after an unprecedented degree of coordination and sacrifice by moderates in the Democratic Party.

While Bernie Sanders will never be president, his two campaigns have transformed the Democratic Party and this country. Old orthodoxies about government spending and foreign policy have crumbled as a result of the unceasing efforts by an old socialist. And while there is more work to be done—Medicare for All remaining the most prominent item on Bernie's still-extensive to-do list—so many of the policies and ideas that were thought to be beyond the bounds of the possible when Bernie was first elected to the Senate are now squarely within the mainstream of American politics.

Politics for Bernie Sanders is not only about policy. It is about fighting. For him it is a personal struggle for a better way of life for this country. It is a fight with members of both the Republican and Democratic parties but also often extends to progressive activists, his staff, and even himself. That fight is who Bernie Sanders is. Without it, he wouldn't be Bernie.

He will never compromise his core belief that a coalition of working-class Americans of all races and ethnicities and religions can bring about a political revolution. In that conversation in 2018, Obama was wrong that Bernie could change himself. But he was right in another way. Bernie Sanders will never see the promised land himself, but he has still managed to move this country in a more progressive direction than any other person who failed to win the White House.

Acknowledgments

OVER FOUR YEARS I WORKED FOR THE MOST PRINCIPLED person I could ever imagine running for president. Thank you, Senator, for giving me this opportunity and letting me go on this adventure with you. Above all else thank you for letting me help you change the course of history and make our country a better and more progressive place.

Thank you to Jane, for your warmth and for always being there with great advice.

Thank you to the campaign's senior team. There is not another group I would want to go into battle with: Senator Nina Turner, Faiz Shakir, Jeff Weaver, Arianna Jones, Rene Spellman, Analilia Mejia, Sarah Badawi, Warren "the Regulator" Gunnels, Josh Orton, Mike Casca, Sarah Ford, Tim Tagaris, Chuck Roche, David Sirota, Robin Curran, Josh Miller-Lewis, Georgia Parke, Claire Sandberg, and my partner in crime, Jean-Michel Picher. Also, our early state directors: Misty Rebik, Shannon Jackson, Sarah Michelsen, and Jessica Bright.

Also thank you to Ann Clancy, Nate Ober, and Lindsay Adams for keeping everything running smoothly for me.

Michaeleen Crowell, Caryn Compton, Katie Van Haste, Jacob Gillison, Lori Kearns, Matt Duss, Katie Thomas, and everyone in

Bernie's Senate office for being the best staff in the US Senate and always being there to answer the phone when I called.

A special thank you to the Bernie 2020 advance family. Yes, the book was dedicated to them, but they deserve to be mentioned twice.

As I once wrote, if you aren't around presidential campaigns, it's easy to ignore the work of advance, because they are supposed to be invisible. When they are publicly recognized it is most often for the pictures they create.

But advance is so much more. Advancers give up their lives and go out on the road living in crappy hotel rooms, never in the same place for very long. They go from city to city making sure everything is in place when the circus comes to town.

They scout the sites, set up the rallies, make sure everyone can hear and see. They make sure the press has access. They make sure attendees are safe. They make sure the pictures look good. They make sure we are picked up at the airport and we have hotel rooms waiting for us. They make sure the motorcade knows where to go and has parking. After eighteen hours on the road and three events, having a Diet Snapple Peach Tea or Diet Coke waiting on the nightstand of my hotel room was always the nicest touch.

You all have been my family on the road. I love you all.

Will Lippincott has not only been my agent for more than a decade, but also someone I am honored to call a friend.

Luke Dempsey worked obscenely hard to help me think through and craft the proposal.

It was Dan Gerstle at Liveright whose editing brought this book to life.

Finally, to my wife, Julie. During the campaign, she knew that Bernie and the movement were my top priority. She gave up so much for me to have this opportunity and I can never repay her.

Notes

1. Adam Geller, "Sanders' Early Life in Brooklyn Taught Lessons, Some Tough," Associated Press, July 21, 2019, https://apnews.com/article/bernie-sanders-donald-trump-ap-top-news-politics-vermont-0f9858ee5d3540e3aa1faabf54bd38b0.
2. Tim Murphy, "I Don't Know Who 'I' Am": Bernie Sanders' Brutally Honest Mayoral Memos," *Mother Jones*, May 9, 2019.
3. Shane Goldmacher, "Bernie Sanders Raises $10 Million in Less Than a Week," *New York Times*, February 25, 2019.
4. Russell Banks, "Bernie Sanders, the Socialist Mayor," *The Atlantic*, October 5, 2015. This piece was written in 1985 but not published for thirty years.
5. David R. Runkel, *Campaign for President: The Managers Look at '88* (Institute of Politics, John F. Kennedy School of Government, Harvard University, Auburn House, 1989).
6. Deepa Seetharaman and Emily Glazer, "How Mark Zuckerberg Learned Politics," *Wall Street Journal*, October 16, 2020.
7. Jeremy Merrill, "A Mysterious Facebook Group Is Using Bernie Sanders' Image to Urge Democrats to Vote for the Green Party," Vice, November 6, 2018.
8. Jonathan Martin, "Bernie Sanders Courts Black Voters Anew," *New York Times*, April 5, 2018.
9. Susan Davis, "Why 2020 Democrats Are Lining Up for Clyburn's 'World Famous' Fish Fry," NPR, June 14, 2019, https://www.npr.org/2019/06/14/732330671/why-2020-democrats-are-lining-up-for-clyburns-world-famous-fish-fry.
10. Briahna Joy Gray, "Hear the Bern Episode 1: Bernie Gets Personal," *Hear the Bern* podcast, April 10, 2019.
11. Banks, "Bernie Sanders, the Socialist Mayor." As previously noted, the profile was written in 1985 but did not appear in print until 2015.
12. Dareh Gregorian, Benjy Sarlin, and Vaughn Hillyard, "Kamala Harris Walks Back Her Hand-Up Moment on Health Insurance in Democratic Debate," NBC News, June 28, 2019, https://www.nbcnews.com/politics/2020-election/kamala-harris-walks-back-her-hand-moment-health-insurance-democratic-n1024756.

13. Geller, "Sanders' Early Life in Brooklyn Taught Lessons."
14. Ibid.
15. Gregory Krieg, Kate Sullivan, and Tami Luhby, "Bernie Sanders Leads Caravan into Canada to Purchase Cheaper Insulin with American Prices Rising," CNN, July 28, 2019, https://www.cnn.com/2019/07/28/politics/bernie-sanders-canada-cheaper-insulin-cnntv/index.html.
16. Sydney Ember, "Why Bernie Sanders Stood Out at the Iowa State Fair," *New York Times*, August 12, 2019.
17. Jonathan Martin and Sydney Ember, "Architects of Bernie Sanders's 2016 Race Part Ways with 2020 Campaign," *New York Times*, February 26, 2019.
18. Sean Sullivan and David Weigel, "Sen. Bernie Sanders to Be Endorsed by Rep. Alexandria Ocasio-Cortez, an Influential Voice Among Young Liberals," *Washington Post*, October 16, 2019.
19. Christopher Graff, "Socialist in Congress Goes Where Democrats, Republicans Fear to Tread," *Los Angeles Times*, September 8, 1991.
20. Banks, "Bernie Sanders, the Socialist Mayor."
21. "A Letter from Bernard Sanders, 1972," February 3, 2019, https://twitter.com/Jehane94/status/109.209.2395716558850.
22. Michael Knight, "Vermont Socialist Plans Mayoralty with a Bias Toward the Poor," *New York Times*, March 8, 1981.
23. Jon Margolis, "Bernie of Burlington," *New Republic*, March 14, 1983.
24. Rachel Scott, Cheyenne Haslett, and Sasha Pezenik, "Bernie Sanders Calls His Plan to Fund Medicare for All 'Far More' Progressive Than Elizabeth Warren's," ABC News, November 3, 2019, https://abcnews.go.com/Politics/bernie-sanders-calls-plan-fund-medicare-progressive-elizabeth/story?id=66715246.
25. Harry Reid with Mark Warren, *The Good Fight: Hard Lessons from Searchlight to Washington* (New York: G. P. Putnam's Sons, 2008).
26. Reid Epstein, "Did New Hampshire Fall out of Love with Bernie Sanders?," *New York Times*, November 25, 2019.
27. Caleb Ecarma, "Joe Biden, Revenant, Was an Irresistible Media Story—And It Helped Win Him Super Tuesday," *Vanity Fair*, March 4, 2020.
28. "Some More Info on Bernie Sanders and Judaism," Chabad.org, February 10, 2016.
29. Bernie Sanders, *Our Revolution: A Future to Believe In* (New York: Thomas Dunne Books, 2016), 21–22.
30. Sean Sullivan, "Some Top Sanders Advisers Urge Him to Consider Withdrawing," *Washington Post*, April 4, 2020.

Index